A Psychological Typology
of Successful Entrepreneurs

A Psychological Typology of Successful Entrepreneurs

John B. Miner

QUORUM BOOKS
Westport, Connecticut • London

Library of Congress Cataloging-in-Publication Data

Miner, John B.
    A psychological typology of successful entrepreneurs / John B.
Miner.
      p. cm.
    Includes bibliographical references and indexes.
    ISBN 1–56720–115–6 (alk. paper)
    1. Entrepreneurship—Psychological aspects. 2. Success in
business—Psychological aspects. 3. Businesspeople. I. Title.
HB615.M56   1997
338'.04'019—dc21   97–8854

British Library Cataloguing in Publication Data is available.

Library of Congress Catalog Card Number: 97–8854
ISBN: 1–56720–115–6

First published in 1997

Quorum Books, 88 Post Road West, Westport, CT 06881
An imprint of Greenwood Publishing Group, Inc.

Printed in the United States of America

∞

The paper used in this book complies with the
Permanent Paper Standard issued by the National
Information Standards Organization (Z39.48–1984).

10 9 8 7 6 5 4 3 2 1

Contents

Preface

A Psychological Typology of Successful Entrepreneurs is written primarily for scholars and students with an interest in the field of entrepreneurship. The book presents original theory and research dealing with major issues in that field. Because it is concerned with psychological measurement, industrial/organizational (I/O) psychologists represent an audience as well. The research questions addressed are not ones that have been of significant concern in I/O psychology previously, but they are amenable to the methods of the field. I believe that the problems associated with developing and selecting entrepreneurs will become the focus of major psychological activity in the future. A rationale for this view is presented in the following pages.

A companion volume to this work was published previously under the title *The 4 Routes to Entrepreneurial Success* (Miner, 1996a). That volume is intended for a trade audience and has the objective of helping entrepreneurs and potential entrepreneurs to make career decisions and sharpen their skills. It draws on a data base which partially overlaps the one used here, but the questions addressed and the style of presentation are quite different.

Traditionally, the approach in these matters has been to publish a scholarly, scientific presentation first, and then follow up with a presentation for practitioners, if that seems appropriate. I have reversed that order. For those who may have reserved judgment regarding *The 4 Routes ...* because it lacked a convincing scientific base, I hope that this volume will provide the underpinning needed, and I apologize for not being in a position to produce both books at the same time.

The 4 Routes ... does not contain any statistical analyses. This book contains that information. Insofar as possible, the statistics reported have been kept simple, given that my readers are likely to have widely varying backgrounds in this regard. This has been facilitated, in part at least, because the typological approach to theory construction permits it.

My research on entrepreneurship has extended over many years, and it has been aided by a number of other people. I want to acknowledge the contributions of these people and to thank them. Phase 1 focused on the managerial characteristics of entrepreneurs, and the contributors were Norman R. Smith (University of Oregon), Kenneth G. McCain (University of Oregon and Boise State University), Frederic E. Berman (Georgia State University and Berman Consulting Group), and John E. Oliver (Georgia State University and Valdosta State University). Norman Smith introduced me to the study of entrepreneurship and in many respects served as my mentor within the field for many years.

Phase 2 of the research focused on the measurement of aspects of achievement motivation (later conceptualized as components of the personal achiever and expert idea generator types). Here contributors were Norman Smith, Jeffrey S. Bracker (Arizona State University and University of Louisville), Louis F. Jourdan (Georgia State University), John N. Pearson (Arizona State University), Barbara W. Keats (Arizona State University), John N. O'del (State University of New York at Buffalo and American University), Renato R. Bellu (Kingsborough College of the City University of New York), Connie Goldfarb (Kingsborough College), Per Davidsson (Stockholm School of Economics), Charles G. Porter (State University of New York at Buffalo), and Herbert Sherman (Marist College). Renato Bellu has been a prolific researcher throughout, and his publications have represented a major contribution.

The Phase 3 research focused specifically on the psychological typology. Contributors were John O'del, Chao-Chuan Chen (State University of New York at Buffalo and Rutgers University), Eric Williams (State University of New York at Buffalo and University of Missouri), Juan Carlos Pastor (State University of New York at Buffalo), Susan Stites-Doe (State University of New York at Buffalo), and Carol L. Newcomb (State University of New York at Buffalo).

These people are all professionals who have contributed directly to entrepreneurship research. I also want to acknowledge the joint contribution of two publishers who worked in tandem to make this book possible. These are Eric Valentine, publisher of Quorum Books, and Steven Piersanti, president of Berrett-Koehler Publishers. This book contains certain materials originally published in *The 4 Routes to Entrepreneurial Success*. That this arrangement was possible is a tribute to these two individuals.

This book has been through a number of what are usually referred to as drafts; in this instance, however, a more appropriate term is "makeover." I seriously doubt that those who saw the initial manuscript would recognize it as the progenitor of this volume. Usually, I do not enjoy doing a great deal of rewriting, and this has been no exception. The person who got me through this process is my wife, Barbara Miner, who spent hour after hour working on the computer (actually several generations of computers) bringing this project to fruition. She is to be commended for her perseverance, as well as for her skill.

J. B. M.
Eugene, Oregon

Part I

Developing a
Psychological Typology

Chapter 1

Typologies in Entrepreneurship: Their Role and Value

The title of this book is *A Psychological Typology of Successful Entrepreneurs*. Breaking this title down into its elements, three components can be identified:

1. The books deals with psychological factors—not economic, or sociological, or anthropological.

2. The book presents a typology, indicating that more than one type of person is considered.

3. The book focuses on successful entrepreneurs, those whose ventures have survived and grown.

My interest in this initial chapter is to set the scene for the descriptions of theory and research to follow. What is a typology? What is different about a psychological typology? What is the history of typologies in entrepreneurship? How useful have typologies been in understanding and predicting entrepreneurial success? Are psychological factors, particularly personality factors, likely to make a valuable contribution in entrepreneurship theory? These are the kinds of questions addressed in this chapter.

THE NATURE OF TYPOLOGIES

The literature on typologies is complex and disparate; there is no universal agreement on definitions or approaches (Rich, 1992). Given this diversity it is important for any typologist, such as myself, to specify exactly what definitions and procedures are endorsed. Further, there is a need to document and support these definitions and procedures with references to the existing literature.

First, typologies should be considered to be theories, not merely classification systems. This argument is set forth by Doty and Glick (1994):

typologies are complex theoretical statements that should be subjected to quantitative modeling and rigorous empirical testing (p. 231). . . . contrary to popular belief, typologies are complex theoretical statements developed to predict variance in dependent variables. Typologies [are] differentiated from classification systems because typologies identify ideal types of organizations, whereas classification systems specify decision rules to categorize organizations into mutually exclusive and exhaustive sets. Typological theories [are] shown to meet these important criteria of theories: they have constructs, they predict relationships among the constructs, and these predictions are falsifiable. Further, typological theories may be more complex than traditional theories because they include assertions based on both grand theory and middle-range theory (p. 243).

These conclusions provide logical underpinnings for the approaches taken in this book.

Second, typologies should be clearly distinguished from taxonomies. The theory presented in this book involves a typology, not a taxonomy. Danny Miller (1996) makes this distinction as follows:

Typologies at their best are memorable, neat and evocative. Among the most prominent of these are those of Burns and Stalker (1961), Miles and Snow (1978), and Mintzberg (1979). These scholars differentiated among types of strategies, organizations, or decision-making styles. They make distinctions that furthered theory and had implications for important organizational outcomes . . . Good typologies are more than anything products of inspired synthesis and a strong sense of conceptual esthetics (p. 506).

The second arm of the configurational approach is empirical. Scholars employ methods of numerical taxonomy and an assortment of clustering algorithms and hypothesis testing techniques to identify mutual clusters in the data. . . . Compared to typologies, taxonomies tend to be more firmly based on facts—or at least on quantitative data. Their large sets of variables and sizable samples can disclose important empirical regularities (p. 507).

Too often, taxonomists discover not stable groupings but chance assemblages of attributes. Change their sample a little, or drop a single variable, and the clusters teeter precariously. Alter the grouping algorithm slightly, and an entirely different classification scheme emerges (p. 508).

Another statement along the same lines is provided by Sanchez (1993):

The distinction between typologies and taxonomies, as established in the organizational literature, refers both to the origins and the internal logic of classificatory attempts. While typologies refer to classification of organization in terms of *a priori* conceptual distinctions, empirical taxonomies, or, to avoid redundancy, taxonomies, refer to empirically derived groupings of organizations. Most important, typologies follow to a less or greater extent, Weber's ideal type logic, that is, they accentuate certain characteristics to yield conceptually clear-cut types or classes (p. 75).

Taxonomies of organizations are derived from multivariate analysis of empirical data on multiple dimensions or variables (pp. 75–76).

Let me reiterate that this book is concerned with typology, not taxonomy. Those who wish to explore the taxonomy arm of the configurational approach should consider the previously noted article by Sanchez (1993) and an article on the use of cluster analysis to develop taxonomies by Ketchen and Shook (1996), as well as McKelvey's (1982) comprehensive volume on the subject.

On occasion the term "archetype" is used in the literature in a way that suggests a close association with the types inherent in a typology. Greenwood and Hinings (1993) discuss this approach as follows:

An archetype is defined in terms of two general statements. First, organizational structures and management systems are best understood by analysis of overall patterns rather than by analysis of narrowly drawn sets of organizational properties. This is the "holistic" perspective asserted by Miller and Friesen (1984). Second, patterns are a function of the ideas, beliefs, and values—the components of an "interpretive scheme" (Ransom, Hinings, and Greenwood, 1980)—that underpin and are embodied in organizational structures and systems (p. 1052).

The development of interest in archetypes . . . represents a return to a central thrust of organizational theory, which is the need to understand organizational diversity through typologies (Lammers, 1978; Weber, 1947). The concept of an archetype implies some form of classification. The idea of coherence between the elements of organizational arrangements is central to typologizing, and the classification of organizations is made according to differences and similarities in overall patterns (pp. 1053–1054).

It appears that sets of archetypes and typologies deal with essentially the same approaches. Even though the term "archetype" is not used widely in this book, it is present in the literature, and thus it is important to understand its relation to typology.

TYPOLOGIES SPECIFIC TO ENTREPRENEURSHIP

Typologies are widespread in entrepreneurship and they have played an important role in the development of the field (Gartner, 1985). Entrepreneurial ventures differ widely, and typological theorizing provides a method of understanding this diversity. This theorizing extends over a wide range. The discussion here focuses on approaches that are currently viable. Although it is not exhaustive, my intention is to provide a good sampling of typologies from the present scene. A useful source for approaches of primarily historical interest is Livesay (1982).

Bird (1989), in her extensive review of the entrepreneurship literature, notes four different typologies. We will start with these, and then add others. Building on the *Enterprising Man* research (Collins and Moore, 1964), Smith (1967) proposed a typology that has spawned considerable research, discussion, and emulation. This approach divides entrepreneurs into craftsman and opportunistic types and their firms into rigid and adaptive types. The criteria for these classifications are set forth in Table 1.1. Opportunistic entrepreneurs are expected to head adaptive firms which grow more rapidly. Craftsman entrepreneurs head rigid firms which exhibit less growth.

The research tends to support this typology, but with many qualifications and extensions. The types and their relationships seem real enough (Davidsson, 1988; Smith and Miner, 1983). However, Peterson and Smith (1986) conclude that opportunistic entrepreneurs do not always foster company growth and craftsmen impede it. The role of the craftsman for growth appears to be dependent on the level of economic development of the country and the firm's stage in its life cycle. Milne and Lewis (1982) report studies in Scotland indicating that craftsmen with adaptive firms are common in that country. Among the firms of inventor-entrepreneurs, who appear to represent a third type, the strong correlation between type of entrepreneur and type of firm breaks down almost completely (Miner, Smith, and Bracker, 1992a). Lafuente and Salas (1989) also find more than two entrepreneurial types; in addition to craftsmen they note a group concerned primarily with family welfare, a group of real managers, and a group with a liking for risk and challenge. Of these four, the first two appear to resemble craftsmen and the last two opportunists. Research conducted by Woo, Cooper, and Dunkelberg (1988, 1991) raises serious questions regarding the generalizability of the type of entrepreneur differentiation; their findings suggest it may have limited applications.

Although the Smith (1967) typology is more sociological and economic in nature than psychological, some efforts to relate personality characteristics to it exist. Lessner and Knapp (1974), for instance, found that opportunistic entrepreneurs were characterized by inner directedness, spontaneity, self-acceptance, and acceptance of aggression. Smith and Miner (1983) found no evidence of a relationship between managerial motivation and entrepreneur type, but some limited evidence of a relation with firm type. Subsequent attempts to correlate entrepreneurial motivation, as reflected primarily in achievement motivation, with the Smith (1967) typology have proven fruitless.

Bird's (1989) second illustration of an entrepreneurial typology is that of Kets de Vries (1977). This incorporates the craftsman and opportunistic types, and adds an R&D technical entrepreneur that appears to match the inventor-entrepreneur subsequently more fully described by Miner, Smith, and Bracker (1992a).

A third typology was proposed by Liles (1974). It includes (1) marginal firms which are designed to provide income, but not as an alternative to engineering or management careers; (2) attractive small firms, not intended to grow, but able to provide income equal to professional and managerial careers, and at the same time flexibility of work, lifestyle, and geographical location; and (3) high-potential firms intended to grow rapidly in both sales and profits.

Finally, Bird (1989) notes the rather extensive typology advanced by Vesper (1980, 1990). As initially stated this included 11 types as follows:

1. Solo Self-employed Individuals: mom and pop stores, tradespeople, and professionals who operate with very few employees.

2. Team Builders: individuals who gradually build an organization incrementally by hiring and delegating.

3. Independent Innovators: inventors who create an organization to market an invention in the mode of high-technology start-ups.

4. Pattern Multipliers: those who utilize a pattern over and over again to expand through franchising or chain operations.

5. Economy of Scale Exploiters: entrepreneurs who reduce prices by increasing volume and thus keep the competition out.

6. Capital Aggregators: financial specialists who put together large front-end capital accumulations to establish their ventures.

7. Acquirers: purchasers of a going enterprise or family business entrepreneurs who take over from a previous family member.

8. Buy-Sell Artists: turnaround artists who take over struggling firms, revive them, and sell them at a profit.

9. Conglomerators: acquirers who use the assets of one company to obtain control of another, often diversifying into unrelated businesses.

10. Speculators: investors in fields such as real estate who use these assets to leverage further investments, with or without development of the assets, to be sold later at a profit.

11. Apparent Value Manipulators: the classic arbitrageur who repackages, redefines, or restructures to add apparent value for resale.

The 1990 version of this typology telescopes types 8 through 11 under the Acquirer title. However, a new type Deal-to-Dealers is added; these are people who develop multiple enterprises, some of which are successful and some of which are not. Thus the typology as a whole is reduced to eight.

Table 1.2 describes a three-way typology proposed by Filley and Aldag (1978, 1980). The craft, promotion, and administrative differentiation suggests a variant of the Smith (1967) typology. However, no reference is made to that source, and consequently, this appears to be an independently developed approach. Evidence is presented in support of the three types. They emerge as separate in different studies and show considerable consistency. However, an attempt to relate the typology to psychological characteristics of the lead entrepreneur did not yield results differing from chance.

Covin (1991) focused on strategic posture to identify (1) conservative firms which are risk-aversive, non-innovative and reactive and (2) entrepreneurial

Table 1.1
Criteria Used by Smith (1967) to Classify Entrepreneurs and Their Firms

Entrepreneurial variables	Type of Entrepreneur	
	Craftsman	Opportunistic
Breadth of education and training	Education focused on current business activity	Education involved many different kinds of courses
Breadth in type of jobs held	Jobs were in same type of business as present company	Jobs were not in same type of business as present company
Management reference group	Previously associated mostly with fellow workers	Previously associated with managers and business owners
Management sponsor or multiple role models	A fellow worker provided example for success	The owner of a business provided example for success
High social involvement	Active in professional, trade, or business associations	Active in community associations not related to profession or business
Effective communication ability	Does not communicate well in writing or speeches	Communicates well in writing and speeches
Delegation of authority and responsibility	Finds to do things right one must do them oneself	Believes those at lower levels in the company should handle operations
Universalistic criteria for employee selection	Attempts to hire people has known a long time	Feels there are many people available to work in company
Multiple sources of capital used	Two or fewer sources of capital used	Three or more sources of capital used
Multiple methods of establishing customer relations	Customers gained through prior relations or personal contact	Customers gained neither through prior relations nor personal contact

8

Type of Firm

Firm Variables	Rigid	Adaptive
Varied competitive strategies	Marketing strategies emphasize reputation, quality, and price	Marketing strategies are not limited to the preceding and place value on creativity and innovation
Long-term planning for company initiation	Planning for company done no more than one year before	Planning for company done more than one year before start
Planning for future growth and change	Plans for growth not developed or sales to new customers not anticipated	Plans for growth developed and sales to new customers are anticipated
Employee relations not paternalistic	Feels personally responsible for employees or that they are like children	Does not feel personally responsible for employees or that they are like children
Changed customer mix	Slight change at best	Major change
Additions to product mix	Slight change at best	Major change
Changed production methods	Slight change at best	Major change
Dispersed locations	Slight change at best	Major change
Dispersed markets	Sells in one state only	Sells in more than one state or country
Concrete plans for change	Plans change within five years in only one area at best among customers, products, production methods, and locations	Plans change within five years in two or more areas

Table 1.2
Criteria Used by Filley and Aldag (1978) to Classify Firms

Characteristic	Organization Type		
	Craft	Promotion	Administrative
Objectives	comfort-survival	personal achievement	market adaptation
Policy	traditional	personal	rational
Leadership	craftsman	entrepreneur	professional
Structure	power levels	field of force	rational hierarchy
Staff	housekeeping	technical-personal	technical-coordinative
Functional development	single	successive emphasis	full development
Work-group bonds	fixed roles	interaction-expectation	homogeneity
Innovation	conventional methods	innovation	development
Uncertainty-risk	no perceived risk	uncertainty	risk
Basis for success	benevolent environment	innovation exploitation	planned adaptation to environment
Pattern of growth	non-growth	S-curve	linear

firms which are risk-taking, innovative, and proactive. A strategic posture scale was used to select extreme groups of small firms falling in each category. Research using cluster analysis found two major clusters of conservative firms—low-priced, low-value firms (with very low performance levels), and financially secure, broad-based firms (with quite high performance levels). Two clusters of entrepreneurial firms were also found—incongruous, growth-seeking firms (with low overall performance), and aggressive, high-profile firms (with very high average performance).

A very similar typology is proposed by Baumol (1993, 1995), but now with reference to the nature of the entrepreneur rather than the firm's strategic posture. The first type, with the label "firm-organizing entrepreneur," refers to a person who creates and then organizes and operates a new business, irrespective of whether anything innovative is involved. The second type, the innovating entrepreneur, is a person who transforms inventions and ideas into economically viable entities, whether or not in the process the person creates or operates a firm. Firm-organizing entrepreneurs are said to be basically managers. With regard to the role of psychological factors, in his typology Baumol (1995) has this to say:

the discovery of the attributes of an entrepreneurial personality, is certainly promising. There is no reason to doubt that it can be carried out to some reasonable degree of approximation or that, when done, it will be valuable and enlightening. But the task seems to fall outside the purview of economic theory, both because it is primarily an empirical rather than a theoretical matter, and because it calls for the skills of the psychologists or the sociologist rather than those of the dismal science (p. 22).

Gartner, Mitchell, and Vesper (1989) have developed a taxonomy which has certain characteristics of a typology and which thus deserves mention here. The components were created by applying cluster analysis to a lengthy questionnaire, but the questions themselves were a product of considerable qualitative study and theorizing; thus the conceptual input to the final result was greater than in most taxonomies. The types were:

1. Escaping to Something New—entering a completely new line of business to get away from a previous job.

2. Putting the Deal Together—using contacts, an entrepreneur assembles a business which will assure that all involved—suppliers, wholesalers, retailers, etc.—will come out winners.

3. Roll-Over Skills/Contacts—obtaining expertise by working in one business, and then using the skills and contacts obtained in the new venture.

4. Purchasing a Firm—acquiring the needed capital, and then purchasing a firm with the intent of achieving a turnaround.

5. Leveraging Expertise—working with partners to enter an established market which

the lead entrepreneur understands well because of outstanding accomplishments in the technical field involved.

6. Aggressive Service—directing professional expertise to the task of creating a very aggressive, service-oriented firm in a specialized area.

7. Pursuing the Unique Idea—being the first to enter a new market based on a new idea or product.

8. Methodical Organizing—planning the new venture in such a way that an existing product or service can be introduced with a new twist.

OVERVIEW OF THE TYPOLOGIES

These eight typologies, taken as a whole, are very different, although there are some similarities as well. Typologies may be created for various purposes, and thus the field can well entertain several good typologies at the same time. Having a one best typology is not something to which entrepreneurship as a discipline need aspire.

Most typologies have not been researched beyond the studies that contributed to their formation; some have not been researched at all. As theories these formulations need to be tested, and other than the Smith (1967) typology, that simply has not occurred to any meaningful degree. Nevertheless, the ideas inherent in the various typologies have advanced the entrepreneurship field. The field not only has produced an abundance of typologies, but it has benefited from this abundance as well.

But has the particular area of psychological typology moved forward in this process? Not really. Efforts have been made to correlate psychological factors with various types, but only with very limited success. The need to establish psychological definitions of types has been recognized, but little beyond that has occurred. In short, the typology literature has generally acknowledged the significance of psychological typology and even endorsed it. Yet the net result has been much less than the expectations.

At this point a taxonomy proposed by Langan-Fox and Roth (1995) seems relevant. It is a taxonomy based on the usual cluster analysis, it deals only with female entrepreneurs, and it focuses entirely on characteristics related to achievement motivation (McClelland, 1961). Yet it shows what a psychological typology might accomplish. It also points up a problem inherent in most taxonomic analyses in that no cross-validation was carried out in a new sample, thus moving beyond the research that established the taxonomy originally.

The Langan-Fox and Roth (1995) study identified the following types.

1. Managerial Entrepreneurs—although low on achievement motivation, these entrepreneurs are high on the ability to influence and exert power, and resistance to subordination; they have an internal locus of control, considerable job satisfaction, marked activism, a tendency to plan their careers, and little trust in others.

2. Pragmatist Entrepreneurs—generally these entrepreneurs are in the middle on the psy-

chological variables; however, they have a pragmatic interest in passing the business on to children and in making more money.

3. Need Achiever Entrepreneurs—these are the real personal achievers exhibiting a predominant achievement motivation; managerial characteristics are at a minimum.

This is a promising result, but we need to know a great deal about what the psychological approach has had to offer up to this point.

THE PSYCHOLOGICAL FACTOR

In this section my intent is to show the position the field has taken on the results of research using psychological characteristics. Quotes are taken from a large number of research reviews, or position statements presumed to be based on such reviews. The coverage may not be exhaustive, but it is comprehensive. I want to show what various reviewers have had to say on the role of psychological factors in understanding entrepreneurship. The statements start with an early period and work up to the present, because there may have been a change as new research has accumulated. The coverage is non-critical because the objective is to establish what is, not what should be. In any event, my intent is to determine whether a consensus has been obtained, and if so what kind of consensus. Is there reason to believe a fully psychological typology of successful entrepreneurship could be viable? If so, what form should it take?

Let us start with the position stated by Gasse (1982):

Although much progress has been made in the past 15 years, no clear link has been established between the personality characteristics of entrepreneurs and the success of their business ventures. However, present research and research methodology holds great promise for the advancement of our knowledge of entrepreneurship and small business management (p. 66).

Sandberg (1986) has the following to say:

Research on the entrepreneur's psychology has been primarily descriptive and has not established causal relationships between personal characteristics and new venture performance. A high nAch [need for achievement] which characterizes successful entrepreneurs, may just as strongly characterize unsuccessful ones; measurements taken after either outcome may tell little about the entrepreneur's characteristics prior to the attempt. Nor has risk preference proved a distinguished characteristic of entrepreneurs or of successful entrepreneurs. Some distinction can be made between likely successful and likely unsuccessful entrepreneurs on the basis of their locus of control beliefs (p. 42).

Aldrich and Zimmer (1986) are similarly negative:

Personality-based theories of entrepreneurship posit that people's special personal traits make them prone to behaving and succeeding as entrepreneurs. The list of traits is nearly endless but includes internal locus of control, low aversion to risk taking, aggressiveness, ambition, marginality, and a high need for achievement. . . . Three problems plague personality-based approaches to explaining entrepreneurship: empirical research does not find strong evidence supporting such approaches, similar approaches in the leadership field have made little progress in finding a generic ''leadership'' trait, and personality-based models underpredict the true extent of entrepreneurship in the United States (pp. 4–5).

Brockhaus and Horwitz (1986) have the following to say:

The literature appears to support the argument that there is no generic definition of the entrepreneur, or if there is we do not have the psychological instruments to discover it at this time. Most of the attempts to distinguish between entrepreneurs and small business owners or managers have discovered no significant differentiating features. A few general characteristics of the entrepreneur do emerge, however. The entrepreneur does appear to be achievement oriented and, at least in the early stages of the business venture, have internal locus of control. In general, their values approach has been to concentrate on making short-run decisions and solving immediate problems. This tendency . . . could possibly result from the heavy work load assumed by most entrepreneurs (pp. 42–43).

Begley and Boyd (1987) preface their presentation of their own research with the following:

In studies of entrepreneurial characteristics, attributes such as the following recur with regularity: need for achievement, internal locus of control, moderate propensity for risk taking, tolerance for ambiguity, and more recently, Type A behavior. . . . Yet . . . more research is required before the salient features of the entrepreneurial personality can be persuasively proclaimed (p. 80).

Low and MacMillan (1988), in a widely cited review, come to the following conclusions:

Two basic problems with need for achievement are first, the theory is as applicable to salespeople, professionals and managers as it is to entrepreneurs, and second, subsequent research has not validated a link between a high need for achievement and the decision to start a business. . . . internal locus of control has proved to be no more useful than need achievement in differentiating the entrepreneur from the non-entrepreneur. . . . Although some of the empirical findings are contradictory, the overall evidence is that entrepreneurs are moderate risk takers and do not significantly differ from managers or even the general population. . . . the wide variations among entrepreneurs make any attempt to develop a standard psychological profile futile (pp. 147–148).

Gartner (1988) largely echoes this view:

a startling number of traits and characteristics have been attributed to the entrepreneur, and a ''psychological profile'' of the entrepreneur assembled from these studies would portray someone larger than life, full of contradictions, and, conversely, someone so full of traits that (s)he would have to be a sort of generic "Everyman" (p. 21).

Bird and Jelinek (1988) continue the negative trend:

Many early students of entrepreneurship began with a look at the person—his or her personality and motivation or life experiences. Although this approach makes intuitive sense, especially when faced by the strong character and interesting lives of real entrepreneurs, this approach has provided little predictive power and limited insight into the functioning of entrepreneurs (p. 26).

Yet Bird (1989) alone, in her book, comes to a somewhat different conclusion:

The abilities (seen best in terms of prior experiences and education) and motivations (need for achievement, need for control, risk acceptance, etc.) of potential entrepreneurs determine if they will act to form a new venture or acquire an existing business. . . . Together ability and motivation predict (1) the decision to start a new venture, (2) the ability to implement that decision, and (3) the results of that venture. Other factors moderate or influence the impact of abilities and motivations (p. 108).

Davidsson (1989a), reviewing the literature prior to his own research, says:

The above review of empirical results may—despite the admitted inconsistencies—give a spuriously coherent picture of the nature of the entrepreneur/small business manager. In fact, it is not uncommon that researchers complain that there is as much variation within the group as there is between "entrepreneurs" and any group used for comparison. Entrepreneurs thus seem to defy aggregation. This holds for personal characteristics as well as for behavior and performance (p. 43).

Vesper (1990) notes a number of grounds on which the psychological findings are open to dispute, and concludes: "academicians have tried to discover psychological characteristics that discriminate between entrepreneurs and nonentrepreneurs, but the findings have been relatively mixed" (p. 59).

Timmons (1990a) states the following:

Most of the research about entrepreneurs has focused on the influence of genes, family education, career experience, and so forth, but no psychological model has been supported. Successful entrepreneurs seem to be of both sexes, and in many sizes, shapes, colors, and descriptions imaginable. . . . a psychological model of entrepreneurship has not been supported by research. However, behavioral scientists, venture capitalists, investors, and entrepreneurs share the opinion that the eventual success of a new venture will depend a great deal upon the talent and behavior of the lead entrepreneur and of his or her team (pp. 22, 161).

Johnson (1990), in a review of the achievement motivation research, concludes:

The lack of definitive research results regarding the link between achievement motivation and entrepreneurship is more likely the result of flawed research methodology than the absence of a positive relationship. It is concluded, therefore, that the study of this motive in particular and psychological characteristics in general should be continued in entrepreneurship research (p. 50).

Guth (1991) presents a historical summary as follows:

Prior to the middle-1980s, academic research on entrepreneurship was predominantly focused on attempting to discover the personality characteristics of successful entrepreneurs. The thought was that, if characteristics unique to successful entrepreneurs could be discovered, it would be possible to encourage people with those characteristics to become entrepreneurs, and to discourage people without these characteristics from becoming entrepreneurs, thus increasing the amount of successful new venture creation. The objective of this approach to research on entrepreneurship has not been achieved. There appears to be no discoverable pattern of personality characteristics that distinguish successful entrepreneurs from non-entrepreneurs (p. 11).

Shaver and Scott (1991) conclude:

The study of new venture creation began with some reasonable assumptions about the psychological characteristics of "entrepreneurs." Through the years, more and more of these personalogical characteristics have been discarded, debunked, or at the very least, found to have been measured ineffectively. The result has been a tendency to concentrate on almost anything except the individual. . . . But none of these will, alone, create a new venture. For that we need a person, in whose mind all of the possibilities come together, who believes that innovation is possible, and who has the motivation to persist until the job is done. . . . we need a truly psychological perspective on new venture creation (p. 39).

Cooper and Gascón (1992), in a review that deals with psychological and other factors, note:

despite the diversity of approaches to studying entrepreneurial factors and their relation to performance, there do appear to be some common findings. The strongest evidence suggests that ventures are more likely to be successful if they are started by white males who have a high need for achievement, who take explicit steps to manage risk, and who engage in relatively systematic planning involving the input of others (p. 316).

Amit, Glosten, and Muller (1993) provide a review that in many respects echoes Low and MacMillan (1988):

Need for achievement . . . is a characteristic common to many individuals and does not predict an entrepreneurial tendency. . . . Internal locus of control . . . is not a trait exclusive to entrepreneurs and it has also been identified in successful managers. . . . the overall evidence is that entrepreneurs are moderate risk-takers and do not significantly differ from managers in the amount of perceived risk they will bear. . . . entrepreneurs have a significantly greater capacity to tolerate ambiguity than managers. . . . Definitional and methodological problems . . . raise the possibility that observed traits are actually the product of entrepreneurial experience. This makes it difficult to interpret the results (p. 821).

Block and MacMillan (1993) provide an update to MacMillan's earlier conclusions (Low and MacMillan, 1988):

Successful entrepreneurs do have some characteristics in common, including a high energy level, great persistence, resourcefulness, and the desire and ability to be self-directed, together with a reasonably high need for autonomy—a need that is greater in independent entrepreneurs than in corporate entrepreneurs. These characteristics, however, do not distinguish entrepreneurs from other groups of high achievers, nor are they enough to ensure success (p. 8).

Ray (1993) says the following on the subject:

It is widely assumed that there is a universal set of finite and linear personality attributes that determine whether one can be an entrepreneur. This list of attributes typically includes moderate risk taking, internal locus of control, need for achievement, and information seeking. . . . the entrepreneurial personality is important in shaping a venture but . . . there is no ideal-type personality or marginal set of attributes that guarantees success for a new venture (pp. 349, 354).

In 1993, Aldrich and Wiedenmayer provided further commentary beyond Aldrich's earlier statement (Aldrich and Zimmer, 1986):

Previous researchers have reasoned that there must be something distinctive about the background or make-up of entrepreneurs and that research should be able to illuminate these characteristics. Many trips down this ''distinctive differences road have ended in dead ends, however. . . . most of the ''traits'' studies are based on small samples, drawn from unknown populations whose generality is not clear, and limited to cross-sectional designs, thus rendering any causal implications suspect (pp. 146, 185).

Caird (1993), in a review which focuses on specific psychological tests, says:

The results of applying psychological tests shows that entrepreneurs have the following characteristics: a high need for achievement, autonomy, change, dominance; an internal locus of control; characteristics of risk taking, energy, and social adroitness; a preference for learning through action and experimentation; and a preference for intuition and thinking (p. 18).

Eggers (1995), drawing upon Low and MacMillan (1988), says:

entrepreneurs do tend to differ from the mean on psychological variables; however, as yet no generally accepted model of entrepreneurial personality or profile of the typical entrepreneur has emerged. This is primarily because of the mixed results in regard to the value of using psychological characteristics as predictors of success and group member-ship. . . . One key reason for this is that the same traits associated with successful entre-preneurs are also found in successful managers; they are not exclusive to the entrepreneurial population. . . . The current consensus is that psychological traits act in predisposing the individual to entrepreneurial behavior but are not predictors. Thus, over-all this research stream has had little meaningful impact (pp. 167–168).

Finally, Naffziger (1995) concludes:

First, there seems to be an emerging consensus that successful entrepreneurs are different from unsuccessful ones, and that entrepreneurs are different from the population in gen-eral. . . . Additional studies reviewed here confirm that as well or indicate that entrepre-neurs are different from practicing managers. The meaning of the differences and how influential they are in the startup process is yet unclear. Second, if entrepreneurship is part of a person's psychological profile, it is likely to be a combination of traits, some of which have already been measured (e.g., risk taking propensity, locus of control, energy level, and need for achievement) and others that have not been measured to date. Third, given the results to date and the methodologies that have been employed, it is likely that the causes behind the entrepreneurial decision and event are multiple but that personality undoubtedly has some influence (p. 37).

OVERVIEW OF THE REVIEWS OF PSYCHOLOGICAL FACTORS

Consensus does not appear to characterize the reviews. Some are very neg-ative on the psychological research, believing that there is nothing new here of value; some clearly state that certain psychological characteristics have been shown to be associated with entrepreneurship and entrepreneurial success; some stake out a position between these two. In an interdisciplinary field like entre-preneurship, consensus on the contribution of one of the component disciplines is often difficult to achieve; perhaps it is impossible. In any event, the reviews clearly indicate that anyone who wishes to document and support a particular position can find at least one review that will achieve that end. There is indeed a great deal of citing and quoting of prior reviews in the literature, and not always the same reviews.

The literature on psychological characteristics goes back to the 1960s, but not enough research to stimulate a meaningful review occurred until the early 1980s. As the research has been accumulated one would expect the reviews to become more positive, if the field is advancing. Yet this has not happened—positive and negative positions remain roughly equal throughout the period of the reviews. Given that a number of significant studies yielding positive results have been conducted in recent years, this is difficult to understand. It may be due to an overreliance on the conclusions from prior reviews, so that reviews recapitulate each other, even though the field is changing.

None of the reviews utilize the statistical techniques of meta-analysis to synthesize the finding of many studies. This is rather surprising. The body of research is certainly sufficient to support such an approach, using personality characteristics in a global sense. Other fields such as honesty testing, with which I have a special familiarity (Miner, 1996b), resorted to this approach early on and have found it important in defining the value of the psychological factor. Entrepreneurship research clearly would benefit from a meta-analytic approach.

The reviews on occasion contradict one another. They often cite different characteristics that are supported by the research, although an overall idea of what these characteristics are may be obtained from this source. Some of the reviews make statements that are clearly incorrect, at least at the present time. In my opinion the research as a whole is much better done and much more conclusive than many of the reviewers believe. Yet I have been a researcher in the field for over 20 years, and that may influence my reading on the field's research.

A frequent statement takes the form that current psychological research does not yield fully satisfactory results, but nevertheless the approach is promising and warrants further study. There is a frequent feeling that somehow the psychological findings, even if highly valid, have not been put together or packaged in the right way. The potential is there, but something is missing.

Finally, a number of reviewers criticize entrepreneurship researchers for failing to find distinguishing characteristics that set entrepreneurs apart from other groups—especially managers. This is unwarranted criticism insofar as predicting entrepreneurial success is concerned. If one wishes to understand, predict, and influence people toward entrepreneurial success, the only comparison that matters is between successful and less successful or failed entrepreneurs. Other comparisons can help understanding, but they are not a necessary condition for valid prediction. Successful entrepreneurs can fail to differentiate themselves from managers (or even successful managers) and still be distinctly different from unsuccessful entrepreneurs—what really matters.

CONCLUSION

Typologies are theories and as such should be subjected to empirical test. In contrast to taxonomies they have a conceptual origin; they do not derive originally from the analysis of empirical data. The theory discussed and researched in this book is a typology.

Because entrepreneurs come in many varieties, typologies have played an important role in the development of our understanding of entrepreneurship. The field is so structured that it is particularly likely to benefit from typological theorizing. However, research testing the various typologies has not been as extensive as it should be. Furthermore, although the creation of psychological typologies appears promising, little of substance has been accomplished on that specific score.

An extended look at the various reviews dealing with the psychological factor in entrepreneurship research yields little evidence of a consensus. Almost any position would find support somewhere in the diverse array. Furthermore, there is as much diversity in the mid-1990s as there was in the early 1980s when the reviews began. Yet the reviews frequently express a belief that even if the research has been less than successful to date, the identification of psychological characteristics making for entrepreneurial success holds considerable promise.

The remainder of this book describes the psychological theorizing and research in which I personally have been involved for the last ten years. As the story unfolds the reader might well consider applying the judgmental criteria proposed by Gartner (1989). He suggests that researchers on entrepreneurial traits and characteristics should:

1. ground their studies in the context of previous research,
2. articulate a specific theory about the nature of entrepreneurship and its relationship to the entrepreneur,
3. define key ideas and variables,
4. conscientiously identify and select samples, and
5. use current social psychology and personality theory-based measurement instruments or provide construct validity evidence for newly constructed measures (p. 35).

This is the essence of good science. I believe our theorizing and research is in that tradition.

Chapter 2

The Four-Way Psychological Typology

The psychological typology described in this chapter has a mixed conceptual foundation. The first type, the personal achiever, had its origins in prior research as reviewed in the previous chapter, and preceded any of our research. At an earlier point my title for this type was high energy inputer, but the personal achiever designation seems to reflect the origins in achievement motivation more fully.

The second type is the real manager. Again the prior literature was the source of this type, and the type preceded any of our research. The term itself derives from Luthans, Hodgetts, and Rosenkrantz (1988). Thus, both the personal achievers and the real managers were conceptualized a priori.

The third type, the expert idea generator, emerged in part out of our research on technologically innovative entrepreneurs (Miner, Smith, and Bracker, 1989, 1992b, 1994) and from other findings in the field of high technology. But other aspects of the type did not become apparent until the research reported in Chapter 6 was half completed. Thus, this type is only partially conceptually a priori.

Finally, the fourth type, called empathic supersalespeople (or sometimes simply supersalespeople), had its origins entirely in my experience with the subjects of the Chapter 6 research. Again, as with the expert idea generators, this type was established as that research was at its halfway point in terms of sample development. It is conceptually a priori only for the second half of that sample. To the best of my knowledge this type has no links to previous research; it is entirely new.

In the rest of this chapter I describe these four types—the personal achiever, the real manager, the expert idea generator, and the empathic supersalesperson—in general terms. Chapter 3 discusses the career route each type must follow to reach entrepreneurial success (the fit), considers the case where more than one of the types exists in the same person (a complex entrepreneur), and deals with certain considerations related to the domain of the theory.

THE PERSONAL ACHIEVER TYPE

Personal achievers as a group are expected to be characterized by a personality make-up which results in high scores in some ten areas. The exact mix can vary from person to person but these ten are the factors that contribute to the personal achiever designation. Evidence on the importance of these characteristics for entrepreneurship is noted in the previous chapter, and in fact motivational factors of this kind have been incorporated in several comprehensive theories of entrepreneurial firm performance (Herron and Robinson, 1993; Johnson, 1990; Keats and Bracker, 1988).

1. *Motivation for Self-Achievement*. The personality factor that research first established as part of the entrepreneurial character is achievement motivation. We know much more about this factor now, but the linkage to entrepreneurship has been apparent for some time (Steiner and Miner, 1986):

1. Individuals differ in the degree to which achievement is a major source of satisfaction.

2. Highly achievement-motivated people have certain interrelated characteristics of which the following are particularly relevant for *self-achievement*:

    (a)   They are more concerned with achieving success than avoiding failure and thus do not concentrate their energies on warding off adversity.

    (b)   They much prefer situations in which they themselves can influence and control the outcome.

    (c)   They prefer situations involving clear-cut individual responsibility so that if they do succeed that fact can be attributed to their own efforts.

3. These characteristics are inherent in the entrepreneurial job, and thus people with high achievement motivation will be attracted to this type of work and, because they fit its requirement more closely, will be more likely to achieve success (business growth) (pp. 269–270).

The original grounding for this position came from research conducted in the 1960s (McClelland, 1961, 1962, 1965; McClelland and Winter, 1969). For a historical perspective on McClelland's thinking in this area see Miner (1980).

2. *Type A Personality*. A type A person, as distinct from the more placid type B, is aggressively involved in a chronic, incessant struggle to achieve more and more in less and less time, and if required to do so, against the opposing efforts of other things or persons. The link between type A personality and being a personal achiever is evident in this definition. There is also a link to heart disease (Schaubroeck, Ganster, and Kemmerer, 1994; Strube, 1991). However, it is increasingly apparent that there are variations within the type A concept; type As are not all the same (George, 1992; Spector and O'Connell, 1994).

Along these lines also, there is reason to believe that type A entrepreneurs may not be at as high a health risk (Lee, Ashford, and Bobko, 1990). This conclusion is consistent with my own impressions.

3. *Desire for Feedback on Achievements.* This is a component within the global concept of achievement motivation, or a closely related factor, depending on one's point of view. These are people who desire some clear index of the level of their performance, such as the annual dollar volume of sales generated by a business they head. Feedback of this kind has long been recognized for its motivational effects among certain kinds of people (see, for instance, Hackman and Oldham, 1980).

4. *Desire to Plan and Set Goals for Future Achievements.* This, too, may be described as an aspect of achievement motivation, or as a separate but closely allied factor. People like personal achievers often tend to think about the future and anticipate future possibilities. They like to plan, to set personal goals that will signify personal achievement, and to plot paths to these goals. The motivational effects of such goal setting on future accomplishments have been shown to be substantial (Locke and Latham, 1990).

5. *Strong Personal Initiative.* These are people whose achievements result from their own activities; they do not depend upon aid from others to get things accomplished. They are self-starters who do not require the support of people such as a superior or the members of a work group to initiate a course of action. The importance of "I did it myself" is just as manifest in this factor as in strong self-achievement motivation. Initiative is not a major characteristic contributing to managerial talent (Ghiselli, 1971). It is much more consistent with the personal achiever pattern.

6. *Strong Personal Commitment to Their Venture.* Personal achievers may be expected to possess a value-based identification with their ventures that is much like the commitment professionals often feel toward their professions. Probably, this sense of commitment relates to a desire to find out information and learn venture-relevant things as well. Mowday, Porter, and Steers (1982) define organizational commitment as the relative strength of an individual's identification and involvement in a particular organization. Conceptually, it can be characterized by at least three factors—a strong belief in and acceptance of the organization's goals and values, a willingness to exert considerable effort on behalf of the organization, and a strong desire to maintain membership in the organization. All three are congruent with the personal achiever designation.

7. *Desire to Obtain Information and Learn.* As manifested in the personal achiever, this is not the scholarly dedication of the intellectual; nor is it a love of learning, any learning, for its own sake. It is a very practical and pragmatic desire to acquire any and all information that will make the venture more successful. These people will work very hard to find out things that they believe will contribute to running the business more effectively. The importance of learning of this kind as new ventures develop is discussed at length in Woo, Daellenbach, and Nicholls-Nixon (1994).

8. *Internal Locus of Control.* Locus of control refers to people's perception of the extent to which control over events resides within themselves or is outside of them and beyond their influence. If people believe that they personally have control over what happens to them in life, they are considered to have an internal locus of control; they believe control is within themselves and that therefore they control their own destiny. This in turn makes planning possible, and contributes to the formulation of effective strategies (Miller, Kets de Vries, and Toulouse, 1982). An internal locus of control serves to facilitate throwing oneself into an endeavor, consistent with the personal achiever concept. There are also people who feel there is little they can do to affect what will happen to them. These individuals have an external locus of control; they believe control of events is outside of their influence and that they have little or no control over their own destiny. An external locus of control such as this does not fit with being a personal achiever.

9. *High Value Placed on Careers in Which Personal Goals, Individual Accomplishments, and the Demands of the Work Itself Govern.* This is in large part an individualistic ethic. These are people who believe a really good job is one where they set their own goals (not have them set for them), strive to accomplish those goals as they see fit (not as someone else prescribes), and live or die by the extent to which they correctly figure out what the task requires (not in terms of criteria established by others). For the personal achiever, careers of this kind are good careers. Research indicates that values of this kind clearly differentiate many entrepreneurs from corporate managers (Fagenson, 1993).

10. *Low Value Placed on Careers in Which Peer Groups Govern.* This is the opposite of a communal ethic. Personal achievers may be expected to shy away from participation in work groups that might pressure them into a course of action or make decisions for them. They believe in personal causation and personal responsibility. In an ideal work situation one can clearly identify who did the work and who should get the credit. To the extent group processes interfere with this they are to be avoided.

THE REAL MANAGER TYPE

Entrepreneurs carry the titles of top managers such as president and chief executive officer. Yet on psychological measures most of them do not score like top managers at all; they show much less evidence of managerial effectiveness on the average (Smith and Miner, 1983; Berman and Miner, 1985). If we look at corporate managers, and compare them to entrepreneurs on measures that are oriented toward entrepreneurship, we find that these managers do not look much like successful entrepreneurs either (Miner, 1990). How then can the real manager designation be used to specify a psychological pattern that contributes to entrepreneurial success?

One possibility is that many real manager entrepreneurs have at least one other pattern that is at a high level in addition to being real managers. What might happen is that entrepreneurs grow their firms in the early years utilizing other talents. Then as the operation becomes big enough, the real manager pattern begins to kick in. In some cases where the other talents do not exist, there may be partners who take up the slack. Also, a venture may have already completed its early stages of growth and reached the point where it is big enough to be managed; then being a real manager could help a great deal. This would be true of many purchased firms and of family businesses. Corporate ventures which operate in the context of a larger organization would also appear to benefit from the skills of a real manager (Stevenson and Jarillo, 1990). There are ventures as well which start big and need to be managed. They are well capitalized and they are able to employ many people from day one. The point is that, under the right circumstances, being a real manager and being a successful entrepreneur are not incompatible.

Because managing and managerial effectiveness have been studied extensively, it is possible to specify a number of factors that would be expected to contribute to a strong real manager pattern (Ghiselli, 1971; Miner, 1993). As a result, the real manager pattern contains some 13 different components. In a few cases these are related and may be partially overlapping, but there is enough range in personality represented here so that one person found to be a real manager need not be identical to another.

1. *High Supervisory Ability.* A person with this characteristic has the capacity to direct the work of others, and to organize and integrate their activities so that the goals of the organization can be attained. Unquestionably, there are variations from situation to situation, so that a person who is a good supervisor in one situation need not be equally good in another. Nevertheless, there is some communality across situations in the capacity to structure and direct the efforts of others, and it is this communality that is included in the concept of supervisory ability.

2. *Strong Self-Assurance.* This quality refers to the extent to which individuals perceive themselves as effective in dealing with problems that confront them. Unless managers have a feeling that they can cope, they are in immediate difficulty. Faith in oneself is essential if a person is to act at all effectively. Self-assurance provides a foundation, a support, which enables the individual to deal with problems. Thus, strong motivation of this kind would be likely to be a source of success.

3. *Strong Need for Occupational Advancement.* We tend to order occupations from the unskilled through the semiskilled, skilled, clerical, sales, middle management, to top management. Within this occupational hierarchy, some individuals are impelled to achieve appointments to high-level positions; these are individuals who need and seek the responsibility and the prestige which is associated with high position. Such people with a strong need for occupational achievement should be motivated to perform better as higher managerial levels come in view.

4. *Strong Need for Self-Actualization.* Some people need, and therefore seek,

the opportunity to utilize their talents to the fullest extent. They wish to be creative through the exercise of their own capabilities, and they feel strongly that those capabilities must not be left unfulfilled, but rather must be made manifest in concrete actions. For such people self-actualization is of paramount importance, and higher-level managerial work offers the discretion to self-actualize. Thus, managerial effectiveness becomes a goal of those who wish to self-actualize.

5. *Weak Need for Job Security*. Because of the uncertainties surrounding tenure in managerial positions, it appears that a need for job security is not an aspect of managerial talent. Those who seek managerial positions must know that they are not secure. To the contrary, it is those who lack a need for job security who are most likely to be attracted to management. Those who seek entry into managerial jobs, and who perform them best, should be people who are comfortable with the insecurities of managerial work, and thus who have a weak need for job security.

6. *Strong Personal Decisiveness*. Managers are frequently in a situation that calls for action, but with little information available. In many situations of this kind, such a long time would be required to collect additional information as to be impractical. Here good managers should utilize the meager information as best they can and make a decision; if they do not, the operations of the organization will be held up, perhaps with serious consequences. This capability is what is meant by strong personal decisiveness. It utilizes a talent that good managers must exhibit.

7. *Positive Attitudes toward Authority*. Managers are expected to behave in ways which do not provoke negative reactions from their superiors; ideally they will elicit positive reactions. They must be in a position to represent their units upward in the organization and to obtain support for their actions at higher levels. Negative attitudes would thwart this. There is a need for unrestricted communication up and down the hierarchy. Thus, positive attitudes toward authority should make for more effective managers.

8. *Desire to Compete with Others*. There is a strong competitive element built into managerial work. This is a function of the pyramidal nature of hierarchic organizations, with fewer and fewer positions present as one ascends the managerial hierarchy. Thus managers must compete for scarce rewards both for themselves and their groups, and those who enjoy doing so are likely to perform better; as a consequence they are likely to be more effective and successful managers.

9. *Desire to Assert Oneself*. Assertive people are inclined to take charge, make decisions, take disciplinary actions when needed, and protect others for whom they feel responsible. They do not lie back and wait for the action to come to them. Rather, they push forth and express their views. They are proactive, rather than reactive. Managing would appear to require this sort of person and in fact management training often attempts to develop this quality. Accordingly, assertiveness appears to be part of managerial talent.

10. *Desire to Exercise Power*. Managers in hierarchies not only interact with people upward (involving attitudes to authority) and laterally with peers (involving desires to compete), but downward as well. Here the need is to exercise power over subordinates, and direct their behavior in a manner consistent with organizational objectives. Managers must tell others what to do when this becomes necessary and enforce their words with appropriate use of positive and negative sanctions. Thus a more favorable attitude toward this type of activity, even an enjoyment of exercising power, should contribute to successful performance as a manager.

11. *Directive in Cognitive Style*. People with this characteristic focus on tasks and technical problems, giving particular attention to facts, rules, and procedures. Ambiguity and a lack of structure are not attractive to them, with the result that they try to reduce both. As managers, they are impersonal and know how to use power. They are forceful, and dislike committees and group decision making. They fit well with structured, goal-oriented organizations where power and authority are used to get things done as quickly as possible.

12. *Desire to Stand Out from the Crowd*. This is a desire to be distinct and different from others. The managerial job requires a person to behave in ways differing in a number of respects from the behavior of others in the same face-to-face group. An incumbent must in this sense stand out from the group and assume a position of high visibility. Managers who enjoy standing out from the crowd in this manner are more likely to meet this role requirement, and thus to prove effective in their work.

13. *Desire to Perform Managerial Tasks*. Individuals of this kind desire to perform the various routine activities associated with managerial work, and to do so in a responsible manner. These activities primarily involve communication and decision-making processes needed to get the work out and to keep on top of environmental demands. Again, desiring to do what the job requires should make for a better manager.

THE EXPERT IDEA GENERATOR TYPE

The number of characteristics used to identify expert idea generators is not as great as might be desired. Of the five factors involved, two are represented by intelligence and a desire to avoid taking risks. These were factors we knew we wanted to consider from the beginning, and two measures of each were incorporated. However, as the concept of an expert idea generator has developed, these have turned out to be supporting factors. They enter into the equation after it is established on other grounds that a person is an expert idea generator. At the core of the pattern itself there are fewer characteristics than there should be. This pattern became clearly evident as a major contributor to entrepreneurial success only after several years of accumulating data. Thus, the number of measures and factors is not very great, and the diversity or variation of characteristics within the pattern is rather limited.

1. *Desire to Personally Innovate.* To a large extent this is a characteristic that causes people to enjoy coming up with new ideas and getting them in play. However, it is also true that original, or novel, or creative, or innovative approaches have a distinctive quality that makes it easier to identify them as one's own, and thus take some personal credit for them. Entrepreneurial innovation can be truly creative in that the idea has not existed before (Kao, 1995). A good source of information on how creativity operates is a book by Runco and Albert (1990).

2. *Conceptual in Cognitive Style.* These are people who love ideas and enjoy solving problems. They have a high tolerance for ambiguity, may take risks, and are often creative. They are insightful and enthusiastic, show concern for others' views, are adaptive and flexible, use intuition, and seek new ideas. Their strong motives include a desire for recognition, a need for independence, and a desire to pursue personal goals. They like loose, decentralized organizational structures. Research indicates that this type of cognitive style can play an important role in determining how entrepreneurs approach their firms (Buttner and Gryskiewicz, 1993).

3. *Belief in New Product Development as a Key Element of Company Strategy.* Whether or not they personally are involved in developing new products and services, and it is very likely that they are involved, these are people who consider new product development important in a company's strategic picture. Relative to such approaches as advertising, delivery, discounts, packaging, price, quality, reciprocity, reputation, sales force, services, and variety, new product development stands very high. If it is not rated as the major strategic factor, it comes close. This is a factor that has been found to be very important in the success of inventor-entrepreneurs and their firms (Miner, Smith, and Bracker, 1992a).

4. *High Intelligence.* Intelligence is a major factor in the career performance of people generally (Herrnstein and Murray, 1994), and thus would be expected to have an impact with all types of entrepreneurs. However, because ideas are at the heart of both intelligence and the expert idea generator type, it plays a particularly crucial role for expert idea generators. Intelligence is considered to involve such capabilities as judgment and reasoning, and the capacity to deal with ideas, abstractions, and concepts. It includes other qualities, too, such as the ability to learn, insightfulness, and the capacity to analyze and to synthesize. General intelligence has often been found to be well predicted by vocabulary tests.

5. *Desire to Avoid Taking Risks.* There have been those who have argued that entrepreneurs should be high risk takers, and there have been others who took the view that a 50–50 risk was more their style. With regard to even the latter view Raynor (in Atkinson and Raynor, 1974) has this to say:

Decisions of success-oriented individuals should not consist of a series of immediate risks in which there is a 50–50 chance of failure, but rather should reflect a much lower degree of risk. . . . since immediate failure has the consequence of failure to achieve the career goal (operating a successful company) through loss of the opportunity to continue its pursuit (pp. 146–147).

In this view entrepreneurs may be much more risk avoiders than many have envisioned. This is particularly important for expert idea generators because their enthusiasm for ideas and innovation may lead them into actions that threaten the venture. For the venture to survive, some counterforce must operate to restrain this enthusiasm; this is the role of a desire to avoid taking risks. Research indicates that entrepreneurs as a group are not pronounced risk takers (Palich and Bagby, 1995).

THE EMPATHIC SUPERSALESPERSON TYPE

Empathic supersalespeople make their ventures work because they can sell sufficient product or services to generate the cash flow needed to keep the firm afloat, and sometimes a great deal more. They do this by catering to the needs of clients or customers, thus helping them to cope with a problem. This service emphasis may be set in contrast to a sales procedure that emphasizes managing the customer into a sale through processes of heavy persuasion and the use of power. One approach focuses on the concerns of the customer, the other focuses somewhat more on the concerns of the salesperson (Oakes, 1990).

The empathic supersalesperson pattern is not something we had in mind at the beginning of our studies. It came into focus gradually as the research progressed and we saw more and more entrepreneurs of this type. As a consequence, there are not a large number of characteristics involved and the test battery is somewhat deficient in this area. Relying on happenstance, it is surprising that we were able to establish that high scores on even as many as five factors contribute to the pattern. When the research began there was nothing in the literature to suggest these empathic supersalespeople would emerge as a distinct type.

1. *Empathic in Cognitive Style*. Empathic people enjoy pleasing others, dislike dealing with problems that require them to face the unpleasant, are responsive and sympathetic to other people's problems, emphasize the human aspects in dealing with managerial concerns, and view problems of inefficiency and ineffectiveness largely in terms of interpersonal and human difficulties. They acquire information by sensing, listening, and interacting with people and they evaluate information by using their feelings and instincts. They have little tolerance for ambiguity. In general they are sociable, friendly, and supportive. They have a talent for building teams, encourage participation at work, like to hold meetings, and are action oriented. Acceptance by others and avoidance of conflict are important to them. Entrepreneurs with this characteristic would be expected to be good at forging strategic alliances outside their ventures (Eisenhardt and Schoonhoven, 1996).

2. *Desire to Help Others*. Inherent in the empathic style is the idea of enjoying being of service to and helping others. However, this characteristic can be embedded in a larger desire for positive social interaction generally. Yet there are people whose social needs are in large part restricted to situations where they can help others. This is the kind of motivation that characterizes the helping professions and it is in fact a major requirement of much professional work. These are people who want to assist people with their problems and do for them what they cannot do for themselves.

This desire to help others with their problems may arise entirely out of a strong concern for others, a warm and understanding need to be of service to those who require assistance. It may also on occasion be tinged with a sense of internal satisfaction on the part of the people doing the helping that stems from the recognition that they are strong enough to give help rather than having to receive it (McClelland, 1975). Either way, the desire to help comes through and customers are motivated to return the favor by buying the product.

3. *High Value Attached to Social Processes*. This characteristic reflects the person's work values. These people consider various kinds of social processes to have a great deal of importance in their lives. They value such things as making a contribution to society, having co-workers who are pleasant and agreeable, being valued as a person and thus having the esteem of others, having the opportunity to meet people and interact with them, and receiving recognition from others for doing a good job. In short, their value systems incorporate a strong emphasis on social interaction and relationships with other people. This in turn facilitates the sales process.

4. *Strong Need for Harmonious Social Relationships*. These are people who not only derive satisfaction from friendly personal relations with others, but may actually need good relations to feel at ease and secure. Their self-esteem can be dependent on how others regard them and relate to them. Thus they are concerned about what others think and they are sensitive to what people around them feel. Encouraging those with whom they work to participate in decision making and to offer new ideas or a different approach to a problem comes easily to them. When describing a person they find very difficult to work with, they are likely to say:

You may be a very poor coworker, you may be frustrating, inefficient, or lazy. But the coworker role is just one of many, and that doesn't mean that you might not be quite pleasant or worthwhile in other respects (Fiedler and Garcia, 1987, p. 76).

There is thus a tendency to see the best in others, and to feel that doing one's work efficiently is not the only basis for defining a person's worth. This on occasion can produce problems in the leadership role, but it makes for positive relationships with customers and helps to cement a sale.

5. *Belief in the Sales Force as a Key Element of Company Strategy*. Whether they personally are part of the sales force or not, these are individuals who

consider a sales force to be an important means of implementing company strategies. Relative to approaches such as advertising, delivery, discounts, new product development, packaging, price, quality, reciprocity, reputation, services, and variety, the sales force stands very high in their minds. It may not be the single most dominant approach, but if not, it is not far behind.

CONCLUSION

The four-way psychological typology as set forth here contains the following:

1. The personal achiever type, with 10 inherent characteristics.
2. The real manager type, with 13 inherent characteristics.
3. The expert idea generator type, with five inherent characteristics.
4. The empathic supersalesperson type, with five inherent characteristics.

All four types are hypothesized to contribute to reaching entrepreneurial success with a venture that experiences substantial growth. This is the typology which guided our research and which that research tested. It is by no means "carved in stone." Subsequent work may well add more inherent characteristics to the four lists.

Chapter 3 extends the theory by considering the routes to success that fit each type, and the pitfalls that exist along those routes. Hypotheses dealing with the case where multiple types exist in the same person are set forth. Chapter 3 also uses the theory in an attempt to move toward a definition of entrepreneurship.

Chapter 3

Theoretical Extensions of the Typology

A good typology will possess "added value" in that it serves to generate additional hypotheses beyond the core typology itself. The idea that entrepreneurs of each type must follow career routes that fit their psychological make-up if they are to reach success is an instance of this added value; so, too, are the other theoretical extensions and hypotheses considered in this chapter.

The subject of entrepreneurial careers has received increasing attention recently (see, for instance, Dyer, 1992, 1994). My approach to this topic is that the career route should implement the special talents of the entrepreneur, and only if this is done is career success likely to be reached. Thus, personal achievers should follow an achieving route, real managers a managing route, expert idea generators an idea-generating route, and empathic supersalespeople a selling route. Put somewhat differently, each type should actualize its potential or "do their own thing." To the extent, and for whatever reason, this does not occur, the theory anticipates a lower level of success, trending into failure.

This is a fit or congruence formulation. Such theories propose a fit among various factors including personality, strategy, organizational structure, and environment. This type of formulation regarding firm success is widely utilized in the entrepreneurship field, although it is not always labeled using the fit terminology (Bouchikhi, 1993; Carsrud, Olm, and Thomas, 1989; Duchesneau and Gartner, 1990; Ginn and Sexton, 1990; Naman and Slevin, 1993; Slevin and Covin, 1990).

The fit considered here is between personality type and the behavior an entrepreneur exhibits in his or her relationship with the venture. Over time this behavior becomes a career route. The personality-career route relationship is mediated by the entrepreneur's strategy for the firm. This strategy is a reflection of the entrepreneur's personality. More often than not it is a growth strategy of some kind (McDougall and Robinson, 1990; Mosakowski, 1993). It may be implicit or explicit.

The following discussions are intended to flesh out the four career routes and are based on my experience in working with a large number of entrepreneurs whose personality types were known to me.

THE ACHIEVING ROUTE (THE FIT FOR THE PERSONAL ACHIEVER TYPE)

Personal achievers are best described as traditional or classic entrepreneurs. They should take on an entrepreneurial role because their talents will not be utilized fully in any other capacity. Certainly, they can do other things, especially if they show other patterns above and beyond that of personal achiever. They are particularly likely to perform well in other roles, such as that of a corporate manager, if they see that role as a means to gaining needed experience before entering upon an entrepreneurial career. But ultimately, these people tend to run afoul of other systems, such as the large corporation; not because they have problems with authority necessarily, but because they want to do their own thing and follow their own path. Often they break out into entrepreneurship because an employer will not follow a course that they are absolutely sure will work. Yet just as often they start upon an entrepreneurial career early because they are convinced that no one else can do it as well as they can. They are less likely to come to entrepreneurship from the ranks of the unemployed (Kirchhoff, 1996).

These are extremely hard-working people and as long as it is entrepreneurial in nature, they love their work. They are loath to seek retirement, and may continue to work at their firms well into their 70s and even 80s (Sonnenfeld, 1988). They may in fact refuse to let go, and may relinquish the reins only because a board of directors requires it, or as a result of legal action. The tenacity with which these entrepreneurs can seek to hold onto their firms and their work is amazing.

The personal achiever pattern contains a number of interrelated characteristics, many of which are directly related to entrepreneurial success (Bird, 1989). In some cases the components of the personal achiever pattern are unique to successful entrepreneurship; in some cases they overlap with success in other spheres, but taken as a whole those who score high on this pattern, and no other pattern, would do best to become entrepreneurs. Of the four patterns, this is the only one that is distinctly entrepreneurial in nature.

An analogy to the football quarterback has been proposed by Galbraith (1982); it fits the successful personal achiever well. The idea is that in the early stages of a venture, structuring the work and the organization is not important. Success comes from energy, commitment, confidence, esprit de corps, and in fact a belief that structuring would be harmful. The leader, as quarterback, is an active doer as well. Early on they establish new ways and serve as team leaders.

Later on they become recruiters, schedulers, budgeters, and anything else the venture may require. Managing in the usual sense is only a small part of the process. There are many things to be done, few people to do them, and even fewer who have any specialized expertise in an area. The personal achiever thus becomes the company expert in many areas simply because someone has to handle them, and energy more than initial knowledge comes to be the deter- mining factor. One learns very rapidly under these circumstances.

The achieving route is one of doing, as much or more than managing, han- dling crises as best one can when they arise, and thus constantly putting out fires. But through it all the goal is to make a first down, and then another, and ultimately to score; except that for personal achievers scoring, and winning, is not a matter of field goals and touchdowns, but of dollar volume of sales, num- ber of employees, and profit margins. These people work very hard, put in extremely long hours, and may find themselves in any area of the business at a point in time. They are generalists in the true sense of the word, but they are not necessarily general managers. More often than not they are general doers. They wear many hats, changing them constantly.

Vesper (1980, 1990) describes a number of occupational starting points for entrepreneurs, including school to venture, job to venture, unemployment to venture, home to venture, and sequential entrepreneurship. There are several variants on each theme. However, the important point is that no one of these is especially typical of the personal achiever.

Entrepreneurs of this type need to couple their high energy level with a firm (either initiated or already existing) where they can put that energy to work in a satisfying way. The catalyst for this process is sufficient knowledge of the business to warrant the relationship. This knowledge may be very complex and require a long period of learning, or may be relatively simple and demand only minimal preparation. Either way there is still some level of experience or learn- ing related to the specific business and its industry that is needed. This knowl- edge is rarely complete at the time the entrepreneur-firm relationship is formed, but a complete lack almost guarantees failure.

One approach that personal achievers may use to deal with this problem is to hire the expertise and then learn from this person. This may be a consultant or a full-time employee. The risk here is that the expert has a degree of power inherent in his or her knowledge and this power may be misused. Yet this approach is employed, and sometimes with great success. Another strategy is to work with a partner who knows the business, at least long enough to become knowledgeable oneself. Most personal achievers would prefer not to do this, but it may be necessary. In some fields it is possible to start very small, perhaps as a one-person operation, and grow the business as one learns. Usually, these are relatively simple businesses where the knowledge base is not very complex. Risk is held down by the fact that in the early period the business is so small that there is little to lose.

These are all strategies that involve gaining knowledge after the fact. Much more common is the situation where the entrepreneur gains knowledge through some combination of schooling and non-entrepreneurial work experience prior to entering into the venture. Sometimes the venture idea comes out of this experience; sometimes it precedes it, and the learning is specifically crafted to maximize the return to the venture. Probably, the latter approach is the ideal. In any event the educational aspect of the personal achiever's career route may take a variety of forms. It may vary not only in what is learned (depending on the nature of the business) but also in its length (depending on the complexity of the knowledge base and the strategy utilized).

HOW THE PERSONAL ACHIEVER–ACHIEVING ROUTE FIT CAN FAIL

The possibility exists that personal achievers may be diverted from the achieving route, and end up someplace quite distant from their objective. One such scenario is that they enter upon a venture without a method of providing for the necessary knowledge, misdirect their energies, and because the essential catalyst is lacking, misfire completely. The solution in this instance is to make sure some provision is made to introduce the necessary learning and experience.

At a later point something may happen to divert or prevent a personal achiever from focusing the requisite energy on the business. This can be as simple as a lack of understanding of how the type of person and the approach to firm development must fit. The younger the person the more likely this will occur. Here the solution is some type of intervention that brings about a better fit. Counseling can be very effective. Even personal achievers with considerable experience, and yet a record of something less than full entrepreneurial success, can benefit.

There are also instances in which personal achievers are forced out of the achieving route, or thwarted so that it is not meaningfully available. This often occurs in corporate venturing or turnaround situations where corporate officers, for whatever strategic reasons, step in and limit the full use of the achieving route. In my experience, corporate venturing of one kind or another frequently produces rapid turnover among personal achievers; this appears to be because these entrepreneurs are kept from using their talents. The corporate structure is simply too restrictive of the unstructured achieving route, and something has to give.

However, there are many other factors that can operate to produce a lack of the necessary fit. Bankers or venture capitalists may impose an incongruent approach, thus unwittingly thwarting the venture at an early point. Family members who retain sizable ownership shares may do the same in family businesses. There is also the matter of family time. The achieving route by its very nature requires that substantial amounts of time be devoted to the business. This can produce conflict, and feelings of rejection (Parasuraman, Purohit, and Godshalk, 1996). In my experience divorce is not an infrequent consequence, and this can occur just as often when the entrepreneur is a female as a male.

Once a personal achiever latches onto the achieving route, there is little likelihood that he or she can be diverted from it; it is simply too satisfying of everything the entrepreneur is made of—and too highly reinforced by the mores of a capitalistic society as well. Now, if counseling is to succeed, it must be directed to helping others understand why personal achievers must follow the achieving route and why doing so both produces economic success and is so satisfying to the entrepreneur personally.

Above and beyond all this, there is another problem that arises because, as firms grow the way personal achievers want to grow them, there finally comes a time where the demands of the situation exceed what the personal achiever can provide. After all, the achieving route is an approach for relatively small organizations. With real entrepreneurial success comes a point where systems, structure, hierarchy, managing, and the like are needed. Here the achieving approach simply runs out of gas (Galbraith, 1982; Churchill and Lewis, 1983; Mintzberg, 1984).

This situation has been well described by Dyer (1992):

Like the marathon runners who "hit the wall" of fatigue at a certain point in the race and must overcome exhaustion to finish, some entrepreneurs describe a feeling of "hitting the wall" as their organizations begin to grow and become more complex. At some point in their company's development, they finally realize that they have created a business that they themselves do not fully understand and are unable fully to control. In my experience, this phenomenon seems to occur as an organization grows to have about twenty-five employees and sales of $1 to $3 million. Of course, there are exceptions to this rule, depending on the industry, product line, or company strategy and the entrepreneur's ability to deal with complexity. Still, it seems to be a threshold where the organization either continues to grow and develop or stagnates because the entrepreneur is unable to move to the next level. It appears to be much easier to go from $6 to $10 million in sales than from $1 to $5 million, even though the difference in each case is $4 million (p. 111).

Hitting the wall in this manner can mean the end of growth. The personal achiever simply settles for what he or she can handle using the achieving route and plateaus the business. Alternatively, a personal achiever may try to take the business on up while still using the achieving route. It won't work any longer, but the entrepreneur typically finds that out too late. The result may be bankruptcy, a takeover by creditors, a forced sale, whatever. In any event, the personal achiever loses control of the business and is pushed out.

However, there is one other scenario; that is, to put management and structure into the previously unstructured firm. If the personal achiever is also a real manager, this transition presents few problems. The entrepreneur merely shifts gears, and emphasizes a new aspect of his or her repertoire of talents. But often, this is not possible. At this point the only way for the personal achiever to retain control of the firm is to give up power over day-to-day operations, while retaining strategic control. This may mean bringing in a general manager or it may mean building an effective management team. The key point is that if the entrepreneur cannot introduce managed and structured hierarchy to cope with increased size, someone else has to be induced to do so. With appropriate attention and guidance, personal achievers can handle this transition and retain control, but it is often a delicate balancing act.

It is well to be aware also that the problems are not ended when firms make the shift from achieving to managing. Growth continues, often phenomenal growth. Yet for a number of reasons even these large firms ultimately face the prospect of decline (Levinson, 1994). Just as certain psychological dynamics may constrain the use of the achieving route, other dynamics can impinge upon the use of a managed hierarchy. Miller (1990) has elaborated more specifically with regard to firms coming out of the personal achiever tradition. In these firms there is the risk that strategies will ultimately lead to overexpansion, that goals will extend beyond growth to grandeur, that organizational cultures will take on the character of the gamesman, and that structures will become excessively fractured. A firm is not home-free when the transition from achieving to managed organization is made. Psychological dynamics continue to impose a threat, although of a much different kind.

THE MANAGING ROUTE (THE FIT FOR THE REAL MANAGER TYPE)

It is not uncommon for real managers to pursue a managerial career in a large organization for some time prior to becoming entrepreneurs. Unlike the personal achievers, this is not done primarily for training purposes; it is a career in and of itself, although much learning that is subsequently put to use in the venture may occur. Often the move to entrepreneuring is prompted by the fact that a major opportunity presents itself or on occasion a strictly managerial career runs into difficulties. In recent years, as large corporations have resorted to downsizing, many managers have found themselves unemployed. Starting a business under these circumstances is to be recommended only if one has the appropriate characteristics. Being a good manager only is unlikely to be enough.

The managing route within entrepreneurship means finding or starting a venture large enough to utilize managerial skills. Within entrepreneurship the managing route is primarily a supplement that makes it possible to avoid "hitting the wall." The fact that a number of ventures are able to keep growing beyond the point where they would be expected to run into difficulty with a personal achiever or expert idea generator or empathic supersalespeople at the helm is now well established (Daily and Dalton, 1992; Osborne, 1994; Willard, Krueger, and Feeser, 1992). One way this occurs is that the entrepreneur has a complex personality make-up, and one of the strong patterns present is that of the real manager.

Being a real manager is also valuable to those pursuing a career in corporate venturing, but again as a supplement to other patterns. The real manager capability is valuable in bridging the culture gap between corporate management and venture operations. Not surprisingly, real managers can make the transition to company management rather easily should they sell their firm and accept an employment contract with the purchaser. Personal achievers, in contrast, often have a great deal of difficulty with this type of transition.

Once established in a venture of some size, what the real manager brings to the organization is a capacity to manage it into substantial growth. Standardized procedures are introduced, the organization structure is stabilized, managers are developed, systems are put in place, and so on. This is the managing route in entrepreneurship. It is the process of institutionalizing the venture. Real managers are very good at this, and if they are to grow beyond the small business category, ventures absolutely need real managers who are following the managing route.

Another aspect of real managers is that they can be quite effective in sales occupations. Our research has often found that within a particular company the sales managers are the managers that exhibit the strongest managerial pattern. This tie between managing and sales appears to occur because both managing and selling involve influencing other people to do what one wishes. A manager tends to have more authority that can be brought to bear in this process, but this is not universally true. There are sales situations where the salesperson has considerable leverage. Reciprocity situations, for instance, almost require that a buyer purchase from a particular source; all that is needed is to make it very clear that reciprocity is expected.

In any event real managers can be very effective at selling if the context is one where they can manage people into buying their product or service. They certainly do not sell in the same way that empathic supersalespeople do and by no means are all true managers attracted to a sales career. But if such an attraction does develop, they can often bring their managerial skills to bear in the sales process and achieve considerable success.

HOW THE REAL MANAGER–MANAGING ROUTE FIT CAN FAIL

Managers, even highly motivated and talented managers, need to know how to go about managing. The best way to gain this kind of experience is to manage for someone else for a while. There are other ways, but this is the preferred route for an entrepreneur. Those who do not learn how to manage, and there is a substantial knowledge component here, are not going to achieve the necessary fit even if they are real managers. A major problem is that if one has never managed, it is very difficult to achieve the requisite skills. You have to learn managing while doing it, in most cases. The work that we have done on how managers cope with ineffective performance in subordinates provides a good example (Miner, 1985). Management training programs and some MBA programs often try to teach managing to people that have never actually experienced the subject matter. The result can be catastrophic. The point is that the real manager-managing fit can go wrong because entrepreneurial managers move too quickly into managing. They do not yet know what they are doing.

A related problem arises when entrepreneurs try to manage ventures that are still too small to experience benefits from the managerial approach. Building a substantial amount of structure and using highly standardized systems in very small firms can yield major problems; the achieving approach is to be preferred. Partners of a different ilk and the presence of a supplementary pattern such as that of the personal achiever can head off this problem. But without these, real managers tend to manage very small firms into either failure or bare survival simply because their firms are not yet ready for their particular talents. Managing is not the route to success when there is very little to manage.

When firms are at a size where there are sufficient employees to manage, and the managing route is now appropriate for real managers, things can still go astray. One tendency is for real managers who have established an affinity for selling to continue down the selling route, when a delicate shift from managing customers to managing employees would contribute more to the firm, given its current state of growth. Normally, people with management potential like to manage, and will seek it out. This is not always true among the very young, however, who have not yet learned to tie their managerial yearnings to actual managerial work. Thus it is possible for real managers to strive for some other use of their talents than managing. The alignment can go wrong, with the result that real managers attempt to become empathic supersalespeople or personal achievers, or expert idea generators (which they are not) and as a result go astray. It is essential that real managers stick to the use of their managerial talents as their firms continue to grow.

Finally, as companies continue to grow under the impetus of a real manager, there comes a time when their trajectory leads to a strategy that is best described as technical tinkering, to goals which move very close to impossible perfection, to an organizational culture that is technocratically dominated, and to a highly rigid structure (Miller, 1990). The result is that the potential for adjustment to environmental change is lost and the firm becomes at risk. After many years, heavily managed firms can lose the capacity for adaptation; this is not always true, and it is certainly not a subject for concern in the early years, but it can pose a threat later on.

A major factor here seems to be whether the company has accumulated extensive knowledge of its industry and thus the capacity to predict changes. Real managers who continue to keep on top of their technologies, their markets, and changes in their human resource bases do not get caught in this focusing trajectory—they can adapt, and do. Thus an important guideline for the real manager is to stay sufficiently attentive to the environment outside the company, to learn new things, and to run the organization in such a way as to be continually ready for change.

THE IDEA GENERATING ROUTE (THE FIT FOR THE EXPERT IDEA GENERATOR TYPE)

Expert idea generators are, as the name would imply, people who have ideas, and act on them. They may be inventors who think up new products and pursue their development, but they may have innovative ideas of many other kinds as well. These can involve market niches, ways of obtaining competitive advantage, innovations in administrative process, or any other factor in which a capacity to think better can contribute to business success.

In some cases these are people who become tremendously enthused about their ideas and devote a great deal of energy to implementing them. Unlike the personal achiever, however, who devotes huge amounts of energy to the venture as a whole, expert idea generators focus their energy more narrowly on the idea itself. If the idea fails and the venture moves off in other directions, they tend to lose interest. Alternatively, their energies in support of ideas may be focused primarily on persuading others to implement what they have created. Here the emphasis is on raising capital, getting potential implementers involved, obtaining government support, and the like. Thus expert idea generators may or may not be strong on personal follow-through. This factor, in and of itself, is not a key to their success. Those whose ideas are so compelling, or whose persuasion is so effective that others will bid in on the venture, can do just as well as those whose enthusiasm for what they have created leads them to invest a great deal of personal energy in it.

Many of these firms have their origins in corporate venturing. They may begin with ideas that are spawned by someone within a larger corporation and end up encompassed within an entirely owned corporate venture, or there may be a spin-off of the venture, or an independent breakaway. In the high-technology area in particular, large capital needs and the importance of technological backing may foster considerable early corporate or government involvements (Burgelman and Sayles, 1986; Roberts, 1991). However, the idea generating route is not limited to high technology, and it can well involve an independent start-up.

The distinguishing characteristic of expert idea generators is that they are experts at something. That means there has to be a period during which they become experts, and then an opportunity to think of ways to put this expertise to work in novel and creative ways. Often they are able to take their thinking to the frontiers of knowledge in an area, and then because they know enough to understand where the frontiers are located, they can go one step beyond. This one step has the potential for giving a sizable competitive advantage, simply because no one else is operating quite this way.

The idea generating career route must contain a period in which people are educated up to the point of being an expert. Formal education would appear to offer major advantages in this regard. Here the emphasis is entirely on learning, and material is presented with the learning objective in mind. More informal learning on the job is less economical simply because it is interspersed with a great deal of doing as well, and perhaps some irrelevant learning in addition. On the other hand, there are many important aspects of business that are not taught in school. Certain whole fields of business activity simply are not to be found in educational curricula.

In any event, because of the time needed for a great deal of learning, expert idea generators tend to be somewhat older than other entrepreneurs. They also tend to dislike, and shy away from, highly structured and regulated employment situations. They need the freedom to think for themselves, to have ideas even if not very good ones, which they later must discard. This freedom to create and try out ideas is crucial. The idea generating route requires that this opportunity exist. Often what pushes expert idea generators into entrepreneurship is that they feel stifled where they are.

As noted previously, by no means do all expert idea generators find entrepreneurship, nor should they find it. In this respect empathic supersalespeople, real managers, and expert idea generators have something in common. Typically, expert idea generators become involved in their ventures because they want to follow the idea generating route and thus have the freedom to develop their ideas. Entrepreneurship can offer that. However, if they can find this same freedom elsewhere, they may never have the need to become entrepreneurs. Many academic settings, research laboratories, professional firms, and the like do offer this freedom. Thus, a big factor in the entrepreneurial decision for people of this type is whether they already have a work situation that permits them to use their talents. It is not infrequent that what appears to be a very positive work setting begins to go bad for some reason, and becomes more restrictive. At that point the transition to one's own venture becomes almost automatic. It is the only apparent way to follow the idea generating trajectory.

Expert idea generators have in common with personal achievers the fact that they can put a tremendous amount of energy into their ventures. However, there is a big if—only if they are in the process of developing, testing, implementing an idea that is important to them, or a set of ideas. Some work better with partners, often partners that add other psychological patterns, or areas of expertise to the business. As the firm grows to greater size, the need for managerial skills becomes important in exactly the same way it does for the personal achiever. Expert idea generators can "hit the wall" too.

All these considerations suggest that people of this type would benefit from the possession of multiple patterns. This is in fact true. Following the idea generating route appears to be more successful when the person has other capabilities to bring to bear as well. However, those whose entrepreneurial talents are limited to the expert idea generator pattern alone can follow the idea generating route to success by focusing on the visionary role in the firm. They are particularly helped by partners, with whom they are unlikely to have major difficulties. Many also appear to benefit from some type of backing by a parent corporation, a relative, an angel, or anyone else who can provide resources while imposing relatively few restrictions on the entrepreneur's freedom (Freear, Sohl,

and Wetzel, 1995). Backing of this kind may in fact be essential to carry out
the ideas. One hears of a number of benevolent benefactors in talking to expert
idea generators.

HOW THE EXPERT IDEA GENERATOR–IDEA
GENERATING ROUTE FIT CAN FAIL

If one wishes to keep expert idea generators from following the idea generating route, the best way is to stifle their ideas. This can be accomplished by
introducing a work climate for them that does the following:

1. Stresses that there is only one best way of doing things.
2. Reacts quickly and negatively to any expression of new ideas.
3. Opposes anything that is not easy to understand.
4. Emphasizes that new ideas bring only trouble.
5. Sees that rewards never go to people who produce new ideas.
6. Keeps people with new ideas under tight control and, if that does not work, ostracizes
   them.

This formulation draws upon Taylor (1972) and also on a more recent statement set forth by McCaskey (1982). Expert idea generators escape to entrepreneurship to avoid these kinds of unfavorable climates. If they have successful
ventures this escape does in fact accomplish its goal. However, an escape to
entrepreneuring can be doomed, also. Corporate ventures, family businesses,
situations where equity is lost to investors and venture capitalists—all of these
can produce climates just as negative for ideas as the one described above. Even
a solely owned start-up can stifle ideas if there are no resources to carry the
ideas out. This is why benevolent benefactors can be so important for expert
idea generators.

Without doubt the most important factor contributing to a separation of the
expert idea generator from the idea generating route is the existence of an in-
hibiting climate for the venture. It is difficult if not impossible for the entrepreneur to do his or her thing in these situations. Another difficulty that may arise
is that the entrepreneur does not become a full-fledged expert—the ideas that
are generated are, so-to-speak, "half-baked." This can happen in a number of
ways—not taking enough time to become expert; poor education; learning on
the job, which does not expose a person to the really important information;
and so on.

Learning within a family business can be particularly risky in this regard. If
the business has gotten behind in some way, and the learning that is really
needed does not exist within it, one can learn by rising within the family business, and never get to be a full-scale expert. The problem is that such people

may come to think they have reached expert knowledge because they have never been exposed to anything else beyond what the family business has to offer.

It is also possible for the expert idea generator to get diverted from the idea generating route on an entirely voluntary basis. There are entrepreneurs who become expert in one area and then think they see an opportunity in another area, thus leaving their area of expertise. An example would be a banker, with small business loan experience, who is really a financial expert, faced with an opportunity to purchase a business in some other area such as manufacturing. The ideas of a financial nature that this person could bring to bear simply will not be sufficient in the new area. Similarly, it is important that expert idea generators remain in the visionary role, implementing ideas in which they believe. If they are drawn heavily into general management or sales, especially if a brain child of theirs is not involved, they can get diverted from the idea generating route, and trouble is to be expected.

For all of these reasons, and perhaps more that we are not aware of, expert idea generators who exhibit only this pattern are a vulnerable lot. Their firms may well suffer during recession, and ups and downs often seem to occur. This is not always true, and indeed some expert idea generators hit upon a great idea and never stop growing. However, periodic vulnerability appears more common. Yet these firms seem to survive. The reason is that, faced with a problem, these are people who can think their way out.

What seems to happen is that, being dependent on the ideas of a single person, these firms do not diversify easily, simply because they have to stay within the field of expertise of the lead entrepreneur. Because they do not diversify, they are vulnerable to both economic recession and even better ideas stemming from the competition. Yet at the same time they do have a true visionary, ready to come up with problem-solutions that can reverse any downward trend. More often than not reversal does occur.

This brings us to the problem of risk taking. We have seen that expert idea generators need to be risk-avoidant, but sometimes this is not part of the mix. There is ample reason to believe that a major factor in small company failure is the adoption of a strategic stance which places the entire company at high risk, frequently in connection with some large-scale new activity that puts the company as currently constituted on the line. The argument that effective entrepreneurs must avoid risks does not mean that they do not take what others perceive as risks, however. Uncertainty exists in the eyes of the beholder; to be successful, entrepreneurs must avoid risk to the degree possible, wherever they see it. Yet the ideal situation for an entrepreneur is one where others perceive that a high degree of risk exists, and thus high rewards are warranted, and the entrepreneur with his or her knowledge sees practically no risk at all.

On the other hand, it cannot be denied that successful entrepreneurs do on occasion take what anyone, including themselves, would view as risks. This appears to happen not out of any desire to gamble or to take risks per se, but because some other strong motive, such as a desire to introduce innovative solutions, drives behavior, transcends the desire to avoid taking risks, and results as a side effect in a certain amount of risk-taking behavior.

Many entrepreneurs are extremely cautious and want to be absolutely sure before they take the plunge. This becomes crucial for expert idea generators because their ideas can be quite outlandish. These are people who think up things that others would never think of. They have no referents to compare against; they can be very far out in left field indeed. Furthermore, their enthusiasms can carry them away. Creative ideas have some redeeming social value; crazy ideas do not. The difference is very hard to establish when one is riding on a wave of inspirational zeal. Thus a tendency to avoid risks, to counteract the enthusiasm, to hold back and wait, to be absolutely sure the idea will work, is essential if the expert idea generator is actually to achieve success. As many of these people will tell you, creative ideas are a dime a dozen; what really matters is figuring out which ones will sell. The world of high technology, for instance, is littered with investors who were sold on an idea by a "great genius" who never did take time to think through exactly how the idea might be brought to market (and in fact did not really care much about such mundane things). Handling risks of this kind is crucial to effectively pursue the idea generating route.

What happens to the idea generating route over the long haul? According to Miller (1990), there is a risk that these firms will essentially retire into themselves. Invention becomes not only the name of the game but the only game; it serves as an end in itself, while client needs are ignored. In this scenario the company's strategy becomes one of high-technology escapism, its goal a kind of technical utopia. The culture moves to that of a think tank, rather than a competitive firm, and the structure of the organization disintegrates into chaos. What is described here is a company that mirrors the innovation of the expert idea generator, but now without the pragmatism that comes with a desire to avoid risks. It is as if success has stripped off the risk-avoidance feature. In all likelihood this is a pitfall that can come into play at any point in the thinking trajectory.

THE SELLING ROUTE (THE FIT FOR THE EMPATHIC SUPERSALESPERSON TYPE)

There is nothing that says empathic supersalespeople have to become entrepreneurs to utilize their talents and achieve satisfaction. Opportunity and the pressure of circumstances may move certain empathic supersalespeople into the entrepreneurial domain, but many others remain employed by corporations throughout their careers, or work in occupations such as manufacturer's representative, real estate sales, and the like, which are best described as semi-entrepreneurial in nature. Certainly, the ties to entrepreneurship are there and it seems to come naturally for many empathic supersalespeople to move over into some type of venture, but these people can function well in various organizational contexts as well.

Supersalespeople usually find sales and marketing at an early age. Their careers frequently run through this route, although this is not universally the case. Ultimately, however, they get heavily involved in the sales process. Because selling is not easily learned in school, they are likely to have fewer years of education, and more years of sales experience. They tend to learn on the job, rather than through formal education. To the extent their education permits, they often take courses in marketing and communications which relate to the selling process.

Knowledge of the business is important, but beyond that a person who is to be the premier salesperson should be familiar with the product or service being sold. For empathic supersalespeople, this product or service familiarity typically is obtained on the job, selling. Usually, there is a start in a junior sales position with another company. In the case of family businesses, they often work their way up through sales and marketing positions within the firm, however, and it is not unheard of to start a venture directly out of school selling it into growth from a very small beginning.

A major problem for people who fit this pattern is that they are likely to be continually pulled back into administration and operations. This is less troublesome if the firm is limited to wholesaling or retailing because there is less by way of operations to be drawn into, but it exists even there. To the extent empathic supersalespeople are not selling, their talent is wasted, they are not following the appropriate route, and the business suffers. This consequence may be compounded because under certain circumstances these people can be overly softhearted, with the result that receivables are not collected, discipline is lax, and the business is simply not very well managed.

This means that for the selling route to work, some backup to handle the sales that the lead entrepreneur brings in must exist. One way is to utilize a partner or partners; unlike personal achievers, empathic supersalespeople do not mind partners; in fact, they rather enjoy them. Such a partner should complement the empathic supersalesperson, having expertise in finance, the technology of manufacture, purchasing, and the like. Ventures where the entrepreneur is following the selling route need this backup person or team at a very early point in their development, however; much earlier than when the achieving route is being followed. If there is no provision for backup, either the entrepreneur is constantly drawn back into the business or the company cannot effectively fill the orders that are generated. This problem becomes less acute if the empathic supersalesperson is also a real manager, a particularly happy circumstance that can obviate the need for backup. Yet the probabilities are that this situation is not likely to occur often.

Developing a cohesive team to handle backup activities is particularly attractive to most empathic supersalespeople. They enjoy the social interaction, and they have no special need to feel that they alone are responsible for successful outcomes. To many who possess this pattern, working with and developing teams seems to come quite naturally; they are by nature participative, sharing people. Examples of successful team efforts are contained in Stewart (1989) who deals with entrepreneurial applications, and more broadly in Katzenbach and Smith (1993). Not infrequently, these teams extend beyond the firm itself into an external network (Aldrich, 1995).

HOW THE EMPATHIC SUPERSALESPERSON–SELLING ROUTE FIT CAN FAIL

As with any other entrepreneurial route, those following the selling strategy can get off track if they do not have the necessary knowledge. Since this route requires backup in the areas of administration and operations, it is unlikely that empathic supersalespeople would have more than a rudimentary knowledge there. However, they need to be much better informed regarding the products or services they are selling. They need the schooling and/or experience, typically sales experience, to make intelligent decisions and represent themselves to clients or customers effectively. Some people simply start their venture too soon, before they have learned enough, and fail as a result. This is a particular problem when coming out of school; such people may think they know more than they really do. It pays to be patient and develop a strategy for learning. Where can a person go to study or work and obtain the best possible information regarding what is to be sold and how to sell it?

Just as personal achievers may face difficulties when they get separated from the achieving route, empathic supersalespeople may run into trouble when they do not devote their efforts to selling. People may inadvertently voluntarily separate themselves from the selling route because they believe their role should now become more managerial. At the other extreme, other people, or the pressure of circumstances, may force a divergence; health problems may make it impossible to get out and sell, for instance. One type of pressure that personal achievers often face, however, is much less of a problem for empathic supersalespeople. That is pressure from family members outside the firm. If one enjoys social relationships, family interaction is just as attractive as customer interaction. Battles over family time are much less likely, accordingly.

Empathic supersalespeople have to spend a particularly large amount of time out selling if a recession hits and they are in an industry where consumer spending patterns tend to fluctuate widely with the business cycle. The natural reaction of people like this when business begins to fall off is to get out to their customers to see what is going on and to attempt to expand sales. Those who do not respond in this manner may suffer severely.

It is also true that there is a limit to the growth an empathic supersalesperson can generate alone. Something very much like the hitting the wall that personal achievers describe occurs, yet there are differences too. Firms that follow the selling route have to have real managers much earlier than those that are following the achieving route. Thus when they get up to a size where the supersalesperson cannot do all the selling anymore, they already have the structure to go on. If they did not, they would never have gotten even to this point. On the other hand, there is a need for the entrepreneur to shift over to handling a limited number of key accounts, while developing a sales force which adds new business and provides for continued growth, or hiring representatives to do this.

The problem is that it is very hard to give these people breathing room. They do not seem to work as hard and as long and with as much dedication as the supersalesperson. Turnover can become excessive. A glitch may develop at this point, and it may take a while to go away. If it does not, the firm plateaus at what the supersalesperson can sell. If this in turn causes that person to become disillusioned, he or she may withdraw from selling or even the business as a whole. Either way the empathic supersalesperson–selling route fit is severed and the firm is likely to go into a tailspin. Reaching the limit of one's own personal sales ability can be a very difficult time for both the individual and the company. Using sales teams can be very helpful at this point.

It is hard to pinpoint exactly when the problem point occurs in the growth of a firm. In working with empathic supersalespeople it is often not too difficult to get a feel for when this limit is around the corner, or already there. But in terms of dollar volume of sales, that point can extend over a wide range. The problem is inherent in the size and time of each sale. Many separate small sales may get a person to the limit quite rapidly, and a dollar amount well below $1 million a year. Large sales are likely to take more time, but at the point that they do occur, may yield many millions of dollars. Furthermore, some large sales in certain markets do not take a great deal of time. Overall there is much to be said for selling big ticket items when pursuing the selling route.

Assuming, however, that a company gets over this glitch, develops a full-fledged sales force, and grows and grows—can a bountiful future last forever using the selling route? According to Miller (1990), probably not. What may well happen eventually is that the company becomes decoupled from the demands of its market and begins to drift. Empathic supersalespeople are no longer challenged, they lose interest, and they come to believe the system will continue to work well even without their efforts. Bland proliferation of products comes to replace brilliant marketing strategies. Market share is no longer the goal, only quarterly numbers. The organizational culture becomes insipid and overly political. Structuring falls entirely to the backup administrators and becomes oppressively bureaucratic. The message that the supersalesperson entrepreneur can never become complacent and get separated from selling remains clear.

COMBINING MULTIPLE TYPES TO FORM THE COMPLEX ENTREPRENEUR

The key hypothesis here is that possessing multiple psychological patterns, and thus having the potential to follow more than one route, creates a major advantage for an entrepreneur. There is strength in diversity of capability. Those with two strong psychological patterns have an advantage over those with only one. Those with three strong patterns are even further endowed. Those with four such patterns, although rare, have a singular competitive advantage. What being a complex entrepreneur, in the sense of having multiple psychological patterns and thus the potential for following multiple routes, brings to the table is a capacity for diversity. A range of talents can be brought to bear depending on the particular needs of the enterprise. This can occur in a sequential manner in that one psychological pattern may be mobilized after another, as the needs of the enterprise change. It can also occur in a concomitant manner as these needs spread, with growth, across several domains.

The best way to explain how these complex entrepreneurs utilize their multiple talents is to draw upon examples. Chapter 4 provides more comprehensive cases, but for present purposes a synopsis showing how multiple talents are brought to bear is sufficient.

LS is one of those rare individuals who possesses all four strong patterns. For a considerable period of time LS was an empathic supersalesperson following the selling route. His other patterns were largely left dormant in this period. With increasing sales, and particularly after he took charge, the company began to grow. His role as a visionary expanded and his skills as an expert idea generator became engaged. At first, as a business owner, LS operated largely as a personal achiever getting his ideas in motion, but even then the family business was large enough to utilize his skills as a real manager to some extent as well. Gradually, he appears to be managing more and more and selling less and less; now he manages the sales process, rather than being the top salesman, and he manages most other aspects of the business as well.

A somewhat similar sequence emerges in the case of LB, who did most of the selling when she first bought the business and it was small; she still does a good deal through her networking. But as the company has grown to surpass 100 employees, there is more and more to manage. LB's real manager pattern has been increasingly called into play. In addition, throughout her entrepreneurial career she has been an innovator, in the tradition of expert idea generators, thinking her way to competitive advantage.

RD started as a professional, but his strong personal achiever tendencies rapidly carried him into entrepreneurship, and ultimately out of his accounting practice completely. As his group of businesses grew, now to some 300 employees, managing this diverse array became more and more essential. That is where the real manager pattern came to dominate his behavior. It has now been quite some time since he shifted gears from a predominantly personal achiever to a real manager who uses sophisticated control and information systems to guide his small empire. However, the fact that he could handle this transition within himself has been a major factor in the smooth growth of his business overall.

In the case of JM, the venture initially engaged his expert idea generator pattern. Here was a Ph.D. biologist with many ideas entering into a newly created industry which was far from being well-defined at the time. There was plenty of room to think one's way to success. But as the company grew, and a network of regulations became established, there was a need to manage further growth. Again, having the real manager pattern within himself served JM well. People like this do not have to rely on others to get the managing done. It comes naturally to them at the point where it is needed.

RP, on the other hand, does not have the real manager pattern available to him. He is an empathic supersalesperson who has sold a large part of his company's business, much of it of a big ticket nature. He also is an expert idea generator in a very technologically sophisticated industry. These patterns have combined, working hand-in-hand, to generate very rapid growth, to a point where the need to manage the business has entered into the picture. RP is not that person, but he has gone out and found a general manager to handle the managing for him. This is what a multiple pattern person of this type must do to keep the venture from plateauing, and to grasp the opportunity that his selling and thinking capabilities have created.

In contrast to RP, BC possesses the real manager pattern to handle growth, but for other reasons a sequential mobilization of multiple patterns has not yet occurred. The problem is that the company is not yet big enough to require full-scale managing, and BC already has the personal achiever capability to operate a venture of the current size. The result is that her real manager pattern has been diverted into managed selling. At the same time, as an expert idea generator, she is working to find the vision that will propel her venture into more rapid growth. Thus, she is currently using all three patterns at once—the personal achiever pattern to operate and continue to grow the enterprise, the real manager pattern to consummate sales, and the expert idea generator pattern to find new niches for growth. If all this works out as it should, BC will be devoting most of her energies to managing a much expanded business in a few short years. Then the sequential use of patterns should occur.

Although normal practice defines complexity as being the possession of two or more strong psychological patterns, it is also possible to simply add up the scores on all four patterns, and then to use this combined score to establish who is a complex entrepreneur. Although the ramifications of this approach to defining complexity are best left to Chapter 5, where the operationalization of constructs is considered, the fact that complexity can be defined in this manner needs to be noted here. The rationale for this combined score procedure is that it taps a person's multiple talents even when some of these are insufficient to break into the zone that clearly would define an individual as of a particular type. Of the case examples considered in this chapter, LS, LB, RD, JM, and BC are all complex entrepreneurs by either definition. Only RP meets the multiple pattern definition, but not the combined score.

This whole matter of complexity, sequential use of patterns, multiple patterns and routes, and combined score definitions is new. I know of nothing in the literature on entrepreneurship that deals with such concerns. Yet the ideas involved appear to be very powerful. They take into account the full range of a person's entrepreneurial strengths. The risk of failure is minimized because the more patterns present at a high level, the greater the possibility that the entrepreneur can diversify from within. Having multiple patterns means that an entrepreneur personally can, if necessary, range across a large number of activities when the venture is at various stages of growth. They can control more and need to delegate less. As a consequence, complex entrepreneurs, by whatever definition, should have very little need for partners.

DEFINING AND PRECLUDING ENTREPRENEURSHIP

Definitions of entrepreneurship abound. There really is no universal statement. Yet in recent years there has been a tendency to incorporate either the fact of or the intention to build an enterprise or grow an organization into these definitions. Examples are the discussions by Timmons (1990a) and by Sexton and Bowman-Upton (1991). Writers such as these emphasize that a major feature of the entrepreneur is some kind of growth orientation that leads, in the case of successful applications, to the employment of a number of other people; without this there really is no entrepreneurship.

Yet, in many cases this growth orientation seems to have a rather low priority, if it exists at all. These firms have less than five employees and annual sales tend to be under the $1 million figure, on occasion well under. Yet some are quite profitable in percentage terms. On the surface these appear to be firms that, because they are brand new or because they had run afoul of economic cycles, simply have not been able to grow to any size as yet. However, as the situation becomes clearer, it is apparent that either as a result of conscious decisions or of unconscious factors, a true growth orientation is not present. The entrepreneur might well desire to sell more product or services, and there certainly is no specific intent to keep profitability at a low level, but the idea of building an organization staffed with employees has much less appeal. In a number of cases these are professionals independently practicing their professions. In other cases they are sales people operating as independent manufacturers' representatives or selling a particular type of product or service on their own. All are start-ups.

Firms of this kind clearly present a problem for any discussion of entrepreneurship. They are more frequent than is widely recognized. Certainly, some definitions of entrepreneurship would include these firms, but a large number focusing on growth orientation would not. It is important to establish how these professional and sales practices should be handled, however, and how the entrepreneurial patterns and career routes relate to them.

What these private practices offer is an opportunity to achieve independence and to experience the satisfaction of utilizing one's special skills and expertise (Schein, 1994). These are people who want to *do* what they know how to do and are good at, not to *manage* and *grow* it. They are mostly concerned with keeping the practice in operation as a vehicle for the application of their particular talents. Thus the goal of firm growth is subordinated to that of continuing survival. Here the firm and the individual become almost entirely one. There is no question that these people are self-employed, and that they are a significant factor in the economy (Kirchhoff, 1996). But there is a question whether they should be designated as entrepreneurs.

It is not always easy to identify a professional or sales practice without having information extending over a considerable period of time. Information of this kind is not likely to appear in résumés or job descriptions. Tests are less useful for this purpose than interviews and listening to people's stories.

You cannot assume that because a person is a professional, a practice is what that person wants. At the beginning it is often difficult to project growth of any kind simply by looking at fledgling companies from the outside. However, a knowledge of the attitudes and aspirations of the entrepreneurs can clearly indicate where they and their firms are headed. The same sort of conclusion holds for those who start out as salespeople. Simply initiating a venture by selling something is insufficient to establish one way or another whether a sales practice is involved. What is differentiating is whether a strong growth orientation exists in the entrepreneur.

If one contrasts growth-oriented entrepreneurs—whether professional or sales—with private practitioners, what stands out is that the two are trying to accomplish different things. People with professional practices use these practices to carry on the activities associated with their profession, many of which were learned during their prior professional education and on-the-job experience. Their primary motivations are professional in nature—to acquire knowledge and expertise; to practice independently without having someone tell them what to do; to establish a reputation as an effective professional, thereby achieving status in the field; to help clients solve their problems and achieve their goals; and to devote themselves to the standards and ethics of their profession. A study which focused on labor arbitrators, most of whom were originally trained as lawyers, makes this point well (Miner, Crane, and Vandenberg, 1994). Almost 50 percent of these arbitrators were working entirely in independent private practice, and their dominant motives consistently were those of a professional nature.

The same situation appears to operate among the sales practitioners. They enjoy selling, have learned how to do it well as a result of their prior experience, and they want a work context where they are free to sell in a manner and to the extent they see fit. It is very important to them that they do not have to manage the sales, or any other type of activities, of others.

Extending the four-way typology to professional and sales practices produces the hypothesis that these are people who do not have strong patterns of any kind. The typology is intended to be predictive of entrepreneurial success, and success is defined in terms of growth. Thus, firms that do not grow headed by people who exhibit no growth orientation should not have strong patterns in any area.

Experience indicates, however, that a subset of professional and sales practitioners do have some strong pattern—an expert idea generator with a professional practice; an empathic supersalesperson, or even a real manager who is managing sales, with a sales practice. In these cases the practitioner makes a conscious decision to minimize costs and drive up personal income. Such people have the potential to grow a firm, but at least for the time being preclude that possibility because they believe they will be better served by not doing so. Instead they attempt to increase their charges to clients or expand their personal sales volume while keeping overhead down.

Are professional and sales practices, whether rooted in the lack of any strong pattern or in a desire to minimize overhead, full-blown entrepreneurial ventures? I believe not. The whole concept of a fit between psychological pattern and career route leading to success simply misses the mark in these cases. When growth is restricted, as it is in practices of this kind, the career route cannot play itself out fully. Also, other considerations of a non-entrepreneurial nature, such as professional motivation, come to play an important role. Some definitions of entrepreneurship, such as those which place primary stress on creating value, surely would incorporate practices of a professional or sales nature. There is no question that these firms can add value to a society, and they can be a source of wealth. What they do not do is build an organization, add jobs, and grow an enterprise. If these factors are part of the way entrepreneurship is defined, then the practices do not belong there.

This should not be taken to imply that these practices are any the less important or attractive as a source of employment. They are merely different. They offer freedom and the satisfaction of doing what one wants to do. They can bring monetary rewards that are the equal of those provided by larger ventures. But this is not full-blown entrepreneurship, with all its responsibilities for meeting payroll and the like.

CONCLUSION

This chapter extends the four-way typology with a series of related hypotheses. Personal achievers must follow the achieving route if they are to reach success. Real managers must follow the managing route if they are to reach success. Expert idea generators must follow the idea generating route if they are to reach success. Empathic supersalespeople must follow the selling route if they are to reach success. Complex entrepreneurs have a special potential for success, and this potential increases the more types of talent they can bring to bear. Professional and sales practices are not growth oriented and thus fall outside the domain of the theory; one major reason for this lack of growth orientation is a failure to possess any of the four psychological types. The four-way typology is embedded in a larger theoretical structure which adds value beyond the typology itself.

The following chapter attempts to consolidate the ideas presented in Chapters 2 and 3 via the medium of case examples.

Chapter 4

Case Examples Illustrating the Typology and Its Extensions

A PERSONAL ACHIEVER FOLLOWING THE ACHIEVING ROUTE

Darwin Dennison at DINE Systems. Dennison founded DINE Systems while continuing to work as a professor in the Department of Health Behavioral Sciences at the State University of New York at Buffalo. The development and strategic planning work in which he is most involved occurs during breaks in the academic calendar—in the summer, the spring, and between semesters. The company is a software publishing firm specializing in nutrient analysis and diet improvement. Products are marketed to both health professionals and direct consumers. Since its beginning the company has received income from research grants obtained from both the federal government and the state. Early on it operated in a technology development center, or incubator, subsequently moving to a commercial facility.

DINE has grown at a rate of approximately two employees per year to its current size of 20. Revenues now approximate $1 million and the company is profitable. There have been some ups and downs, but the research grants provide a good buffer against recession. The company is moving increasingly into consumer markets and there are plans for continued expansion; R&D remains important, but less so than in the past. Overall this is a major success story, although DINE is still small, as are its competitors.

Dennison has been president of the company from its beginning. His psychological profile indicates average strength as a manager and even more as a generator of new ideas, but it is the energy he puts into his company and his work that comes through as most characteristic. He is highly motivated to achieve on his own, to set goals and plan for future company growth, and to compare his performance against various indexes of success along the way. To his way of thinking, what others in positions of power do and chance events have very little to do with his outcomes. What really matters is what he does, and that incites him to do the best he possibly can. He has a large amount of nervous energy and maintains a rather high level of tension, but he likes to be challenged and would be uncomfortable not being active, if not even somewhat driven. Knowledge is important to him, especially as it relates to his profession and his business. He has a strong personal commitment to both. Work which permits a high degree of individual effort and accomplishment is what really turns him on; group endeavor where decisions are shared is not very attractive.

As is typical of personal achievers like this, Dennison throws himself completely into all aspects of his work. He writes books, articles, research proposals, and the software. He is a strong proponent of the free enterprise system and of reward based on individual performance. He has not stopped learning since he obtained his doctorate in health education from West Virginia University a number of years ago; currently, he is immersed in managerial accounting. When conflicts emerge within the company, he steps in with a solution. Crises are not allowed to get out of hand. Plans are in place for future growth. Dennison is involved in every aspect of his business including financing, with a Small Business Administration loan, and quality control which is absolutely critical. He himself is well-informed in a number of technological areas, but consultants provide needed expertise as well. Market planning and development are a particular concern. Sales and marketing are not part of his background and there is a need for help in this area. Characteristically, Dennison recognizes the need and has moved to meet the challenge by hiring those who can help him. Like many people with advanced degrees, he prefers people who are both bright and well educated. DINE has a quality senior management team consisting, in addition to himself, of Thomas Golaszewski, Dominic Galante, Barry Williams, Roberta Burstein-Markel, and Deborah Weese, all of whom have graduate degrees. He does not mind paying to get what he wants. His goal is not personal wealth, but a successful, competitive business and the reputation that goes with it.

Up to now it has been possible to run DINE, and to grow it, with a highly personal style. There are not a lot of rules, procedures, standardized systems, and the like. There is outside competition, but the company is at the forefront in technological innovation and with a large number of overweight people as well as hypertensives, diabetics, athletes, and others concerned with improving diets in the population, the market is there. Accordingly, the company should be able to grow and prosper for some time under the kind of high personal achiever system that Dennison finds so compatible.

A REAL MANAGER FOLLOWING THE MANAGING ROUTE

Paul Shine at AIM Corrugated Container Corporation. AIM is a second-generation family business with Paul Shine as its president and Kevin Shine as its vice president of operations. Paul was an accountant previously with Arthur Andersen, and Kevin had a law practice. It has been only a few years since control shifted from the father to the sons.

The business was started to sell surplus and misprinted boxes. It now manufactures corrugated boxes, displays, signs, and other products from sheets of corrugated board which it purchases. It markets within a 150-mile radius of the Buffalo plant, selling primarily to the furniture, printing, food service, and metal manufacturing industries. The plant itself is technologically advanced and highly computerized. Flat sheets are cut, creased, slotted, and folded by machine, and then glued, taped, stitched, and printed as needed. Much of the work is customized. The major competitive advantage is in high-quality products, and service which provides for delivery times well below the industry average. The company has its own trucks to expedite delivery.

AIM operates in a very competitive industry and has been hurt by the closing of manufacturing plants as a result of the business downturn in its market area. Nevertheless, there has been steady growth in sales—to $7 million a year currently—and in the number of employees—to 55. Recently, in particular there has been substantial sales growth, after several years at a plateau. The firm has been profitable in every year but its first, and has provided a comfortable income to the Shine family over the years.

Paul Shine is above the entrepreneurial average as both a personal achiever and an empathic supersalesperson. But his greatest entrepreneurial strength is as a real manager. He is a directive manager, which means he focuses on facts and prefers structure, is action oriented, decisive, and looks for speed, efficiency, and results. Accomplishing difficult tasks and exercising power and control come easily to such people. They are not always comfortable with this style but they tend to use it, and very effectively. Shine is highly competitive, he wants to win and drives hard to get his company to the top. He tends to structure the work of those who report to him, giving them a clear picture of what he expects. Although it is sometimes difficult to do so, he can take charge and put pressure on those who do not perform. These are the signs of a good manager, and are entirely consistent with his position as president of the company. They also fit with the kind of person who tends to manage the sales process.

As both a real manager and to a degree an empathic salesman as well, it is not surprising that Shine has devoted his talents heavily to the sales and marketing aspects of the business in recent years. He handles a number of accounts himself simply because these are people who have become used to dealing with him, but he keeps on top of what his sales staff is doing as well. Much of the process of negotiating prices falls to him. Although his brother Kevin now handles the operations end, he had set up many of the systems there originally. The two have worked together to continue the rapid delivery and high-quality service which have given AIM its competitive advantage over the years. This has paid off in that the company is able to position itself at a price level which permits an entirely adequate profit margin. There are problems in that the expensive equipment could be run for longer hours and the sales staff could be utilized more effectively, but Shine is working on these. The company is growing once again and it is making money. There is every reason to believe that company growth will be managed into the future, just as it has been in the past.

AN EXPERT IDEA GENERATOR FOLLOWING THE IDEA GENERATING ROUTE

Margaret O'Connor at Air Charter Service. Air Charter Service was formed when O'Connor and her husband purchased the assets of a prior company. It is an on-demand aircraft charter company governed under Part 135 of the Federal Aviation Rules. It flies passengers to destinations extending from New England to Michigan and as far south as Washington, DC. In addition to the charter business operating from its Western New York point of origin, the firm acts as an aircraft broker by getting airplanes to fill company needs, provides aircraft management by handling planes for companies, and serves as an air ambulance when people need an organ transplant. A small proportion of the business involves handling cargo. Most customers are businesspeople and professionals.

The company has six employees including four pilots. It does close to $400,000 in annual business now and in a few short years has become profitable. It is expanding steadily. Peggy O'Connor is the majority owner, president, and visionary. She grew up in aviation, both of her parents being pilots. For nine years she worked for American Airlines as a flight attendant, supervisor, and emergency procedures training instructor.

O'Connor is particularly strong as an expert idea generator. That is her number one entrepreneurial pattern, and fits with her role as company visionary. However, she is well above the entrepreneurial average on all three of the other patterns as well. As an idea person she is constantly generating new ways of doing things and innovative solutions to company problems. She loves the challenge of thinking her way to competitive advantage. Among her talents is a keen capacity to judge the abilities and potential of other people. Thus she is able to develop her plans for change in ways that factor in the strengths and weaknesses of others. Compromise, when necessary, is no problem. She tends to look at the big picture and to leave small details to others. Timing is important to her, and she gives a great deal of thought to exactly when it would be best to undertake specific initiatives. She wants to win very much, but she is willing to bide her time and wait for opportunities. Thus she is far from being a gambler; it is important to think things out so that any risk is reduced to the barest minimum.

Although Air Charter Service started by owning its own plane, it has now shifted to a strategy whereby it utilizes the unused time of planes owned by corporations. This leasing approach has given the company a sizable cost advantage and permits a schedule of charges which is not only below that of the competition, but permits significant margins as well. Since adopting this strategic thrust, the company has grown very rapidly. Much of this growth has been created by a marketing and sales campaign that has tripled the customer base and become a model for an industry that, until recently, has lacked innovative approaches in this area.

There have been a number of other changes, many of them unusual for a company this size. A computer now provides instant price quotes. Ground transportation for passengers (rental car, taxi, or limousine) is arranged in advance and confirmed by radio from the aircraft prior to landing. A turbo jet has been added to the fleet recently which, because it can fly to destinations more rapidly than the planes of competitors, has generated a considerable amount of new business. The organ transplant business in particular has increased. The company is consolidating what previously were dispersed operations at the Niagara Falls Airport. A bid has also been submitted to manage that airport. Things are indeed moving very rapidly. O'Connor is looking into a number of other opportunities as well, including a major expansion into Canada and building facilities, some of which would be rented out, at the Buffalo Airport. She is thoroughly enjoying the process of seeing her ideas become realities.

AN EMPATHIC SUPERSALESPERSON FOLLOWING THE SELLING ROUTE

Richard Page at Woodstream Nurseries. Woodstream Nurseries was started by two partners who went to college together. After about 10 years Page bought his partner out and the latter left the business. Since that time the company has grown a great deal. The largest business sector is in contract landscaping, which includes design and construction. The company also does a good business in wholesaling to other nurseries and to institutions. Maintenance services such as snow plowing are provided, and the company owns two retail outlets which are contributing an increasing share to total sales. The firm's market area extends throughout Western New York including Buffalo and Rochester.

The number of employees varies with the season. It has grown to 85 during the summer months; during the winter offseason it is about 25. Sales are now up to well over $2 million a year. The company has remained profitable almost every year, although, as is typical where retail sales are an important component, margins have not been large.

In recent years Page has made an effort to cut back on his activities, due to some health problems, but he continues as president and also making sales to customers, particularly in the contract landscaping area. His forte is as an empathic supersalesman. There is some strength as well in expert idea generation which is reflected primarily in the design work he does in connection with making landscaping sales and in planning for the business. Although Page may well have been a high personal achiever at one time, and still shows some strong vestiges of that pattern, this is not a major characteristic at the present time.

What is most pronounced is the desire to interact with other people, both inside and outside the business. He is spontaneous, persuasive, empathic, loyal, grasps the values of others, and draws out other people's feelings. Telling people unpleasant things does not come easily to him. He likes to create a friendly, agreeable atmosphere which usually means seeing the best in other people. Being personally liked and valued by others is important. He prefers a certain loose, informal type of control which seems to be conducive to building team spirit and trust. Helping others to deal with their problems is important to him. One of his company's most important strategies is said to be the effective use of a good sales force. Giving these people, and other employees as well, full credit for what they accomplish is simply part of his nature.

Page has always been a major factor in the company's sales growth. He is out of the office much of the time talking to customers and potential customers. This is when he is in his element, and he does very well at it. Even when he does not seem to be selling, or perhaps even realize it, he is. He is very active in various trade associations, in the Buffalo Executives Association, and in other business or business-related groups. This networking brings in a lot of work for the company.

A by-product of this style, however, is that the company needs people to manage the business, handle financial affairs, and provide expert advice. It is to Page's credit that he recognized this need early on and did something to take care of it. He has put together a strong management team that has stayed with him. He meets with them as a group often and the discussion is very much two-way. He is in the process of releasing part of his ownership to this group. There is a lot of delegation. This extends to his accounting and legal advisors who have remained the same over a number of years. The structure that has emerged is one where Page himself does the outside networking, the planning, and a not-inconsiderable amount of the selling, while a team of managers and experts actually run the business on a day-to-day basis.

A COMPLEX ENTREPRENEUR WITH TWO STRONG PATTERNS FOLLOWING THE ACHIEVING AND MANAGING ROUTES CONCOMITANTLY

Richard DiVita at the DiVita Group of Companies. For many years DiVita, with a professional degree from Canisius College, operated an accounting practice which served many small businesses. Gradually, he began collecting companies and running them. Some he bought, some he started, some he has operated with one or more partners, and some have been subsequently sold. The accounting practice itself ultimately came to reside in the latter category. The DiVita Group is a holding company that over the years has maintained ownership in a wide range of enterprises including hotels and restaurants, electrical distributorships, real estate ventures, fluid power distribution firms, car washes, gas wells, and financial consultants. The most recent additions are a machine shop, a hotel and conference center, and a small inn and restaurant. DiVita has his children and other relatives in management positions in many of these companies. In most cases he holds at least a 51 percent interest.

Earnings from these holdings have fluctuated considerably. At present, sales are running at over $21 million a year and there are some 300 employees. The company is sufficiently diversified so that when one company is facing a downturn in business, others take up the slack. There have been failures in the past, but the successes far outweigh them. Overall this has been a highly profitable small conglomerate for a number of years.

The strong patterns that distinguish DiVita and characterize his personal style are those of personal achiever and to a somewhat lesser extent real manager. These factors are clearly evident in the way he runs his holding company. He is above the entrepreneurial average as an empathic supersalesman as well, but this factor is less pronounced, and it is less manifest in his business, although certainly not non-existent.

As a personal achiever DiVita is strongly oriented toward personal accomplishment, desires information on how well he is doing, and likes to plan for future goal achievement. He is a person who predicates his behavior on the assumption that what he does is what really makes a difference. Although he is in an overall sense rather relaxed, he thinks about the problems of his company constantly and finds it difficult to unwind. He constantly looks for opportunities that he can exploit in some way. More than anything else he is a self-starter. He enjoys learning whatever is related to the success of his business, and is indeed fully committed to both his profession as an accountant and his firm. Consistent with his desire for at least 51 percent ownership, he wants to make his own decisions and certainly does not wish to turn control over what he does to others. In short, he wants to be his own boss.

On the real manager side, DiVita manifests a number of strengths. He is a take-charge person who enjoys being in control. He is a highly competitive person who wants to win. Exercising power over others is something that he is comfortable with. Standing out in situations where he makes presentations or rises above others around him is attractive. Perhaps consistent with his accounting background, doing the routine, day-to-day things that managerial work requires comes rather easily. All in all he has many of the characteristics of an effective manager. In addition he is a rather social person who appreciates the role of a sales force in a business. Furthermore, he enjoys helping people in any way he can, especially members of his family.

The personal achiever pattern is most manifest in the multiple businesses, the buying and selling, the starting and shutting down, the juggling of family members into and out of various companies as appropriate. There is a great deal going on here every day. Plus there are partners to deal with in various businesses, and new business opportunities to consider all the time. Part of the strength of all this comes from the fact that DiVita owns a considerable amount of real estate and other assets. He talks about letting go and turning the various businesses over to his children, but he keeps getting into new business ventures at the same time. This does not yet sound like a person who is ready to smell the roses.

As a manager DiVita's greatest strength comes from his highly analytical background in accounting. He develops and uses a wide range of financial controls. The result is that he knows exactly how every business is doing all the time. When there is any evidence of decline, he is in a position to cut costs immediately. There are clear plans for each business and any departure from plan brings action. Because he is so knowledgeable regarding the financial aspects of his businesses, he is able to take steps to keep taxes to a minimum. Sales and acquisitions are based on well-managed information systems. Furthermore, DiVita has no problem in cutting costs and personnel when this seems needed. Yet he also knows how to pump more money into a venture when the data appear to warrant it. This is how he remains competitive and profitable with a diversified industry base containing an array of companies, none of which, with the exception of the restaurants that were his original family business, are within his area of special expertise.

A COMPLEX ENTREPRENEUR WITH ALL FOUR STRONG PATTERNS FOLLOWING VARIOUS ROUTES CONCOMITANTLY AND SEQUENTIALLY

Leon Smith at Niagara Lubricant Company. Niagara Lubricant was founded by Smith's grandfather and subsequently run by his grandmother and later his father before he took over. It is a compounder and blender of lubricants as well as a distributor of major brands. Products include metalworking fluids, greases, gear oil, hydraulic oil, rust preventatives, recycled industrial oils, and the like. At times in the past the company has been a distributorship only, but it is now heavily involved in manufacturing; it sells to industrial users of its products.

Both sales and profits have been up and down over the years, although there were long periods when business was very good indeed. In the period before Smith took over from his father, however, the company was not doing well and it was almost sold. In fact, it was Smith's last-minute decision to try to keep the company afloat that rescued it from being bought out by a competitor. At this time it was not profitable and had run up substantial debt. Problems included a lack of financial controls, poor inventory controls, no marketing strategy, incorrect information from the computer system, the wrong product and market emphasis, and generally laissez-faire management. In recent years many of these factors have been corrected, and Niagara Lubricant has returned to profitability. Its sales are now up to $5.5 million a year and there are 28 employees.

Smith is one of those rare entrepreneurs whose profile exhibits high scores in all four areas. He is best characterized as a real manager, but he is only slightly less a personal achiever and again slightly less still an expert idea generator. He is an empathic supersalesman as well, but this factor is not quite as pronounced. As a manager he is characterized by a strong emphasis on efficiency and the use of controls; he is highly competitive (he was a championship golfer at one time) and finds it easy to organize the work of others. Decisions present no problems for him and he is secure in himself. There is no question that he runs his company.

As a personal achiever Smith's achievement drive is manifested in considerable pride in what he is able to accomplish. He likes to plan, and he believes planning is worthwhile because he, not others or mere chance, determines his own destiny. He brings a tremendous amount of energy to everything he does, and that produces a good deal of tension. He wants to make the key decisions regarding what he does at work, utilizing his own goals and plans as a guide. It is easy for him to become totally immersed in his company and its needs.

He loves to do things differently and introduce changes. In this sense he is a classic idea generator. Figuring out new ways to solve problems, new marketing strategies and niches, new products to introduce—these are the things he enjoys most about his position. Although he did not finish college, he is very bright and this gives him an advantage in thinking up ways to outsmart the competition.

As a salesman Smith tends to manage the sale in many instances, but there is also a softer side to his approach. He really wants to help people and this comes through in his dealings with customers. He also tends to find the best in others; being hypercritical is not at all his way. Sales and marketing strategy is something he understands, and he views it as the most important factor in his company's success. For a number of years he was in fact the number one salesman at Niagara Lubricant. That was before he put on another hat, became a full-time manager, and ultimately president of the company.

It is apparent that Smith is a complex person, and that complexity is clearly evident in the things he has done in turning his company around and moving it forward. For a time the company was in automotive and coolant applications; that has shifted to the industrial market. Manufacturing has been reemphasized with the move into a new facility and the purchase of another manufacturing company. Major technological advances in chemical engineering have changed the way products are made and several new products have been introduced. A machine that takes used oils and other petroleum-based fluids and recycles them back to their original quality is now on stream. This is part of the company's planned move in the environmental area.

A human resource consultant has been brought in to assist with staffing. A number of new people have been hired as a result, the objective being to create a managerial team that would compensate for Smith's own weaknesses on the financial and technical sides. Salespeople have been added as well and the sales compensation program has been redesigned. There is more training as well.

A variety of management systems have been introduced to give Smith a better handle on what is happening in the company. Financial controls are now in place, the computer system has been improved, and inventory is moving out more quickly. Change is everywhere and it is being managed efficiently. This requires a great deal of time and effort, but for a person like Smith that is no problem at all. Above all there is a plan in place and the company is now being managed so as to make that plan a reality.

Although all four patterns and all four routes manifest themselves in this case example, there has been a shift over time so that the personal selling route has been emphasized less and the other three routes have been emphasized more.

A PRACTITIONER WHO HAS NO STRONG PATTERN

Robert Caldwell at RW Caldwell Associates. RW Caldwell Associates is really mostly Robert Caldwell. There are part-time professionals and full-time clerical assistants, but the firm has never had more than four people working for it. Nevertheless, it provides Caldwell with a comfortable living, and an opportunity to do what he enjoys.

The firm offers outplacement services to individuals and groups who are sponsored by their former employers. It makes available training in the job search process, including assistance in writing résumés, interview skills development, resources for locating hidden job markets, and administrative support during a job search. The latter may include the provision of office space from which to conduct a search. Payments for the service are made by the relatively larger companies in the Western New York area which are the firm's clients. Many of these companies have been reducing force for a number of years. Most of the business is outplacement of individuals, but a small percentage stems from the conduct of group workshops. There are also opportunities in preretirement counseling and the placement of spouses who relocate to the Buffalo area business community. There is national-level competition in the area, but RW Caldwell Associates has something of an advantage in that it is a locally owned and operated business with considerable experience in the proximate business community.

Caldwell has a master's degree in industrial and labor relations and was employed for many years by Bethlehem Steel Corporation, primarily in the human resource area. He started in labor relations and worked his way up to manage human resources in the huge Lackawanna plant. As that plant subsequently shut down, he handled outplacement for the company. His firm represents an extension of what he did at Bethlehem on the company side. He is by training and by long experience a human resource professional.

Insofar as the entrepreneurial patterns are concerned, Caldwell does not exhibit any to a marked degree. He is first and foremost a professional, who has established a small company to house his professional practice. Nevertheless, he does possess certain strengths that aid him in his work. His achievement drive is strong; consequently he is ambitious and takes considerable pride in his accomplishments. Knowing how well he is doing is important to him, and he believes that what he does, not the actions of powerful people or the luck of the draw, determines how things will turn out. He works hard at his profession, is personally committed to it, and believes in its ethical principles. Contributing to the welfare of society and of other people is important to him. In his relations with others he is warm, supportive, sensitive, and a good listener. Other people's problems are his problems. He is a very intelligent person who can indeed figure out ways of assisting those who have lost their jobs. Yet he is not a risk taker. His approach tends first and foremost to be a conservative one. Only when he is quite sure of what will work in a particular situation will he proceed.

These characteristics have stood Caldwell in good stead over the years. Over a seven-year period he has helped more than 400 people from 70 different companies. They range from hourly employees to chief executive officers. He does find jobs for them, and he knows how to introduce his clients to new careers. Furthermore, he tends to place people in positions where they stay and prosper; that is where his conservatism pays off. He does not recommend that his clients jump at the first opportunity, only at the right opportunity.

ANOTHER PRACTITIONER WITH NO STRONG PATTERN

Sherill Sutton at Sassy Graphics Inc. Sutton is a graphic designer with a degree in textile design from Buffalo State College. Sassy Graphics Inc. is the vehicle for her design activities. Prior to starting the company she worked at her profession, learning on the job, with two printing firms. However, she found that rather confining, and now would not consider working for someone else.

Sassy Graphics is a graphic design studio which produces brochures, newsletters, letterheads, logo designs, catalogs, menus, annual reports, even books. Services include creative/concepting, layout, typesetting, mechanicals, copywriting, illustration, photography, and desktop publishing. The work is split about equally between art service, which is done on a project basis in-house, and resale, which is largely printing purchased from outside sources. Clients are heavily concentrated in various membership and professional organizations, but extend to education, tourism, retail, business-to-business, and manufacturing.

The studio has operated with from two to four employees throughout its existence. Annual sales are under $.5 million. By most business standards it has not been very profitable, but it has provided its owner with a reasonable income and security over the years. Sutton, in combination with various groups of partners, has started several other small businesses aimed at promoting various products that display her designs. The only one now operating is a signature retail store in a ski area, which sells sportswear and gift items with her original designs imprinted or embroidered on them.

Sutton is not particularly high on any of the psychological patterns, but she shows some positive strengths within all four. She is firmly convinced that she controls her own destiny. Time pressures and deadlines drive her to the point where she is somewhat stressed out. She is a self-starter who shows evidence of considerable initiative. Other people are important to her, she is very much aware of their feelings, and disagreements with them tend to bother her. All this does not quite add up to an empathic supersalesperson, but some of the qualities are present. Her managerial characteristics include considerable self-confidence, competitiveness, and decisiveness. She is creative and likes to try new things.

However, it is in the area of professional motivation that Sutton exhibits the most pronounced characteristics. She is strongly committed to her work, and identifies with her profession as a creative artist and designer. She does other things, but this is really what she is. Also, she is very independent, with the result that she sticks by her own ideas and conceptualizations. That is why she no longer wants to work with a partner, or for anyone but herself either.

Sassy Graphics will do roughly 800 jobs in a year, and Sutton works with many of these clients to produce creative solutions to their needs. That is what she enjoys. There is an obvious sales/service requirement and she does her best to rise to that. In terms of promotion, she will provide a portfolio of her more creative work, showing examples to clients of what she can do for them. Cold-call sales for her company are not much fun, and she rarely does it. She can be very creative, however, in thinking up new ways to promote the studio. To really grow the organization, it would be necessary to hire people to handle marketing, finances, administration, and the like, but then it would be necessary to devote one's energies to managing these people to see that they are doing their work correctly. In the past, many did not seem to, and that produced all kinds of problems. Because all this is not particularly attractive to her, Sutton stays small enough, trying to delegate what she can, while leaving ample time to do the creative design work for clients that she loves.

CONCLUSION

These case histories are introduced in an effort to make the theoretical concepts of Chapters 2 and 3 more real and more meaningful. Additional cases of this kind are contained in Miner (1996a), and the reader should consult this source for a better understanding.

All of these cases have been reviewed by the entrepreneurs involved for authenticity and for acceptability. These are real entrepreneurs and their firms. I have learned a great deal from these entrepreneurs and their experiences. In the early years they made a major contribution to the typology and to the overall theory.

Part II

Applying the Typology

Chapter 5

Operationalizing the Constructs of the Typology

The tests and questionnaires described in this chapter were selected almost 10 years ago, as the research described in Chapter 6 was getting under way. Some were included not so much because of their psychometric qualities as because they were short, easily scored, and thus useful as experimental exercises to be incorporated in a development program for entrepreneurs. I am not sure that I would use the same instruments today. However, this is the test battery employed in our research, and it appears to cover the characteristics set forth in Chapter 2 quite well.

MEASURES AND SCORES FOR THE PERSONAL ACHIEVER TYPE

1. Strong Motivation for Self-Achievement

(a) *Lynn Achievement Motivation Questionnaire* (Lynn, 1969; Hines, 1973). This is an eight-item measure developed through factor analysis of a larger item pool. It yields a single score for achievement motivation which has been shown to distinguish entrepreneurs from other groups. The score is characterized as follows:

the achievement scale covers several of the central components of McClelland's concept, viz. consciousness of time, dislike of waste and commitment to work, efficiency and achievement. Some of the other traits which McClelland has regarded as characteristic of achievement motivation are not included in the questionnaire (Lynn, 1969, pp. 532–533).

The measure continues to be used in research on achievement motivation, and is now probably best considered an index of conscious achieving values (Langan-Fox and Roth, 1995).

Hines (1973) indicates that individuals with a score of 6 or more can be assumed to have strong achievement motivation. Using this figure as a guide, the scores on the instrument were converted as follows:

$$0 \text{ to } 5 = 0$$
$$6 \text{ and } 7 = 1$$
$$8 = 2$$

(b) *Miner Sentence Completion Scale—Form T: Self Achievement Subscale* (Miner, 1986, 1993). The Self Achievement subscale is one of five 8-item measures contained in the larger 40-item instrument. It is modeled after one of the five aspects of the achievement situation specified by McClelland (1961). A sentence completion format is used, rather than that of the Thematic Apperception Test employed by McClelland; the projective character of the instrument is retained, however. Each response to an item is characterized using guidelines and examples presented in the *Scoring Guide* (Miner, 1986). These item scores can be −1, 0, or +1, and thus the subscale scores can range from −8 to +8. Reported scorer reliability is .96 and test-retest reliability .91 (Miner, 1993). Validity has been established against various criteria of entrepreneurial firm growth, and the subscale also differentiates between entrepreneurs and managers.

The Self Achievement subscale is a measure of the desire to achieve through one's own efforts; it is described as follows:

The key consideration here is being able to attribute success, or failure, to personal causation, the concept of individual responsibility. Entrepreneurs must be pulled into the task situation continually so that they do not simply avoid pressures and anxieties involved by escaping from the work context. The major source of this pull is an intrinsic desire to achieve through one's own efforts and ability, and to experience the enhanced self-esteem that such achievement permits—to be able to say ''I did it myself.'' Good team members who are highly cooperative and prefer to share the credit for accomplishments tend to lack this intense desire to achieve through one's own efforts and accordingly lack the drive that makes a task system dynamic and growing (Miner, 1993, p. 19).

On the norms for this subscale, established among a group of entrepreneurs who had founded their own businesses, a score of +2 was at the 50th percentile and of +4 at the 75th percentile (Miner, 1986). These values were used in the score conversions—

$$-8 \text{ to } +1 = 0$$
$$+2 \text{ and } +3 = 1$$
$$+4 \text{ to } +8 = 2$$

2. Type A Personality

(a) *Individual Behavior Activity Profile* (abbreviated) (Matteson and Ivancevich, 1982a, 1982b). The authors describe this as a short test designed to assess the extent to which a person is prone toward either type A or B. It contains 15 items, each of which yields a score varying from 0 (strong type B) to 5 (strong type A); thus the total score can range from 0 to 75. As measured by this instrument—

Major facets of type A behavior include a chronic sense of time urgency, a hard-driving and competitive orientation which probably includes some hostility, a strong dislike for being idle, and chronic impatience for situations which are seen as blocking efforts to get things accomplished (Matteson and Ivancevich, 1982a, pp. 131–132).

The authors indicate that scores of 60 or above are indicative of strong type A behaviors and scores of 45 to 59 indicate moderate type A behaviors. Thus—

$$0 \text{ to } 44 = 0$$
$$45 \text{ to } 59 = 1$$
$$60 \text{ to } 75 = 2$$

(b) *Rose Tension Discharge Rate Scale* (Matteson and Ivancevich, 1983; Rose, Jenkins, and Hurst, 1978). The 6 items of the Tension Discharge Rate Scale each utilize a 7-point response format; the single score can vary from 6 to 42, with the higher values indicating a tendency to hold onto tension. Reliability as reflected in coefficient alpha averages .85. The instrument is related to measures of the coronary prone behavior pattern and to the existence of a variety of health problems. Matteson and Ivancevich (1983) have the following to say regarding the characteristic measured—

in spite of the label, it is not entirely clear what TDR is measuring. It may be simply a measure of perceived total work stress. On the other hand, it may be a much subtler measure of an important adaptive or coping attribute related to the ability to dissipate tension efficiently—tension that otherwise would remain with the individual and be a contributor to various negative outcomes (p. 544).

Either way, the measure appears to tap into the type A behavior syndrome in some manner.

The authors say that scores above 24 are increasingly indicative of a tendency to hold tension in and not discharge it. Using this value as a cutting point, score conversions were established as follows—

$$6 \text{ to } 24 = 0$$
$$25 \text{ to } 30 = 1$$
$$31 \text{ to } 42 = 2$$

3. Desire for Feedback on Achievements

Miner Sentence Completion Scale—Form T: Feedback of Results Subscale (Miner, 1986, 1993). Like the Self Achievement subscale, this is an 8-item measure and scores can range from −8 to +8. Scorer reliability is .94 and test-retest reliability .66. Higher scores have been found to be predictive of firm growth and also to differentiate entrepreneurs from managers. The rationale for the measure is as follows:

True entrepreneurs desire some clear index of the level of their performance. They do not enjoy being unsure whether they have performed well or not. Feedback on the level and results of one's performance is necessary in order to attribute any degree of success (or failure) to one's efforts. It is crucial to know whether one has succeeded or failed, and feedback is the means to that end. An individual who is lacking in the desire for performance feedback is inevitably less concerned about achievement as well. An entrepreneur must be motivated to actively seek out results-oriented feedback in terms of measures such as profitability, productive output, wastage, course grades and the like if a sense of self achievement is to be attained (Miner, 1993, p. 20).

In the normative sample of founding entrepreneurs the 50th and 75th percentiles on the Feedback of Results subscale are at scores of 0 and +2 respectively. This converts to—

$$-8 \text{ to } -1 = 0$$
$$0 \text{ and } +1 = 1$$
$$+2 \text{ to } +8 = 2$$

4. Desire to Plan and Set Goals for Future Achievements

Miner Sentence Completion Scale—Form T: Planning for the Future Subscale (Miner, 1986, 1993). This is the third and final subscale from Form T used to measure a personal achiever characteristic. Again scores may vary from −8 to +8. The scorer reliability is .91 and the test-retest value .78. The Planning for the Future measure differentiates entrepreneurs from managers, predicts firm growth, and is related to the use of formal planning. The implications of the index for entrepreneurs are as follows:

Effective entrepreneurship requires a desire to think about the future and anticipate future possibilities. Entrepreneurs must be pulled by the prospect of anticipated future rewards (expectancies), and therefore must approach their work with a strong future orientation. There needs to be a desire to plan, to set personal goals that will signify personal achievement, and to plot paths to goal achievement. This implies a minimal expectation, or fear, of future failure. Without this type of future orientation the gleam in the entrepreneur's eyes tends to dull, and the motivational incentive of striving for a future goal is lost. The entrepreneurial organization loses power (Miner, 1993, pp. 20–21).

The 50th percentile in the normative sample is at a score of +1 and the 75th percentile is at +3. Using this in the score conversion process yields the following—

$$-8 \text{ to } 0 = 0$$
$$+1 \text{ and } +2 = 1$$
$$+3 \text{ to } +8 = 2$$

5. Strong Personal Initiative

Ghiselli Self-Description Inventory: Initiative (Ghiselli, 1971). The initiative measure uses 17 items from the overall 64 items of the adjective checklist Self-Description Inventory. Because the items are weighted (from 2 to 5), the maximum possible score is 51. Evidence presented by Ghiselli (1971) clearly supports the contention that this is a measure of initiative. This characteristic is described as follows:

initiative . . . can be said to have two aspects; one involves the beginning of actions, and the other the capacity to note and to discover new means of goal achievement. The first aspect is comprised both of the ability to act independently, and of the ability to initiate actions without stimulation and support from others. The second aspect has to do with the capacity to see courses of action and implementations that are not readily apparent to others. Both aspects have the property of being self-generative. Initiative does not imply the capacity to maintain motivation or to sustain goal-oriented activity in the face of frustration. Rather, a person who possesses a high degree of initiative is an inaugurator or originator, one who opens up new fields and who conceives of novel ways of doing things (p. 49).

The normative information for the Self-Description Inventory derives from a sample of the general employed population, not from a group of entrepreneurs. Thus, the scores would be expected to be somewhat lower than in an entrepreneurial sample. The 75th percentile score is 38 and the 90th percentile 41. These appear to provide the best indicators of strong personal initiative for conversion purposes—

$$0 \text{ to } 37 = 0$$
$$38 \text{ to } 40 = 1$$
$$41 \text{ to } 51 = 2$$

6. Strong Personal Commitment to the Venture

Miner Sentence Completion Scale—Form P: Professional Commitment Subscale (Miner, 1981, 1993). Like Form T, Form P is a sentence completion measure and utilizes five 8-item subscales. The Professional Commitment subscale was originally constructed to measure commitment to one's profession among professionals. However, because of the projective nature of the instrument, the items are rather general in nature and would appear to deal with any type of commitment, including commitment to an organization or venture. This close association between professional and organizational commitment has been demonstrated by Wallace (1993). The subscale has a scorer reliability of .98 and has shown considerable validity as a predictor of professional success. It has not been used within the entrepreneurial domain previously. The rationale for the relevance of the measure for the professions is as follows:

Professional careers are intended to be of a life-long nature. There is a substantial investment in training and this is expedient only if the individual is to utilize this training over many years. Thus there must be a strong emotional tie to the profession that keeps members in it. This is achieved through value-based identification. This professional commitment also serves to keep members responsive to the profession's ethical norms. Without such an identification, individuals may leave the profession in search of greater opportunities prior to the time the training investment is recovered, and they may also act in "unprofessional" ways, perhaps to the point of being expelled from the profession. Professional identification or commitment is a crucial ingredient in the profession's survival (Miner, 1993, p. 17).

It is easy to see how a similar type of commitment operates with regard to ventures to which entrepreneurs develop long-term attachments. Personal achievers often use analogies which liken their venture to a baby to which they have given birth.

The normative information for the Professional Commitment subscale derives from professionals, not entrepreneurs. Among professionals, a score of +2 is at the 75th percentile, and this value was used as a basis for converting scores—

$$-8 \text{ to } +1 = 0$$
$$+2 \text{ and } +3 = 1$$
$$+4 \text{ to } +8 = 2$$

7. Desire to Obtain Information and Learn

Miner Sentence Completion Scale—Form P: Acquiring Knowledge Subscale (Miner, 1981, 1993). Although acquiring knowledge is an important component of professional motivation, it is also very important to the personal achiever. In the one case the knowledge is highly specialized, in the other it is generalized, but the need for knowledge of some kind is no less significant. The Acquiring Knowledge subscale, again because of its projective nature, tends to deal with knowledge per se, not any specific type. The scorer reliability for the subscale is .90, and it has been shown to relate to professional success indexes. It has not been studied previously in relation to entrepreneurship. In the context of the professions the Acquiring Knowledge measure operates as follows:

In the professions the essence of the work is that technical expertise be developed, transmitted, and used in the service of clients, patients, students, or other users of professional services. Accordingly to do professional work well a professional must want to learn what needs to be learned to provide an expert service. Those who do not want to acquire knowledge, or who find doing so distasteful for some reason, will fall short of others' performance expectations. Their work is likely to be lacking in the key ingredient of professional expertise (Miner, 1993, p. 16).

Within entrepreneurship the knowledge and learning involved are quite different, but it is equally crucial that information be acquired and learning occur.

Among professionals the 75th percentile is at a score of +2 and the 90th percentile at a score of +4. Using these values for conversion, we obtain—

$$-8 \text{ to } +1 = 0$$
$$+2 \text{ and } +3 = 1$$
$$+4 \text{ to } +8 = 2$$

8. Internal Locus of Control

(a) *Matteson and Ivancevich Internal-External Scale* (Matteson and Ivancevich, 1982a). The scale asks for agreement or disagreement with 8 statements which posit external beliefs. The internal-external differential derives from a single score which is described as follows—

locus of control is a personality characteristic which may serve to moderate some aspects of the stress relationship. Locus of control refers to your perception of the extent to which control over events resides within you or is outside of you and beyond your influence. If you believe that you have a good deal of control over what happens to you in life, you are what is known as an *internal*, meaning you believe control is within you. If, on the other hand, you feel there is little you can do to affect what will happen to you, you are an *external*, meaning you believe control of events is outside of your influence (p. 126).

A person who agrees with 6 or more statements is said to be an external, and agreement with 2 or less indicates an internal; those in between exhibit no clear pattern. We used this guidance to create conversion scores of—

$$5 \text{ to } 8 = 0$$
$$3 \text{ and } 4 = 1$$
$$0 \text{ to } 2 = 2$$

(b) *Levenson Internal-External Instrument: Internal Control Scale* (Levenson, 1972, 1974). The Levenson instrument contains 24 items which break down into three 8-item scales determined by factor analysis. The items for each scale are distributed throughout the instrument, and responses are given using a 6-point format ranging from strongly disagree (1) to strongly agree (6). Thus, a scale may have a score varying from 8 to 48. The test-retest reliability of the Internal Control scale is .64. Levenson (1974) describes her locus of control instrument in the following terms:

[It] measures the extent to which people believe they exercise control over their lives (internally controlled) or the degree to which they feel their destinies are beyond their own control and are determined by fate, chance, or powerful others (externally controlled). . . . people who believe the world is unordered (chance) . . . behave and think differently from people who believe the world is ordered but that powerful others are in control. In the latter case a potential for control exists. . . . Furthermore, . . . a person who believes that chance is in control . . . is cognitively and behaviorally different from one who feels that he himself is not in control (pp. 377–378).

The author reports a mean score of 35 in a diversified sample, but no additional normative information is available. With this mean in mind, scores on the Internal Control scale were converted as follows—

$$8 \text{ to } 39 = 0$$
$$40 \text{ to } 42 = 1$$
$$43 \text{ to } 48 = 2$$

(c) *Levenson Internal-External Control Instrument: Powerful Other External Control Scale* (Levenson, 1972, 1974). The Powerful Other index has a test-retest reliability of .74 and is negatively correlated with the internal scale. Personal achievers would be expected to have low scores, and thus the scale is reversed in setting up conversion scores. The mean reported in the diversified sample is 17. The conversion was—

$$18 \text{ to } 48 = 0$$
$$14 \text{ to } 17 = 1$$
$$8 \text{ to } 13 = 2$$

(d) *Levenson Internal-External Control Instrument: Chance External Control Scale* (Levenson, 1972, 1974). The Chance Control measure has a test-retest reliability of .78. It is negatively correlated with the internal scale and strongly positively correlated with the powerful others measure ($r=.59$). The mean value in the diversified sample is 14. With this as a guide, the following score conversions were used—

$$16 \text{ to } 48 = 0$$
$$13 \text{ to } 15 = 1$$
$$8 \text{ to } 12 = 2$$

9. High Value Placed on Careers in Which Personal Goals, Individual Accomplishments, and the Demands of the Work Itself Govern

Oliver Organization Description Questionnaire: T Score obtained for an ideal work situation (Oliver, 1981, 1982; Miner, 1993). The T Score utilizes 15 items from a 43-item instrument which discriminate task organizations from those of a hierarchic, professional, and group nature. The items ask respondents to describe aspects of their work in terms of one of the four organizational forms. T Scores can vary from 0 to 15. The test-retest reliability of the score is .84. Oliver (1982, p. 857) describes the task organizational form as follows:

Task organizations are those in which most individual positions possess relatively large degrees of autonomy, skill variety, task identity and significance, and knowledge of results that are designed into the work. Individual goal-setting is used to induce commitment and performance. Success is achieved through the incumbent's own efforts, abilities, and motivation rather than by chance or compliance. Examples from literature include entrepreneurial organizations, venture teams, commissioned sales organizations, and enriched job settings (Collins and Moore, 1964; Hackman and Oldham, 1980; Herzberg, 1976; Locke, 1967; McClelland, Atkinson, Clark, and Lowell, 1953).

The instructions used to obtain a T Score for an ideal work situation were:

Please complete this second copy of the Oliver Organization Description Questionnaire in the same way as you did before. However, this time you should answer, not by selecting the response which best describes your present situation, but by selecting the response which *best describes your ideal work situation*. What would the organization be like if you were free to choose exactly what characteristics you wanted in the work situation. Responding in this way could conceivably produce a result much the same as for your present work situation. However, for most of us there are real differences between the world in which we do work and the one in which we would like to work—under ideal circumstances.

Scores obtained in this manner reflect values which may guide careers over long periods of time.

Oliver (1981) provides normative data for a broad sample which includes people working in all four organizational forms. Within this group the 90th percentile is at a score of 10 and the 75th percentile at a score of 7. Based on these results, the following conversions were selected—

0 to 4 = 0
5 to 9 = 1
10 to 15 = 2

10. Low Value Placed on Careers in Which Peer Groups Govern

Oliver Organization Description Questionnaire: G Score obtained for an ideal work situation (Oliver, 1981, 1982; Miner, 1993). The G Score used is comparable to the T Score noted previously in every respect except that now it is the low end of the scale that is characteristic of personal achievers and the test-retest reliability is .77. Oliver (1982, p. 857) describes the group organizational form in the following terms:

Organizations in the group domain exhibit democratic processes of decision making and task assignment, emergent situationally-variable leadership that must conform to the will of the majority or group consensus, and interdependent tasks requiring cooperation and overlapping skills. Satisfying group relationships are coupled with work that would have little motivational potential if arranged as a set of individual tasks but that allows the group to assume total responsibility. Personnel selection and discipline are accomplished by the group, and compensation is based on group productivity (Bramlette, Jewell, and Mescon, 1977; Trist and Bamforth, 1951; Walton, 1972).

This is not the type of work situation that personal achievers would be expected to value and to which they would be attracted. This raises an interesting question with regard to partners. In general they prefer not to have partners, and they tend to get rid of them as quickly as possible in the early stages of a venture (Collins and Moore, 1964). Personal achievers do not like to operate in a peer group setting, where the group, rather than they themselves, is in control. Thus, they will suffer partners only when they have to.

In Oliver's (1981) broad sample the 25th percentile on the G Score is at 1 and the 50th percentile is at 3. With these values in mind, conversion scores were established as follows—

$$5 \text{ to } 15 = 0$$
$$2 \text{ to } 4 = 1$$
$$0 \text{ and } 1 = 2$$

The Personal Achiever Score. This score is based on 15 measures each of which converts to scores of 0, 1, or 2. Thus, the personal achiever score may vary from 0 to 30. In all cases the conversion scores are based on information provided by others, usually the test authors. The objective is to be absolutely sure that scores of 1, and particularly of 2, are not awarded unless there is strong evidence for the presence of the characteristic. The conversion score approach is comparable to using standard scores to equalize the instruments, but has the advantage that it is not tied to any single sample, which if made up of successful entrepreneurs could yield highly skewed distributions on many of the variables.

The reliabilities of the measures are noted where available, but in certain cases

Table 5.1
Distribution of Personal Achiever Scores in a Sample of 100 Established Entrepreneurs

Personal Achiever Score	Frequency and Percent	Cumulative Percent
0-4	0	0
5	1	1
6	1	2
7	3	5
8	3	8
9	5	13
10	8	21
11	8	29
12	8	37
13	8	45
14	12	57
15	7	64
16	7	71
17	7	78
18	1	79
19	10	89
20	5	94
21	2	96
22	2	98
23	1	99
24	1	100
25-30	0	100

this information has not been reported in the literature. Nevertheless, the reported reliabilities are entirely satisfactory, and the personal achiever score is based on a total of 131 items from the 15 measures. It appears unlikely that unreliability of such a measure would represent a problem.

The mean personal achiever score in a sample of 100 established entrepreneurs (see Chapter 6) is 14.1 and the standard deviation 4.2. The distribution of these scores is given in Table 5.1. Scores of 17 or higher are considered indicative of the personal achiever type.

Elsewhere (Miner, 1996a) these same 15 measures are grouped under 7 characteristics, instead of 10, and rather than using each score separately to calculate the personal achiever score, the average score within each of the 7 characteristics was employed (and rounded to 0, 1, or 2). Using this procedure the highest possible score is 14 and the personal achiever type is defined as a person with a score of 8 or above. The objective in doing this was to simplify the typology for use by an audience without professional training.

Using this approach, the converted scores from MSCS—T: Self Achievement,

Lynn, Individual Behavior Activity Profile, and Rose tests were averaged to yield an index labeled "Need to Achieve"; MSCS—P: Professional Commitment and Acquiring Knowledge converted scores were averaged to yield an index labeled "Strong Personal Commitment to Their Organization"; Matteson and Ivancevich Internal-External and the three Levenson measure converted scores were averaged to yield "Belief That One Person Can Make a Difference"; and the Oliver T and G converted scores were averaged to yield "Belief That Work Should Be Guided by Personal Goals, Not Those of Others." The other converted scores remained unchanged. Thus, using the numbering of this chapter, the seven characteristics were measured as follows—

1a, 1b, 2a, and 2b

3

4

5

6 and 7

8a, b, c, and d

9 and 10

This procedure tended to bring together measures which in the literature and in my experience are positively correlated (the conversion scores), although in no case at a high level (above .60).

MEASURES AND SCORES FOR THE REAL MANAGER TYPE

1. High Supervisory Ability

Ghiselli Self-Description Inventory: Supervisory Ability (Ghiselli, 1971). The Supervisory Ability measure uses 24 items from the 64-item instrument. These have weights from 1 to 4 and the maximum possible score is 54. This is the best predictor of managerial talent among the Self-Description Inventory measures. Ghiselli (1971) has the following to say about supervisory ability:

If an organization is to function effectively its human parts must operate together in an integrated fashion, and this integration is to be achieved by the guidance and direction provided by managers. . . . the most effective organizational machinery . . . is an authoritarian structure of individuals . . . this consists of a hierarchy of individuals, a series of superiors and subordinates, ranging from the president or managing director at the top to the line workers at the bottom. In an organization, then, each person, save the individual who occupies the top spot, has his activities supervised by some other person. The purpose of the supervisory scale is to measure [this] capacity to direct the work of others, and to organize and integrate their activities so that the goal of the work group can be attained.

The finding that supervisory ability is such a significant aspect of managerial talent, a quality which plays an important role in determining the efficacy with which managers perform their executive and administrative duties, gives further substance to the ever-growing emphasis that people are the stuff of the organization (pp. 39, 44).

In the normative sample for the general population the 75th percentile is at a score of 36 and the 90th percentile at 40. Using these values for guidance, conversion scores were established as follows—

$$0 \text{ to } 36 = 0$$
$$37 \text{ to } 39 = 1$$
$$40 \text{ to } 54 = 2$$

2. Strong Self-Assurance

Ghiselli Self-Description Inventory: Self-Assurance (Ghiselli, 1971). This measure is the second longest for the Self-Description Inventory, using 31 of the 64 items. However, the item weights are only 1 and 2 so that the maximum score is 46. As an index of managerial talent self-assurance is the fifth highest among the seven predictors noted by Ghiselli (1971) He has this to say about the measure:

There are some persons who see themselves as being sound in judgment and able to cope with almost any situation, whereas there are others who think of themselves as being slow to grasp things, making many mistakes, and being generally inept. The former are high in self-assurance, and the latter are low. [It] differentiates ... those managers who see themselves as captains (or at least first mates) of industry from those who see themselves as mere cogs in the organizational machinery, and those who see themselves as winners from those who see themselves as losers.

... the empirically obtained findings ... indicate without question that self-assurance must be included within the domain of managerial talent. However, they also show that the contribution of self-assurance to managerial success is not an overwhelming one. On the basis of what is indicated by the findings from our managers, line supervisors, and line workers, we can only take this trait to be a secondary aspect of managerial talent (pp. 57, 60).

The norms for the SDI for the general population place a score of 33 at the 75th percentile on the self-assurance measure and a score of 35 at the 90th percentile. Based on these values, the conversions were—

$$0 \text{ to } 32 = 0$$
$$33 \text{ to } 35 = 1$$
$$36 \text{ to } 46 = 2$$

3. Strong Need for Occupational Advancement

Ghiselli Self-Description Inventory: Need for Occupational Achievement (Ghiselli, 1971). Although called an achievement motivation index, this is in fact an upward mobility measure. It contains 20 items but the weights can be sizable, varying from 1 to 6. Thus the score can rise to 66. The research indicates this is the second best predictor of managerial talent, behind supervisory ability. The following comments are relevant:

managers . . . are people who are ambitious, ambitious in the sense that they are impelled to seek high positions in their organizations. Furthermore, those managers who perform their executive and administrative functions exceptionally well are held to be even more ambitious, for it is said that they strive to outperform their colleagues in order to achieve even higher positions. . . . the need for occupational achievement [is] a significant aspect of managerial talent. It reflects a fundamental desire for achievement, and for the opportunity to accomplish it.

All in all, it seems quite clear not only that the need for occupational achievement necessarily must be considered to be a part of managerial talent, but also that it is a most important part. Those who seek entry into management, and those who achieve the greatest degree of success in it, have a strong desire to achieve high position (Ghiselli, 1971, pp. 81–82).

The 75th percentile on the population norms is at a score of 49 and the 90th percentile at 53. These figures have been used to produce conversions as follows—

0 to 49 = 0
50 to 53 = 1
54 to 66 = 2

4. Strong Need for Self-Actualization

Ghiselli Self-Description Inventory: Need for Self-Actualization (Ghiselli, 1971). This is a relatively short measure, with only 12 items included. The weights are 1 or 2 and the top score 18. As an index of managerial talent, this self-actualization scale is the fourth highest, somewhat better as a predictor than self-assurance. Ghiselli (1971) describes the measure as follows:

The scale for the measurement of the strength of the need for self-actualization is intended to provide an indication of the extent to which the individual needs and wants to utilize his talents to the fullest. . . . they must utilize their talents in something they believe to be worthwhile, in an activity which is important, and in which achievement is of consequence to society.

The findings of the present investigation support the view that self-actualization is indeed a significant part of managerial talent. Not only are managers distinguished from supervisors and workers in terms of average scores and in degree of relationship between scores and success, but in addition, for managers the relationship between scores and success is at least moderate in magnitude. Creativity and self-realization, then, clearly plays a definite part in determining who will enter management, and who will attain success in it (pp. 82–83, 85).

The norms for this measure put the 75th percentile at a score of 13 and the 90th percentile at 15. This information has been used in establishing conversion scores as follows—

0 to 13 = 0
14 and 15 = 1
16 to 18 = 2

5. Weak Need for Job Security

Ghiselli Self-Description Inventory: Need for Job Security (Ghiselli, 1971). The need for job security scale is reversed so that a low need or the lack of a need contributes to managerial talent. The scale uses 17 of the 64 SDI items. Weights range from 1 to 3 and the maximum score is 23. Of the seven characteristics said to be important for managerial talent this is the least important; the relationship is the lowest. Concerning the Need for Job Security scale Ghiselli (1971) indicates:

Scores of the strength of the need for security . . . differentiate people in terms of the extent to which they are fearful of their circumstances and want protection from adverse forces. However, the relationship is in a negative direction so that it is those managers who have a strong need for job security who are less likely to be successful. . . . it is the lack of the need for job security which is a part of managerial talent. Those who seek entry into managerial jobs, and those who perform them best, tend to be people who have little need for job security (pp. 91, 93).

Again, based on the population norms the 10th percentile score occurs at 6 and the 25th percentile at 8. Thus—

9 to 23 = 0
7 and 8 = 1
0 to 6 = 2

6. Strong Personal Decisiveness

Ghiselli Self-Description Inventory: Decisiveness (Ghiselli, 1971). Although seven aspects of managerial talent are noted using the SDI, only six are used as characteristics of the real manager entrepreneur. The Intelligence scale is incorporated under the expert idea generator type with the other intelligence test. The measure of decisiveness has 21 items. With weights of 1, 2, or 3 this translates to a maximum score of 34. As an index of managerial talent decisiveness rates rather low, next only to the lack of need for security. Ghiselli (1971) says:

The decisiveness scale is intended to measure two different approaches to problem-solving. Those who fall at the high end of the scale tend to decisive behavior, and those at the lower end tend to cautious behavior.

If the decisiveness scale is valid, then it ought to differentiate those in occupations which require quick and forcible action from those which rather need planning and analysis. . . . [people] in line management positions, which involve the making of exec-utive decisions, earn higher scores than do those in staff positions, which involve analysis and planning. . . . Thus, the factual results support our logic that decisiveness is a man-agerial trait; yet, it is not a trait that can be considered to be a prime aspect of managerial talent, for its association with success is only limited. We shall therefore have to consider it a secondary quality (pp. 62–63, 65).

The reported 75th percentile score is 27 and the 90th percentile score is 29. These values were used in establishing conversion scores for the Decisiveness scale—

$$0 \text{ to } 26 = 0$$
$$27 \text{ to } 29 = 1$$
$$30 \text{ to } 34 = 2$$

7. Positive Attitudes toward Authority

Miner Sentence Completion Scale—Form H: Authority Figures Subscale (Miner, 1964, 1989, 1993). The Authority Figures measure is one of seven five-item subscales contained in the 35-item instrument (an additional five items are not scored). The approach in Form H is the same as with Forms T and P, but the items are completely different and measure different variables. The median scorer reliability from a number of sources for the Authority Figures subscale is .92 and the best estimate of the test-retest reliability is .67. The subscale differentiates managers from non-managers and predicts managerial success in many instances, although among the subscales of Form H it yields significant validity less often than five of the six other subscales. The rationale inherent in the measure is as follows:

Managers must be in a position to represent their groups upward in the organization and to obtain support for their actions at higher levels. This requires a good relationship between manager and superior. It follows that managers should have a generally positive attitude toward those holding positions of authority over them, if they are to meet this particular role requirement. If managers do, in fact, like and respect their bosses, it will be much easier to work with the superiors in the numerous instances where cooperative endeavor is necessary. Any tendency to generalized hatred, distaste, or anxiety in dealing with people in positions of authority will make it extremely difficult to meet managerial job demands. Interactions with superiors will either be minimal or filled with so much negative feeling that the necessary positive reactions and support cannot possibly be attained (Miner, 1993, pp. 11–12).

The norms used to guide conversion scoring were for managers in medium and large sized corporations (Miner, 1989). The 90th percentile was at a score of +3, the 75th percentile at +2, and the 50th percentile at +1. Thus—

$$-5 \text{ to } +1 = 0$$
$$+2 = 1$$
$$+3 \text{ to } +5 = 2$$

8. Desire to Compete with Others

(a) *Miner Sentence Completion Scale—Form H: Competitive Situations Subscale* (Miner, 1964, 1989, 1993). There are two measures of competitiveness in the MSCS—H, of which this is the more general. The best estimate of scorer reliability is .91 and of test-retest reliability .76. As with the other subscales of the MSCS—H, both concurrent and predictive validity are well established. The Competitive Situations subscale, in fact, has been the most consistently valid across studies of the seven subscale measures. The idea behind both competitiveness scales is the following—

Managers must characteristically strive to win for themselves and their groups, and accept such challenges as managers at a comparable level may introduce. On occasion challenges may come from below, particularly from among one's own subordinates. In order to meet the competitive role requirement, a person should be favorably disposed toward engaging in competition. Managers should ideally enjoy rivalry of this kind and be motivated to seek it whenever possible. If they are unwilling to fight for position, status, advancement, and their ideas, they are unlikely to succeed. It may well be that such a manager will be ignored so consistently that the whole unit disappears from the organization chart, or is merged into or subordinated to some other unit. Any generalized tendency to associate unpleasant emotion, such as anxiety and depression, with performance in competitive situations, will almost surely result in behavior that falls short of role demands (Miner, 1993, p. 12).

The corporate manager norms for Competitive Situations place the 90th percentile at +2 and the 75th percentile at +1, with the 50th percentile down at −1. The conversions are—

$$-5 \text{ to } 0 = 0$$
$$+1 = 1$$
$$+2 \text{ to } +5 = 2$$

(b) *Miner Sentence Completion Scale—Form H: Competitive Games Subscale* (Miner, 1964, 1989, 1993). This measure is intended to deal with the same constructs as Competitive Situations; its rationale is identical. However, the items all refer to games of various sorts; items of this specific type are not included in the Competitive Situations subscale. Because this is a projective test, the fact that the items focus on something other than managerial competition is to be expected, and should not represent a problem. The validity evidence supports this conclusion, although Competitive Games yields validity less frequently than Competitive Situations—it ranks fifth among the seven subscales. The median scorer reliability is .94 and the test-retest correlation is .79.

The managers in the corporate sample tend to obtain higher scores on Competitive Games, with the 90th percentile at +3, the 75th percentile at +2, and the 50th percentile at +1. This is used to convert as follows—

$$-5 \text{ to } +2 = 0$$
$$+3 = 1$$
$$+4 \text{ and } +5 = 2$$

9. Desire to Assert Oneself

Miner Sentence Completion Scale—Form H: Assertive Role Subscale (Masculine Role) (Miner, 1964, 1989, 1993). Until the early 1970s this subscale was referred to as Masculine Role (Miner, 1973a). The change in name was introduced because it became evident that many women possess this type of motivation, and thus a label which appeared to indicate a characteristic of males was misleading. However, the conceptual foundation involved is the traditional male role as it existed in the United States during and prior to the 1950s. Although this masculinity-femininity aspect of motivation is less frequently noted in the literature of the 1960s and beyond, there are significant exceptions; see, for example, Ghiselli (1971) and Hofstede (1980). Clearly, changing gender role patterns have had a significant impact over the years.

The Assertive Role index has a scorer reliability of .91 and a test-retest figure of .86. Validity evidence is strong; this is the third most frequently valid of the seven subscales. Thus, in spite of changes in values and family structures, this factor continues to have an important impact on managerial success. The processes underlying the Assertive Role index are hypothesized to operate as follows:

there appears to be considerable similarity between the requirements of the managerial role and the more general demands of the masculine, father role. Both sets of expectations emphasize taking charge, making decisions, taking disciplinary action when necessary, and protecting other members of the group (family). Thus, one of the more common role requirements of the managerial job is that the incumbent behave in this essentially masculine manner. In fact, a major means of demonstrating masculinity has been to assume a position of managerial responsibility. . . . The job appears to require an individual who obtains pleasure from performing as prescribed by this culturally defined male role, and who is therefore highly motivated to act in accordance with this particular behavior model. The behavior involved may well give the appearance of being somewhat macho.

This motivation would be expected to arise out of a strong and stable father identification during the formative years, whether in males or females (Miner, 1993, p. 13).

Among corporate managers the norms indicate a 90th percentile score of +2 for Assertive Role, a 75th percentile score of +1, and a 50th percentile of 0. Based on these figures conversion scores were calculated using the following equations—

$$-5 \text{ to } +1 = 0$$
$$+2 = 1$$
$$+3 \text{ to } +5 = 2$$

10. Desire to Exercise Power

Miner Sentence Completion Scale—Form H: Imposing Wishes Subscale (Miner, 1964, 1989, 1993). Scorer reliability for this subscale is .83 and test-retest reliability .75. In terms of validity this is one of the best MSCS—H subscales. It comes in just behind Competitive Situations among the seven subscales in the frequency with which it predicts relevant criteria. The rationale for Imposing Wishes has been set forth as follows—

Managers must tell others what to do. . . . The individual who finds such behavior difficult and emotionally disturbing, who does not wish to impose upon others or believes it is wrong to utilize power, would not be expected to meet this particular role requirement. On the other hand, a more favorable attitude toward this type of activity, perhaps even an enjoyment of exercising power, should contribute to successful performance as a manager. In the typical situation subordinates must be actively induced to perform in a manner conducive to attaining organizational goals, and the person placed in a position of authority over them ideally desires to behave in ways intended to achieve this objective (Miner, 1993, p. 12).

On the corporate manager norms both the 75th and 90th percentile fall at a score of +2 and the 50th percentile at +1. The conversion scores were—

$$-5 \text{ to } +1 = 0$$
$$+2 = 1$$
$$+3 \text{ to } +5 = 2$$

11. Directive in Cognitive Style

Decision Style Inventory: Directive (Rowe and Mason, 1987). The DSI is a 20-item measure with four alternatives for each item which are to be ranked. The test-retest reliability for the total instrument is .70. The directive measure, in contrast to the other three—analytical, conceptual, and behavioral—is the best predictor of managerial success. The meaning of the directive score, which can range from 20 to 160, is described by Rowe and Mason (1987) as follows:

This style is characterized by its practical orientation and its emphasis on the "here and now." People with this style tend to use data that focus on specific facts and to prefer structure. They are action oriented and decisive and look for speed, efficiency, and results. People with this style can be autocratic and exercise power and control. Their focus is short range, and they tend to have the drive and energy needed to accomplish difficult tasks. They also focus on problems internal to the organization. Interestingly, they sometimes feel insecure and want status to protect their position (p. 45).

Rowe and Mason (1987) present score ranges for the directive style indicating that a particular score reflects a style that is very dominant, dominant, backup, or least preferred. The very dominant range is 90 to 160 and the dominant 82 to 89. Thus, the conversions used were—

$$20 \text{ to } 81 = 0$$
$$82 \text{ to } 89 = 1$$
$$90 \text{ to } 160 = 2$$

Another measure that might have been used to get at the directive in cognitive style is the Thinking score from the *Problem-Solving Questionnaire* (Slocum and Hellriegel, 1983). Since this measure was part of the test battery, this score was available. It was not used in the present instance, however, because the way the instrument is scored, the Thinking index is the direct obverse of that for Feeling. Thus, the two scores are not independent of one another. Since the Feeling score seemed to fit the empathic supersalespeople well, and was needed there because of the limited number of measures available to us, Thinking was not used to operationalize the directive cognitive style of the real manager type.

12. Desire to Stand Out from the Crowd

Miner Sentence Completion Scale—Form H: Standing out from Group Subscale (Miner, 1964, 1989, 1993). The scorer reliability for this subscale is .91 and the test-retest value .85. Although the Standing Out from Group measure has demonstrated good validity in predicting managerial criteria, significant results are obtained with this measure less frequently than with any other subscale of Form H. The idea behind the subscale is the following:

Managers cannot use the actions of . . . their subordinates, as guides for their behavior. Rather they must deviate from the immediate group and do things which will inevitably invite attention, discussion, and perhaps criticism from those who report to them. The managerial role requires that an individual assume a position of considerable importance insofar as the motives and emotions of other people are concerned. When this prospect is viewed as unattractive, when the idea of standing out from the group, of behaving in a different manner, and of being highly visible elicits feelings of unpleasantness, then behavior appropriate to the role will occur much less often than would otherwise be the case. It is the person who enjoys being at the center of attention and who prefers to deviate to some degree from others in a group, who is most likely to meet the demands of the managerial job in this area. Such a person will wish to gain visibility and will have many of the characteristics of a good actor. Certainly a manager is frequently "on stage" (Miner, 1993, pp. 13–14).

A score of +3 is at the 90th percentile among the corporate managers, while +2 is at the 75th percentile and the +1 at the 50th percentile. This translates as follows—

$$-5 \text{ to } +1 = 0$$
$$+2 = 1$$
$$+3 \text{ to } +5 = 2$$

13. Desire to Perform Managerial Tasks

Miner Sentence Completion Scale—Form H: Routine Administrative Functions Subscale (Miner, 1964, 1989, 1993). This subscale has a scorer reliability of .90 and a test-retest correlation of .86. Among the seven subscales, it stands squarely in the middle in terms of the extent to which significant results against managerial criteria have been obtained. It turns out to be a reasonably good predictor. The apparent reason is inherent in the following:

The basic concern is with communication and decision-making processes needed to get the work out. . . . The things that have to be done must actually be done. These functions range from constructing budget estimates to serving on committees, to talking on the telephone, to filling out employee rating forms and salary change recommendations. There are administrative requirements of this kind in all managerial work, although the specific activities will vary somewhat from one situation to another. To meet these prescriptions managers must at least be willing to face this type of routine, and ideally they will gain some satisfaction from it. If, on the other hand, such behavior is consistently viewed with apprehension or loathing, a person's chances of success in management would appear to be considerably less (Miner, 1993, p. 14).

The corporate manager norms indicate scores of +3, +2, and +1 for the 90th, 75th, and 50th percentiles respectively. The conversion scores are—

$$-5 \text{ to } +1 = 0$$
$$+2 = 1$$
$$+3 \text{ to } +5 = 2$$

The Real Manager Score. In this instance the total score for the real managers, based on 14 different measures, can vary from 0 to 28, using the conversion scores each of which can be 0, 1, or 2. Again these conversion scores derive from data outside our own studies of entrepreneurs. The number of items used to obtain these scores totals to 180, and where reliability is reported it is entirely satisfactory, ergo, there appears to be no problem in terms of reliability.

The mean real manager score in the Chapter 6 sample of established entrepreneurs is 5.9 and the standard deviation 3.6. The conversion score distribution

Table 5.2
Distribution of Real Manager Scores in a Sample of 100 Established
Entrepreneurs

Real Manager Score	Frequency and Percent	Cumulative Percent
0	1	1
1	5	6
2	12	18
3	13	31
4	15	46
5	8	54
6	5	59
7	8	67
8	10	77
9	9	86
10	3	89
11	3	92
12	3	95
13	1	96
14	2	98
15	1	99
16	1	100
17-28	0	100

is given in Table 5.2. Scores of 8 or higher are considered characteristic of the real manager type. It is evident that, using the present approach with entrepreneurs, very high scores for real managers simply do not occur.

In Miner (1996a) these 14 scores have been grouped into six characteristics—not the 13 used here. Again when this was done, average scores in each of the six areas were calculated from the conversion score source and then rounded to 0, 1, or 2. As before, the objective was to provide a simpler approach for those without professional training in entrepreneurship or psychometrics.

The procedure involved clustering five of the SDI measures—Supervisory Ability, Self-Assurance, Need for Occupational Achievement, Need for Self-Actualization, and Need for Job Security (reverse scoring)—under a heading called "Desire to Be a Corporate Leader." This clustering is based on the consistent finding that these scores are highly correlated and that the measure which yields the highest average correlation with the others is Need for Occupational Achievement. The Decisiveness measure on the SDI is less interrelated with these other measures, and thus is held out as a separate index. On the MSCS—H the Authority Figures subscale remained independent, but the Competitive Situations, Competitive Games, and Assertive Role subscales were averaged as "Desire to Compete." "Desire for Power" was applied to the conceptually similar Imposing Wishes subscale of the MSCS—H and the Directive measure from the Decision Style Inventory. Finally, the Desire to Stand Out from the Crowd designation was applied not only to the MSCS—H subscale Standing Out from the Group, but also to Routine Administrative Functions. The result of all this was a telescoping of measures to yield six characteristics as follows, based on the previous numbering—

$$1, 2, 3, 4, 5$$
$$6$$
$$7$$
$$8a, 8b, 9$$
$$10, 11$$
$$12, 13$$

Again, the clustering was based on intercorrelations reported in the literature and conceptual commonalties. With this procedure in effect scores could range from 0 to 12, any score of 4 or more was considered indicative of the real manager type.

MEASURES AND SCORES FOR THE EXPERT IDEA GENERATOR TYPE

1. Desire to Personally Innovate

Miner Sentence Completion Scale—Form T: Personal Innovation Subscale (Miner, 1986, 1993). Three subscales from Form T were used in the measurement of the personal achiever type (Self Achievement, Feedback of Results, and Planning for the Future). Personal Innovation is similar in format to these three. Scores can range from -8 to $+8$, scorer reliability is .93, and test-retest reliability .76. Validity against entrepreneurial criteria such as firm growth and survival is good. In certain respects this is a characteristic that relates to self-achievement. However, the means of accomplishing a sense of personal causation is quite different. Innovation operates as follows:

For entrepreneurs the pull of individual achievement operates only to the extent the individual can attribute personal causation. . . . creative or innovative approaches have a distinctive quality that makes it easier to identify them as one's own, and thus to take personal credit for them. Those who wish to forego innovation give up this opportunity for attaining a sense of self achievement. Thus a desire to introduce innovation is consistent with the concept of achieving through one's own efforts, and experiencing approval for doing so (Miner, 1993, p. 20).

For many the very act of launching an entrepreneurial venture yields the experience of personal innovation.

On the norms for Personal Innovation, established using a group of business founders, the 50th percentile score is at +3 and the 75th percentile at +5. These values yield conversion scores as follows—

$$-8 \text{ to } +2 = 0$$
$$+3 \text{ and } +4 = 1$$
$$+5 \text{ to } +8 = 2$$

2. Conceptual in Cognitive Style

(a) *Decision Style Inventory: Conceptual* (Rowe and Mason, 1987). This conceptual measure is comparable to the directive measure noted under the real manager pattern. Those with a high conceptual score are described as follows:

This style . . . is characterized by creativity and a broad outlook, although [such people] may rely too much on intuition and feelings. [They are] good at getting along with others, enjoy having discussions, and [are] willing to compromise. [They are] curious and open-minded but want independence and dislike following rules. Conceptual executives are perfectionists, want to see many options, and are concerned about the future. They tend to be creative in finding answers to problems and can easily visualize alternatives and consequences. They tend to closely associate with their organization and value praise, recognition, and independence. They prefer loose control and are willing to share power (Rowe and Mason, 1987, p. 48).

This style in conjunction with the directive style is said to constitute a typical pattern for entrepreneurs.

The very dominant score range for Conceptual is 95 to 160, and the dominant range 87 to 94. This translates as follows—

$$20 \text{ to } 86 = 0$$
$$87 \text{ to } 94 = 1$$
$$95 \text{ to } 60 = 2$$

(b) *Problem Solving Questionnaire: Intuition* (Slocum and Hellriegel, 1983). This score is based on 8 items from the 16-item questionnaire. These eight are items which ask for a response either in terms of the intuition concept or a concept called sensation. Intuition on this instrument and the Rowe and Mason (1987) Conceptual score have the same theoretical origins and tend to be positively correlated. People who are high scorers on the intuition measure are said by Slocum and Hellriegel (1983) to have the following characteristics:

An intuitive manager is one who likes solving new problems, dislikes doing the same things over and over again, jumps to conclusions, is impatient with routine details, and dislikes taking time for precision. . . . the intuitive person tends to perceive the whole or totality of the world—as it is and as it might change. In problem solving, intuitives tend to:

• Keep the "total" or overall problem continually in mind as the problem-solving process develops.

• As the process unfolds, show a tendency, willingness, and openness to continuously redefine the problem.

- Rely on hunches and unverbalized cues.
- Almost simultaneously consider a variety of alternatives and options.
- Jump around or back and forth in the elements or steps in the problem-solving process.
- Quickly consider and discard alternatives.

. . . the intuitive person is suffocated by stable conditions; he or she seeks out and creates new possibilities. Intuitives may often be found among politicians, speculators, entrepreneurs, stockbrokers, and the like. This type can be extremely valuable to the economy and society by providing a service as initiators and promoters of new enterprises, services, concepts, and other innovations in both the public and private sectors. If the intuitive is oriented more to people than to tangible things, he or she may be exceptionally good at diagnosing the abilities and potential of other individuals (p. 59).

Given that the scale used to measure intuition has sensation as its only alternative, one would want to have a majority of the eight items answered in a manner congruent with the intuition concept to be sure that the style is present. Thus—

$$0 \text{ to } 4 = 0$$
$$5 \text{ and } 6 = 1$$
$$7 \text{ and } 8 = 2$$

3. Belief in New Product Development as a Key Element of Company Strategy

Company Survey: Ranking of Competitive Strategies (Smith, 1967; Miner, Smith, and Bracker, 1992a). The Company Survey is a lengthy questionnaire designed to gather information regarding entrepreneurial firms and their founders, as well as to score the entrepreneurs on Smith's (1967) craftsman-opportunistic dimension and their firms on the rigid-adaptive dimension. Only one item is used to measure belief in the value of new product development:

From the list below, please indicate your three most important marketing strategies.

Advertising	Packaging	Reputation
Delivery	Price	Sales Force
Discounts	Quality	Services
New product development	Reciprocity	Variety

1. _____ 2. _____ 3. _____

Please list the next most important.

4. _____ 5. _____ 6. _____

Miner, Smith, and Bracker (1992a) found this item to be very useful in identifying inventor-entrepreneurs as defined using Smith's (1967) typology. High rankings were consistently given to new product development by these inventors. The item was used to produce conversion scores as follows—

New product development not ranked in top six = 0
New product development ranked 4 to 6   = 1
New product development ranked 1 to 3   = 2

4. High Intelligence

(a) *Ghiselli Self-Description Inventory: Intelligence* (Ghiselli, 1971). The Intelligence measure from the SDI was developed by comparing responses to the adjective checklist items with results from an intelligence test. There are 36 items, of the total 64, that differentiate high- and low-intelligence people. The weights vary from 1 to 4 and the highest possible score is 70. The measure is in fact the third best indicator of managerial talent among the seven noted as truly important. On this ground it could have been incorporated in the real manager score. However, as indicated in Chapter 2, it is even more important as an expert idea generator characteristic. Ghiselli (1971) has the following to say about this measure:

Clearly, intelligence is a very broad domain of cognitive abilities, quite capable of being analyzed into a number of subdomains each fully worthy of being named, defined, and studied on its own merits. But there has been a good deal of value, both practical and theoretical, in dealing with a domain of general intellectual ability, broad in scope and including diverse elements, even though its bounds are far from clear and its components not completely known. At the very least, it gives an overall picture, even though a crude one, of the individual's general level of competence.

Direct evidence of the degree of validity of the intelligence scale is given by the coefficients of correlation between the scores it yields and scores on other measures of intelligence. . . . these coefficients are quite substantial [varying from .52 to .60].

All in all, then, the scores on the intelligence scale seem to provide quite adequate indices of the level of general intellectual ability. Standard intelligence tests obviously are superior, but considering the shortness of the intelligence scale, it does seem to have adequate practical utility (pp. 45–46).

On the general population norms the 75th percentile is at a score of 48 and the 90th percentile at a score of 51. With these values in mind conversion equations were set as follows—

0 to 48 = 0
49 to 51 = 1
52 to 70 = 2

(b) *Vocabulary Test G-T: Forms A and B* (Thorndike, 1942; Thorndike and Gallup, 1944; Miner, 1961, 1973b). Forms A and B of this multiple choice vocabulary test each have 20 items; they were constructed as parallel forms.

Both were used in this instance to give a total of 40 items. This particular test was created originally to be used by public opinion interviewers in conducting surveys where an intelligence measure was desired. The test-retest reliability is in the mid-.80s. The applicability of this instrument as a measure of general intelligence is discussed by Miner (1961):

> the present findings offer rather impressive support to those who have argued for the validity of short vocabulary tests as measures of intelligence. The 20-item tests yield correlations with the more general measures of intelligence which are comparable to those found between the general measures themselves. In the population as a whole the correlation between the short tests and tests of general intelligence appears to be at least .75. This figure compares favorably with that of .83 found for the longer and presumably somewhat more reliable vocabulary tests on which data have been reported previously (p. 159).

Using population data for the 40-item test the 75th percentile falls at a score of 28 and the 90th percentile at 32. The mean score for the professional occupations is 29. Given that the objective in using an index of intelligence in the expert idea generator score was to identify people with a potential for graduate study, conversion scores were established as follows—

$$0 \text{ to } 28 = 0$$
$$29 \text{ to } 33 = 1$$
$$34 \text{ to } 40 = 2$$

5. Desire to Avoid Taking Risks

(a) *Miner Sentence Completion Scale—Form T: Avoiding Risks Subscale* (Miner, 1986, 1993). This is the last of the five MSCS—T subscales. It has a scorer reliability of .94 and a test-retest value of .86. High scores indicative of a desire to avoid taking risks have generally been found to characterize entrepreneurs heading high-growth firms. The rationale for taking a counterintuitive position, and putting stress on the risk-avoiding rather than risk-taking aspects of entrepreneurial personality, is set forth below:

> risk-taking may result in the entrepreneur being forced out of the entrepreneurial situation because of business failure. To avoid this, and continue to experience a sense of self-achievement, the entrepreneur attempts to minimize risk. There is ample evidence that a major reason for small company failure is the adoption of a strategic stance which places the entire company at high risk, frequently in connection with some large-scale new venture that puts the company as currently constituted on the line (Richards, 1973). The argument that effective entrepreneurs must avoid risks does not mean that they do not take what others perceive as risks, however. Uncertainty exists in the eyes of the beholder; to be successful, entrepreneurs must avoid it to the degree possible, wherever they see it. Yet the ideal situation for an entrepreneur is one where others perceive that a high degree of risk exists, and thus high rewards are warranted, and the entrepreneur with his or her knowledge sees practically no risk at all (Miner, 1993, pp. 19–20).

Using the norms for business founders, the 50th percentile score is at $+1$ and the 75th percentile at $+3$ on the Avoiding Risks subscale. Accordingly—

$$-8 \text{ to } 0 = 0$$
$$+1 \text{ and } +2 = 1$$
$$+3 \text{ to } +8 = 2$$

(b) *Shure and Meeker Risk Avoidance Scale* (Shure and Meeker, 1967; Harnett and Cummings, 1980). This measure derives from factor analysis, and we utilized 17 items to which responses are made on a scale of 1 to 3, with the highest scores indicating the most risk avoidance. Items 29, 39, 43, and 47 from the 21-item scale printed in Harnett and Cummings (1980, pp. 95–97) were not used. The scale is part of a much larger instrument that has been employed widely in studies of bargaining behavior. Split-half reliability appears to be in the .70s. Harnett and Cummings indicate the following as regards those who score as risk avoidant on this scale:

High scorers are unadventuresome, exhibit a low activity level, and are unwilling to expose themselves to dangers or to hazard risks of either a material or physical character. . . . In general those subjects who were the most risk adverse . . . asked for the highest initial profits, tended to choose a tougher strategy, and made significantly higher profits. Although the fact that most risk adverse subjects tended to ask for high initial profits supports our earlier research in this area (Harnett et al., 1968), the present finding that risk avoiders tend to use a tough strategy, and make more profit, is not consistent with the earlier data. It thus appears that the risky approach in this study is to expose yourself to the possibility of being "compromised," or taken advantage of, by using some strategy other than a tough strategy (pp. 91, 159).

With 51 as the maximum score for the 17 items, a score of 34 indicates an average response indicating indecision as between risk and no risk. Consequently, conversion scores were set as follows—

$$17 \text{ to } 36 = 0$$
$$37 \text{ to } 40 = 1$$
$$41 \text{ to } 51 = 2$$

The Expert Idea Generator Score. The eight scores on these five characteristics can produce conversion scores ranging from 0 to 16. The number of items involved totals to 138. This, and the level of known reliability for the component scales, suggest that reliability for the expert idea generator score as a whole is entirely acceptable. The mean value for this score in the established entrepreneur sample of Chapter 6 is 4.9 and the standard deviation 2.6. Table 5.3 contains the distribution of conversion scores for this sample. Scores of 6 or higher are indicative of the expert idea generator type.

In Miner (1996a) these scores are grouped into the five characteristics so that the maximum possible value is 10. These characteristics are measured as follows, using the previous numbering—

1
2a, 2b
3
4a, 4b
5a, 5b

A score of 5 or more is sufficient to establish the expert idea generator type using this procedure.

MEASURES AND SCORES FOR THE EMPATHIC SUPERSALESPERSON TYPE

1. Empathic in Cognitive Style

(a) *Decision Style Inventory: Behavioral* (Rowe and Mason, 1987). The behavioral measure is the third, beyond the directive and conceptual, from the Decision Style Inventory to be utilized. A fourth measure, the analytical, was not used in any of the patterns. The behavioral style looks as follows:

This style is the one that is most people oriented of all four. . . . [Such a person] enjoys being involved with people and exchanging views with them. [He or] she is a good listener and is interested in others. Executives with this style also are very supportive, are receptive to suggestions, show warmth, use persuasion, accept loose control, and prefer verbal to written reports. They tend to focus on short-run problems and are action

Table 5.3
Distribution of Expert Idea Generator Scores in a Sample of 100 Established Entrepreneurs

Expert Idea Generator Score	Frequency and Percent	Cumulative Percent
0	3	3
1	5	8
2	8	16
3	16	32
4	13	45
5	22	67
6	12	79
7	8	87
8	4	91
9	1	92
10	3	95
11	3	98
12	1	99
13	1	100
14-16	0	100

oriented. This style is typical of individuals who want acceptance and who are willing to share with others (Rowe and Mason, 1987, p. 49).

Scores in the range of 70 to 160 are said to indicate a very dominant style and scores of 62 to 69 reflect a dominant style. Thus—

$$20 \text{ to } 61 = 0$$
$$62 \text{ to } 69 = 1$$
$$70 \text{ to } 160 = 2$$

(b) *Problem Solving Questionnaire: Feeling* (Slocum and Hellriegel, 1983). Under the Directive in Cognitive Style characteristic for real managers the Thinking score is mentioned as a possible measure. That score is the obverse of the Feeling score, with the same eight items measuring both; thus the two scores are not independent of one another. Accordingly, a decision was made to use the Feeling measure only. This measure and the Behavioral score of Rowe and Mason (1987) are concerned with the same construct. Slocum and Hellriegel (1983) describe that construct as follows:

Feeling managers make decisions based on extremely personal conditions, gossip, hearsay, and so on. These people want to personalize every situation by stressing the uniqueness of the situation and how the individual will respond to the decision. They are aware of other people and their feelings, like harmony, need occasional praise, dislike telling people unpleasant things, tend to be sympathetic, and relate well to most people. Feelers are likely to engage in a high degree of conformity and to accommodate themselves to other people. They tend to make decisions that result in approval from others (peers, subordinates, and superiors). . . . These managers have a strong tendency to avoid problems that are likely to result in disagreements. When avoidance or smoothing of differences is not possible, they are apt to change their positions to ones more acceptable to others. The establishment and maintenance of friendly relations may be more important to them than a concern for achievements, effectiveness, and decision making (p. 61).

Based on the scoring instructions given by Slocum and Hellriegel (1983) conversion scores were established—

$$0 \text{ to } 3 = 0$$
$$4 \text{ and } 5 = 1$$
$$6 \text{ to } 8 = 2$$

2. Desire to Help Others

Miner Sentence Completion Scale—Form P: Providing Help Subscale (Miner, 1981, 1993). This is the third of the Form P subscales used, the other two being employed to measure personal achiever characteristics. Providing Help has a scorer reliability of .91 and has proven valuable as a predictor of various criteria of professional success. This latter appears to result from the nature of the relationship professionals have to their clients, patients, students, and so on, which is discussed as follows:

The professional-client relationship is central to any professional practice. In that relationship the professional is expected to assist the client in achieving desired goals, or in some instances what from a professional perspective is in the client's best interest, even if not consciously desired. As a consequence a professional must want to help others. In certain professions this role requirement is recognized by the designation "helping profession." However, helping in some form is inherent in all professions. Those who are unmotivated to help others lack something as professionals (Miner, 1993, pp. 16–17).

Essentially, the same type of relationship holds for the empathic supersalesperson in dealing with customers. This is why the Providing Help score is relevant in identifying empathic supersalespeople.

On the norms for professionals the 75th percentile score is at $+3$ and the 90th percentile at $+5$. These values provided guidance in establishing the conversion scores—

$$-8 \text{ to } +3 = 0$$
$$+4 = 1$$
$$+5 \text{ to } +8 = 2$$

3. High Value Attached to Social Processes

Elizur Work Values Questionnaire: Social Values Items (5, 7, 8, 18, and 20 of the 24-item measure) (Elizur, 1984; Meindl, Hunt, and Lee, 1989). This index was constructed by selecting the five items from the larger measure that relate to social processes. Responses are given on a 6-point scale ranging from "very unimportant" to "very important." Thus scores can vary from 5 to 30 with the former reflecting a consistent "very important" designation for the social items. A measure of social values derived from the Work Values Questionnaire is envisioned by Elizur (1984), who has the following to say in this regard:

Although material outcomes are more salient, various other outcomes occur that are not of material nature. Most studies include items that ask about relations with people, including colleagues, supervisor, and others. These items relate to social relations, and they are affective outcomes rather than material (p. 381).

A score of 15 on the five items represents an average response of "somewhat important," 10 represents "important," and 5 "very important." In this context conversion equations were established as follows—

$$10 \text{ to } 30 = 0$$
$$8 \text{ and } 9 = 1$$
$$5 \text{ to } 7 = 2$$

4. Strong Need for Harmonious Social Relationships

The Least Preferred Coworker (LPC) Scale (Fiedler and Chemers, 1984). LPC is measured with an 18-item instrument with each item utilizing an 8-point scale. Thus scores can extend from 18 to 144. Low scores are indicative of task motivation and high scores of relationship motivation. Each of these types of motivation can contribute to effective leadership given the right circumstances, although task motivation would seem to be more the norm for corporate managers. Reliability for the scale appears to be good (Miner, 1980). Fiedler and Chemers (1984) provide descriptive information on the relationship motivated person:

High LPC leaders derive major satisfaction from good personal relations with others. . . . In a work setting, relationship-motivated leaders encourage group members to participate in decision making and to offer new ideas or a different approach to a problem. . . . In low control situations . . . high LPC leaders look for support from their group members. They will be considerate of subordinates' feelings, nonpunitive, and concerned with the welfare of the group. The high LPC leaders thus may pay less attention to the task. They can become so concerned with seeking the support of the group that they fail to get the job done. In extremely stressful situations, high LPC leaders may withdraw from the leadership role altogether and not give the direction that the group needs (pp. 22–23).

LPC scores of 64 or less indicate task motivation, scores of 65 to 72 are intermediate, and scores of 73 or above clearly reflect relationship motivation (Fiedler and Chemers, 1984). Accordingly—

$$18 \text{ to } 64 = 0$$
$$65 \text{ to } 72 = 1$$
$$73 \text{ to } 144 = 2$$

5. Belief in the Sales Force as a Key Element of Company Strategy

Company Survey: Ranking of Competitive Strategies (Smith, 1967; Miner, Smith, and Bracker, 1992a). The item used to measure belief in the sales force as a key element of company strategy is the same as was used for the expert idea generator characteristic, belief in new product development as a key element of company strategy. The same 12 strategies are ranked, but here it is the sales force that is of concern, not new product development. The conversion scores were established from this item as follows—

> Sales force not ranked in top six = 0
> Sales force ranked 4 to 6   = 1
> Sales force ranked 1 to 3   = 2

The Empathic Supersalesperson Score. There are six instruments used to measure the five characteristics inherent in the empathic supersalesperson score. Thus conversion scores can go from 0 to 12. The number of items overall is 60, the lowest number of any of the scores for a specific type, but still entirely adequate to support good reliability. The mean score among the 100 entrepreneurs described in Chapter 6 is 4.2 and the standard deviation 2.5. Table 5.4 gives the distribution of conversion scores. Scores of 6 or above are taken to indicate the empathic supersalesperson type.

The grouping used in Miner (1996a) is in terms of the five characteristics as follows—

> 1a, 1b
> 2
> 3
> 4
> 5

Thus, the maximum score is 10, not 12; scores of 5 or more now indicate the type.

Table 5.4
Distribution of Empathic Supersalesperson Scores in a Sample of 100 Established Entrepreneurs

Empathic Supersalesperson Score	Frequency and Percent	Cumulative Percent
0	5	5
1	10	15
2	8	23
3	22	45
4	13	58
5	15	73
6	7	80
7	11	91
8	2	93
9	4	97
10	2	99
11	1	100
12	0	100

MEASURES AND SCORES FOR COMPLEX ENTREPRENEURS

One approach to measuring complexity is simply to add up the number of times a person meets or betters the score that defines the existence of a type. These values for the analyses presented in this book are:

personal achiever	17
real manager	8
expert idea generator	6
empathic supersalesperson	6

Thus, roughly 30 percent of the established entrepreneurs studied in Chapter 6 meet the criterion for each type. This relatively stringent requirement was established to be certain that a person of a given type really did possess a majority of the characteristics inherent in the type. Adding the number of types can yield a score for complexity ranging from 0 to 4. In the sample of 100 there were 27 entrepreneurs with two types, 10 with three types, and 1 with all four types.

As noted in Chapter 3, a combined score for complexity was developed as well. This is the sum of a person's four type scores. It is based on over 500 test items. Although the impact of each type on this score could have been equalized by correcting for the differences in the number of measures involved, this was not done. From the standard deviations it appears that the personal achiever and real manager scores exert a somewhat greater influence than the expert idea generator and empathic supersalesperson scores. This may or may not be entirely appropriate. Table 5.5 presents this combined score distribution. The mean score is 29.1 and the standard deviation 6.8. Scores of 33 and above are used to define a complex entrepreneur from this combined score. This again yields a percentage selected approximating 30.

Using the approach of Miner (1996a) the number of characteristics declines to 23 and with conversion scores extending only to 2, this creates a maximum combined score of 46. Under these conditions the so-called alternative complex entrepreneur score (or combined score) needed to indicate complexity becomes 18 or above, based on the averaging of test scores within characteristics.

CONCLUSION

This has been a lengthy statement of how the characteristics inherent in the types and the various measures were operationalized. This information is used in various ways in the descriptions of the studies which follow. Often it will be necessary to refer back to this source. Insofar as possible, the conversion scores and the scoring systems as a whole are based on information provided by test developers; they utilize internal data from the studies we have conducted as little

Table 5.5
Distribution of Combined Scores for Complex Entrepreneurs in a Sample of 100 Established Entrepreneurs

Combined Complex Entrepreneur Score	Frequency and Percent	Cumulative Percent
0-14	0	0
15	2	2
16-17	0	2
18	1	3
19	2	5
20	3	8
21	3	11
22	4	15
23	9	24
24	5	29
25	7	36
26	5	41
27	5	46
28	3	49
29	6	55
30	3	58
31	3	61
32	8	69
33	6	75
34	3	78
35	5	83
36	5	88
37	2	90
38	3	93
39-40	0	93
41	2	95
42	2	97
43-45	0	97
46	2	99
47	1	100
48-86	0	100

as possible. This is intentional. The objective is to establish what is a high score, and a low one, not based on what we have found within a relatively well-performing entrepreneurial group, but in terms of what the original researchers found in their basic studies—what really are high and low scores overall.

Chapter 6

Testing the Typology: Relation to Success among Established Entrepreneurs

The research described in this chapter is longitudinal in nature, extending over a seven-year period, and utilizes the entire test battery as set forth in Chapter 5. Prior reports on this research utilizing less than the full sample have appeared in several sources (Miner, 1991a, 1996c; Miner and Stites-Doe, 1994). Also, the research has served as a basis for a number of articles which employ the full sample, but provide reports to various audiences in varying degrees of depth (Miner, 1996d, 1996e, 1997a, 1997b, 1997c). The present treatment draws on all of these publications, but supplements them as well.

THE SAMPLE OF ESTABLISHED ENTREPRENEURS

The sample was accumulated using an entrepreneurship development program as a vehicle. This program was operated by the Center for Entrepreneurial Leadership in the School of Management at the State University of New York (SUNY) at Buffalo. The sample consisted of participants from the inception of the program to the end of the seventh year. Thus the number of subjects increased gradually as follows:

Year 1	10
Year 2	9
Year 3	14
Year 4	14
Year 5	16
Year 6	19
Year 7	18

The program's objective was to foster homegrown businesses in a region which had previously suffered from a large-scale withdrawal on the part of corporations whose headquarters were located outside of Western New York (Miner and Stites-Doe, 1994). Established businesses were targeted with the intention of facilitating their growth and expansion. The program extended through an academic year from September to June. It involved presentations on their firms by the entrepreneurs themselves, seminars conducted by various speakers including SUNY/Buffalo faculty members, psychological assessments utilizing the test battery of Chapter 5 followed by individual feedback sessions, and a variety of social networking opportunities. All of this is set forth in much more detail in Chapter 12, which describes the rationale for the program, its content, and the extent to which various features contributed to the goal of business growth.

The nature of the sample of 100 entrepreneurs is best described by reference to the program brochure (Center for Entrepreneurial Leadership, undated). On page 2 the following appears:

The mission of the Center . . . is to enhance the entrepreneurial talents of proven creators and managers of established businesses, improving their prospects for further growth and development. The Center serves the following types of businessmen and businesswomen:

Classic Entrepreneurs—independent profit-seekers who are working to innovatively exploit an identified business opportunity.

Intrapreneurs—innovative managers who are employed to develop new functions or exploit new opportunities as part of a revised strategy within an established business firm.

Change Agents—business persons who are managing renewal efforts within organizations that are striving to remain viable, competitive, and profitable in the face of significant external or internal changes.

This statement casts a very wide net, presumably in order to attract enough participants in the beginning to make the program viable. For the research it specified a broad definition of the term "entrepreneur." In the first two years the statement was determining in that most of those who applied were selected. Subsequently, there was more selection by the policy council (made up of successful local entrepreneurs, plus a few academics). Their emphasis was on more securely established businesses, and somewhat larger ones as well. Eventually, the statement was modified to describe classic entrepreneurs and intrapreneurs, thus placing less emphasis on the change agent category.

What did this broad net produce? The primary ventures with which the participants entered the program could be classified as follows:

Start-ups founded by the entrepreneur	49
Alone	21
With partner(s)	21

Professional or sales practice	7
Family businesses founded by a relative	23
Firms purchased by the entrepreneur	12
Corporate ventures and turnarounds	16
Initiated venture	7
Undertook turnaround	9

Among the start-ups the selection criteria tended to minimize the number of professional and sales practices. A number of firms added or eliminated partners during the course of the study so that the figures on this factor do not necessarily hold for the whole period. The family business entrepreneurs either had taken over from a relative or were in the process of doing so or were scheduled to take over at a later date. There were five instances where two people in the sample came from the same venture, although the two did not always have the same degree of control within the firm.

The important point made by these data is that, because of the way in which the sample was obtained, the definition of entrepreneurship employed is a broad one. Purists who associate entrepreneurship with founding a business may not be pleased with this definition. Nevertheless, there have been benefits inherent in the sample's diversity. It should be noted also that cutting across the designations noted above is the fact that 10 of the ventures incorporated some type of franchise relationship—either of a product name or business format type (Tikoo, 1996). Whatever research results emerge from a sample this diverse would appear to have wide application. On the other hand, the very extent of the diversity could serve to reduce the likelihood of obtaining significant findings.

Of the 100 established entrepreneurs 12 were women. The mean age in the sample is 41.9 years with a standard deviation of 9.4. There were only 9 percent in their 20s where the time available for learning could represent a problem, and only 4 percent over 60 where time to retirement could represent a constraint on continued growth. In all cases these figures are for age at the time of entering the sample.

Similarly, the number of years of education completed at the beginning averaged to 16.0—a college graduate. The standard deviation was 1.9. Only 4 percent did not have some exposure to college and 31 percent had been involved in graduate study including 5 who held a doctorate. There were several who obtained additional education after entering the program, but this is a small minority. Overall, among entrepreneurs generally, this is a well-educated group.

As they entered the program, the firms of these entrepreneurs had an average of 58.3 employees with a standard deviation of 93.3. The range was from 1 to 600. There were 8 instances with fewer than 5 employees, primarily professional and sales practices. At 200 or more employees there were only 6 firms. Thus, in most instances, the firms involved were not very large in the beginning.

This view is reinforced by figures on gross sales for the year prior to entering the program. This value ranged from 0 to $37 million; however, the mean was $4.4 million and the standard deviation $6.2 million. A full 17 percent of the firms were under a half million dollars and only 12 percent at or above the $10 million mark.

The reported profits for these firms averaged at 7 percent for the year preceding entry into the program, but 48 percent of the firms were below 5 percent and only 15 percent of the firms had profits above 15 percent.

Personal income from the firm is affected by a number of factors including inflation and the extent to which income was intentionally put back into business growth. Nevertheless, over the seven-year period the mean income reported on program entry was $85,000 and the standard deviation $59,040. There were only 10 instances of incomes of $25,000 or below, but at the $150,000 level or above the percentage was only 17.

Taking these figures as a whole, the firms and their entrepreneurs would appear to be typical for studies that have been carried out in the past, except that the educational level of the entrepreneurs is higher.

An attempt was made to apply the Smith (1967) typology to these firms. However, because of missing data and because the typology was constructed originally to apply to start-ups, which constituted only roughly 50 percent of these firms, the results must be considered tentative. Nevertheless, for what it is worth, the type of entrepreneur score obtained was −.72, slightly in the craftsman direction. This is very close to what has been obtained in previous studies except for those involving technologically innovative companies, which score much lower (Miner, Smith, and Bracker, 1992a). The type of firm score obtained in this sample was .97, in the adaptive rather than rigid direction. Studies in the past have consistently yielded much more rigid scores. This finding may well reflect the growth potential inherent in our sample, but given the limitations on the scoring, this conclusion must be considered suggestive only. All that can be said with certainty is that the adaptive nature of the firms fits with the program's mission statement emphasizing growth and development.

STUDY DESIGN

The personality test measures were administered as each cohort of participants entered the program, usually during the month of September. Thus, test data were accumulated at seven different points in time over seven years.

Baseline data on the firms of these entrepreneurs were derived from several sources. One was the application form that each participant submitted immediately prior to entering the program. Second, at the time of the September testing each participant completed the Company Survey which provided considerable information on the firms. Finally, over a six-month period, usually starting in October, the participants made a detailed presentation, called a clinic, describing their firms and their performance. From these sources baseline information on number of employees, dollar volume of sales, profit percentage, and a variety of considerations related to these figures were established. Again there were seven data points.

Once an individual was in the data set, follow-up continued until June of the seventh year, at which point the study terminated for all subjects. Testing the typology involved comparing those subjects who did not possess any strong pattern, and thus were not characterized by any of the personality types, with those whose pattern scores were indicative of each of the various types, using indexes of entrepreneurial success subsequent to testing as criteria.

FOLLOW-UP PROCESSES AND SUCCESS MEASURES

The period from testing to the cut-off of data collection could be as long as 6.7 years (for the first-year subjects), and as short as .7 years (for the seventh-year subjects). The average period for a given subject was 3.2 years.

The follow-up processes drew upon a number of sources as follows:

1. The feedback sessions occurring six to seven months after testing, during which the test data were provided to program participants and discussed with them.

2. Clinic follow-up sessions occurring seven to eight months after testing, during which each participant made a second presentation to the class describing what had happened to them and their firms since the initial clinic presentations.

3. Various presentations that some of the subjects made regarding their firms after completing the program; these included invited presentations to entrepreneurship classes at the university and presentations to the Center for Entrepreneurial Leadership Alumni Association.

4. Informal discussions with some of the subjects, at social events such as cocktail parties, CEL graduations, the overnight retreat for new participants, and the like, as well as at chance meetings in the airport, at the university, and around town.

5. Discussions with some subjects that were specifically arranged at some point subsequent to the feedback sessions to focus on specific problem areas; many of these were part of a consulting relationship.

6. Information provided in the local business press dealing with some of the firms and their entrepreneurs.

7. Systematic interviews conducted specifically for the purpose of eliciting follow-up information. There were two rounds of interviews for the first two classes and one round for classes three through six. In most cases the interviews were conducted at the subject's place of business, in a few cases at the university, and if all else failed a telephone interview was employed.[1]

Through these procedures we obtained comprehensive follow-up information on 84 of the 100 entrepreneurs. Of those remaining, five provided test information, but subsequently dropped out of the program and did not return. None made clinic presentations and since accordingly full baseline data were not available, no attempt at follow-up was made. There were also 11 people in the seventh-year class who made their initial clinic presentations rather late in the year and for whom, therefore, the interval between clinic and clinic follow-up was very short. For this class the clinic follow-up report was the primary source of follow-up information, and if the interval involved got much below six months it was considered insufficient to yield reliable data.

When dealing with small firms of the kind represented in this sample the performance of the firm reflects the entrepreneur involved to a substantial degree. As companies become larger, more and more people contribute to company success; the strategies and behaviors of any one individual are diluted, and indexes of aggregate performance have less to say about the work of a specific person. A compelling argument for this interpretation is given in Preisendorfer and Voss (1990), to take one example.

Thus, using indexes of firm performance to evaluate entrepreneur success in a study such as this seems reasonable. However, many such indexes exist and might appropriately be considered (see Lumpkin and Dess, 1996). One approach has been to utilize the simple fact of survival. This says little about growth, which for present purposes represents a major liability, but even more important in a sample selected to contain established firms, failure to survive is a rarity. In fact, there were only three such cases in the sample, although a number of the entrepreneurs became separated from their firms for various reasons.

The most appropriate approach seemed to be to put primary emphasis on annual dollar sales, number of employees, and profitability. Such a procedure encompasses growth and has considerable precedent in the literature (see, for example, Birley and Westhead, 1990). Data on all three factors were obtained for the baseline period. It soon became apparent, however, that some of the entrepreneurs were putting most of the firm's earnings back into the business in an effort to fuel growth, while others were taking these earnings as compensation for themselves while borrowing to fund growth. Perhaps over a larger number of years these processes would equalize out and growth in profits could be used as a success criterion, but in the relatively short term represented by this study profitability did not appear to be very useful. Consequently, only secondary attention was given to it during follow-up.

Accordingly, our primary concern was with changes in number of employees and in gross sales. In prior research with high-tech entrepreneurs these two have correlated at approximately .85 (Miner, Smith, and Bracker, 1994). Although in diversified samples such as this the correlation would be expected to be lower, the two should still be related, and they are at .35 ($p<.01$). Accordingly, one was treated as a proxy for the other, where data on both were not available. Profits were unrelated to number of employees or sales, but were correlated with income at .36 ($p<.01$). Income was uncorrelated with number of employees, but correlated .34 with sales ($p<.01$).

In 86 percent of the cases where follow-up was feasible the individual entrepreneur remained associated with the same firm. Thus it was possible to measure firm growth directly. Under these circumstances four criterion groups could be established:

1. The trend line from baseline to end follow-up was sharply upward on number of employees and/or annual sales. There may have been plateaus, but these were shortly overcome (30 percent).

2. The trend line from baseline to end follow-up was still upward overall, but somewhat more level, and there was considerable volatility in between (31 percent).

3. The trend line from baseline showed growth early on, but a decline set in at the time of recession in the area, which appeared on the evidence to be attributable to that recession; some recovery occurred subsequent to that recession (13 percent).

4. The trend line from baseline to end follow-up was level at best and in some cases showed decline; these firms were clearly not growing and in many cases barely survived through the follow-up period (12 percent).

Among the 14 percent who separated from their firms, establishing growth performance was more difficult. There appeared to be two types involved:

5. The individual did not continue with the original firm, but either sold out or left ultimately to form another entrepreneurial venture. In most cases the new venture was smaller than the original, but not always. In any event, the person stayed an entrepreneur. It is difficult to assess the performance of these second ventures; many had existed for only a short time (7 percent).

6. The individual failed to continue with the original firm, but on leaving either became a student or took a position of a non-entrepreneurial nature. None of these people returned to entrepreneurship over the follow-up period. This is where the few business failures occurred (7 percent).

Because several of these categories yield few cases, and the six categories are not on a single linear scale in any event, categories were combined as follows to yield a three-point scale of entrepreneurial success:

1. Most successful—category (1) constituting the clear growth successes, labeled "Substantial Evidence of Entrepreneurial Success" (30 percent).

2. Next most successful—categories (2) constituting slow growth entrepreneurs, (3) constituting those vulnerable to recession, and (5) constituting those reinvolved in entrepreneurship, labeled "Some Evidence of Entrepreneurial Success" (51 percent).

3. Least successful as entrepreneurs—categories (4) constituting no growth entrepreneurs, and (6) constituting those who separated from entrepreneurship, labeled as "Little Evidence of Entrepreneurial Success" (19 percent).

Note that this scale indicates a predominance of successes consistent with the fact that the sample was selected to contain established entrepreneurs.

THEORY FORMING AND THEORY TESTING

At the beginning of Chapter 2 the conceptual origins of the four-way typology are discussed. The personal achiever and real manager types are a priori, having their conceptual foundations in literature and research which preceded this study. However, the expert idea generator and empathic supersalesperson types are not completely a priori. In the former case, aspects of the type derived from prior research, but other aspects did not; in the latter case, the type arose completely from the data of this research.

The theory-forming phase with regard to these two types was spread over the first four years during which 47 subjects entered the sample. The fourth-year people were particularly influential. At the end of this year the first draft statement of the typology was prepared. A comparison of the initial 47 cases (years 1–4)—the theory-forming sample—with the remaining 53 cases (years 5–7)—the theory-testing sample—may be used to determine if any change occurred, and thus whether the two samples should be combined. Such a comparison is provided in Table 6.1.

The chi-square values consistently provided no evidence of a significant difference between the theory-forming and theory-testing samples. This would clearly be expected for the personal achiever and real manager types, since both of these constructs were formulated a priori. However, for the other theoretical variables, had capitalization on chance been involved in the theory-forming sample, a fall-off in predictive power in the theory-testing sample would have occurred. There is no evidence that this happened. The relationships to success are just as strong at the end of the study as in the beginning. Consequently, it is appropriate to combine the two samples in subsequent analyses.

Table 6.1 contains few cases under the ''Little Evidence of Entrepreneurial Success'' heading. As a result the expected values in the chi-square calculations are low (well under 5). This should not present a problem in this instance because the anticipated consequence of small values is an inflated chi-square value. However, as a check, the chi-squares were recalculated combining the ''Little'' and ''Some Evidence of Entrepreneurial Success'' categories so as to produce a value for $df=1$ with entirely adequate expected frequencies. The chi-squares change little; the conclusion that the samples can be combined continues to receive support.

RESULTS—THE PERSONAL ACHIEVER TYPE

To test the hypothesis, entrepreneurs who were of the personal achiever type were compared, as to their subsequent success, with other entrepreneurs in the sample who had no pattern score high enough to exceed the cutting points (including that for the combined score). Thus, entrepreneurs with and without the specified pattern served as criterion groups. Understand, however, that those who possessed a given pattern, and thus could be identified as of a particular

Table 6.1
Comparison of Theory-Forming and Theory-Testing Samples in Terms of the Theory's Power to Predict Success

Theoretical Variable	Samples	N*	Evidence of Entrepreneurial Success			x^2 (df=2)
			Little	Some	Substantial	
Personal Achiever Type	Theory-Forming	12(1)	2	3	7	3.08
	Theory-Testing	14(2)	0	6	8	$p<.30$
Real Manager Type	Theory-Forming	13(1)	2	4	7	2.64
	Theory-Testing	14(5)	0	7	7	$p<.30$
Expert Idea Generator Type	Theory-Forming	13(2)	1	6	6	.04
	Theory-Testing	14(4)	1	7	6	$p<.90$
Empathic Supersalesperson Type	Theory-Forming	12(0)	0	7	5	1.06
	Theory-Testing	12(3)	1	8	3	$p<.70$
Multiple Types (2 or more)	Theory-Forming	14(1)	1	5	8	.27
	Theory-Testing	18(5)	1	8	9	$p<.90$
High Combined Score	Theory-Forming	12(2)	1	2	9	2.31
	Theory-Testing	13(4)	0	5	8	$p<.50$

*Numbers in parentheses indicate additional cases with no follow-up evidence.

type, could well possess other strong patterns as well. Thus, the differences observed cannot be attributed entirely to the personal achiever type being present.

This procedure serves to determine whether the presence of a set of personality characteristics produces a pattern of subsequent success. On the evidence of Table 6.2, it appears that the personal achiever set of personality characteristics does indeed have this effect in many instances. The data clearly support the conclusion that the personal achiever characteristics taken as a whole operate to produce a type of person who is likely to succeed as an entrepreneur.

Given that the concern here is with a comprehensive typology, determining the predictive power of individual characteristics and tests is not relevant. Table 6.3 does present the intercorrelations among the inherent measures, however. Of the 105 correlations 22 are statistically significant ($p<.05$). All of these significant correlations are in the direction expected. They follow the direction of the conversion process used to construct the personal achiever score. Thus, where significance is found it supports a clustering that is consistent with the theory.

On the other hand, several of the measures have no significant correlations with any other. This is true of the feedback index from the MSCS—T and the Levenson internal locus of control measure. Given that no significant correlations contrary to theory exist, there is no reason to believe that these measures operate to diminish the prediction of success; quite the contrary.

A final point relates to the origin of the entrepreneur's relationship with the firm. When the personal achievers are compared with those who lack a strong pattern, the largest difference in favor of the personal achievers is that they are more likely to be involved with taking over a family business; to only a slightly smaller extent, they are likely to start a business without partners. At the other extreme, personal achievers are not disposed to enter into a professional or sales practice.

RESULTS—THE REAL MANAGER TYPE

Table 6.4 presents the comparisons of the real manager entrepreneurs with the no strong pattern group. The procedure followed is identical to that used with the personal achievers. Again the success differential is very large, although not quite as pronounced as with the personal achievers. The typology is supported with regard to its second component.

Table 6.5 reports the intercorrelations among real manager measures. The high correlations between Ghiselli SDI measures of managerial talent noted previously are immediately evident. In all there are 91 correlations in the table and 20 of these are statistically significant in a direction consistent with theory. In one case, the relationship between SDI supervisory ability and MSCS—H routine functions, the correlation is significant and negative, contrary to theoretical expectations. In addition several of the MSCS—H subscales do not produce a

Table 6.2
Success Subsequent to Testing Obtained by Personal Achiever Types in Comparison with
Entrepreneurs Possessing No Strong Pattern

Evidence of Entrepreneurial Success	No Strong Pattern Present		Personal Achiever Pattern Present	
	N	%	N	%
Substantial	0	0	15	58
Some	10	48	9	34
Little	11	52	2	8
N*	21(6)	100	26(3)	100
x^2 (df=2)		21.00, $p<.01$		

*Numbers in parentheses indicate additional cases with no follow-up evidence.

112

Table 6.3

Intercorrelations of Raw Scores for Personal Achiever Score Measures

Characteristics	1a	1b	2a	2b	3	4	5	6	7	(8a)	8b	(8c)	(8d)	9	(10)
1. Self Achievement															
1a. Lynn	—														
1b. MSCS—T	.19	—													
2. Type A															
2a. IBA Profile	.19	.27**	—												
2b. Rose	.30**	.17	.51**	—											
3. Feedback	.08	.08	-.08	.00	—										
4. Planning	.11	-.05	.04	-.03	-.02	—									
5. Initiative	.20*	.15	.01	.00	.12	.20*	—								
6. Commitment	.23*	.20*	.04	.06	.16	.15	.25*	—							
7. Learning	.26**	.22*	-.15	-.13	.07	.21*	.22*	.28**	—						
8. Locus of Control															
(8a) I-E Scale	.07	.17	-.04	-.02	.14	-.24*	-.02	.06	.05	—					
8b. Internal	-.03	.09	.12	-.06	-.06	-.01	.17	-.04	.06	-.04	—				
(8c) Others	-.06	-.06	-.08	.05	-.13	-.15	-.07	.13	.02	.17	-.13	—			
(8d) Chance	-.04	.00	.01	.03	-.06	-.11	-.02	.15	-.20*	.22*	-.19	.32**	—		
9. Individual Values	-.01	.20*	.23*	-.03	.04	.18	.14	.05	.09	-.07	.07	-.16	-.01	—	
(10) Peer Values	-.07	-.35**	-.06	.09	-.14	-.23*	-.13	-.12	-.21	-.15	-.01	.00	.00	-.51**	—
Mean	6.9	3.1	55.3	28.4	.6	.7	35.0	1.2	1.2	2.6	40.1	19.6	16.0	7.4	3.8
Standard Deviation	1.0	2.3	11.1	7.8	2.2	2.5	7.2	2.4	2.6	1.5	4.0	5.7	4.9	3.1	3.2

*p<.05

**p<.01

( ) Low scores contributing to personal achiever score.

Table 6.4

Success Subsequent to Testing Obtained by Real Manger Types in Comparison with Entrepreneurs Possessing No Strong Pattern

Evidence of Entrepreneurial Success	No Strong Pattern Present		Real Manager Pattern Present	
	N	%	N	%
Substantial	0	0	14	52
Some	10	48	11	41
Little	11	52	2	7
N*	21(6)	100	27(6)	100
x^2 (df=2)		19.71, $p<.01$		

*Numbers in parentheses indicate additional cases with no follow-up evidence.

114

Table 6.5
Intercorrelations of Raw Scores for Real Manager Score Measures

Characteristics	1	2	3	4	(5)	6	7	8a	8b	9	10	11	12	13
1. Supervisory	—													
2. Self-Assurance	.48**	—												
3. Advancement	.55**	.66**	—											
4. Self-Actualization	.40**	.50**	.51**	—										
(5) Security	-.46**	-.33**	-.56**	-.62**	—									
6. Decisiveness	.56**	.41**	.47**	.25*	-.33**	—								
7. Authority	.13	.19	.13	.13	.08	.07	—							
8. Compete														
8a. Situations	.24*	.17	.16	.20*	-.26**	.05	.06	—						
8b. Games	-.05	.05	.12	-.11	-.07	-.04	.00	.17	—					
9. Assert	.01	.18	.07	.10	.07	-.03	.12	.25*	-.04	—				
10. Power	-.06	.07	.03	.05	-.04	-.01	-.05	.04	-.03	.00	—			
11. Directive	-.01	.08	-.01	-.15	.07	.08	-.01	.10	.13	-.04	.25*	—		
12. Stand Out	.10	-.02	.07	-.02	.06	.09	.11	.06	-.09	.19	.00	.01	—	
13. Tasks	-.24*	.03	.04	.06	.02	-.08	-.02	.07	-.01	.11	.00	.11	.11	—
Mean	31.1	27.6	41.3	12.0	8.3	23.6	.4	-.6	.6	-.3	1.1	79.2	1.2	.2
Standard Deviation	6.1	5.3	10.2	2.9	3.8	4.9	1.6	1.8	2.0	1.7	1.5	15.1	1.4	1.6

$*p<.05$

$**p<.01$

( ) Low scores contribute to real manager score.

115

significant relationship with any other of the measures in the table. This is true of Authority Figures, Competitive Games, and Standing Out from Group. Other than the finding as regards the Routine Administrative Functions subscale, there is no cause for concern here. Merely because a measure does not support clustering in accordance with theoretical expectations does not mean it lacks predictive power. In fact, because it is independent, it may very well make a greater contribution to prediction than more closely correlated variables.

Real managers demonstrate few differences from those without a strong pattern insofar as the origin of their venture is concerned. They are, again, less likely to start a professional or sales practice, but the only other meaningful departure is a tendency to start a firm without benefit of partners. As will be documented shortly, personal achiever and real manager scores tend to go together, and the two types may well exist in the same person. This kind of complexity is particularly advantageous for those who wish to start and grow a firm alone.

RESULTS—THE EXPERT IDEA GENERATOR TYPE

The results set forth in Table 6.6 largely mirror those of Table 6.2 and 6.4 The proportion in the "Substantial Evidence of Entrepreneurial Success" category is lower than with either of the other two types, but not significantly so. The differential in comparison to those who lack the expert idea generator pattern, or any pattern, is again quite large and the support for this particular type strong.

In Table 6.7 the evidence for a mild clustering consistent with the theory continues. There are 28 correlations and 9 of them are significant—all in a direction consistent with theoretical expectations. The only measures not showing any significant relationship to another are the two avoiding risk scales; not a surprising finding. Somewhat more surprising is the fact that the two are not related to one another. However, the fact that one is projective in nature and the other self-report may well account for this (Langan-Fox and Roth, 1995).

As to venture origin, the pattern seen previously, where starting firms without partners is elevated above the frequency in the no-pattern group and starting a professional or sales practice is depressed, continues to be typical. However, there is another, rather striking finding: Expert idea generators are particularly likely to undertake a turnaround in the context of corporate venturing. This would appear to be primarily because they have ideas that offer a potential solution to existing problems. If existing ventures, or subsidiaries, or components of the business are in trouble and need to be revived, hiring an expert idea generator and giving that person plenty of freedom to put his or her ideas to work would seem to be a strategy well worth pursuing.

Table 6.6

Success Subsequent to Testing Obtained by Expert Idea Generator Types in Comparison with Entrepreneurs Possessing No Strong Pattern

Evidence of Entrepreneurial Success	No Strong Pattern Present		Expert Idea Generator Pattern Present	
	N	%	N	%
Substantial	0	0	12	45
Some	10	48	13	48
Little	11	52	2	7
N*	21(6)	100	27(6)	100
x^2 (df=2)	17.69, p<.01			

*Numbers in parentheses indicate additional cases with no follow-up evidence.

Table 6.7
Intercorrelations of Raw Scores for Expert Idea Generator Score Measures

Characteristics	1	2a	2b	(3)	4a	4b	5a	5b
1. Innovate	—							
2. Conceptual								
2a. Conceptual	.22*	—						
2b. Intuition	.37**	.32**	—					
(3) New Products	-.03	-.34**	-.28**	—				
4. Intelligence								
4a. Ghiselli	.19	.17	.38**	-.29**	—			
4b. G-T	-.03	.11	.12	-.28**	.37**	—		
5. Avoid Risk								
5a. MSCS-T	-.08	-.02	-.18	.06	-.07	-.06	—	
5b. Shure	-.04	-.03	.08	-.07	.11	-.11	.09	—
Mean	4.0	78.7	4.9	5.7	39.8	25.3	1.8	32.2
Standard Deviation	2.1	16.0	2.0	1.9	7.8	4.6	2.4	5.1

*$p < .05$
**$p < .01$

( ) Low scores contribute to expert idea generator score.

RESULTS—THE EMPATHIC SUPERSALESPERSON TYPE

In contrast with Tables 6.2, 6.4, and 6.6, the data of Table 6.8 suggest a lower frequency in the "Evidence of Substantial Entrepreneurial Success" category. There is still a major difference overall as compared to those who lack a strong pattern, and without question this type takes its place with the other three in the four-way typology based on this evidence. Yet outstanding growth seems a bit harder to come by for these people. These differentials do not reach levels that yield statistical significance in comparisons with the other types, but they are sufficient to be worth noting. The problem appears to be that the firms of empathic supersalespeople are more likely to be hurt by recession.

Table 6.9 contains the intercorrelations for the six empathic supersalesperson measures. Of the 15 correlations 4 are significant. All four are in a direction consistent with theory. There are no measures that do not have at least one significant correlation with another.

The findings on firm origin contain little that is new. Like the other types the expert idea generators exceed the no-pattern group in starting a firm alone and they are less likely to start a professional or sales practice. Of the four types the empathic supersalespeople have the highest frequency of entrepreneurs who start a firm with at least one partner.

RESULTS—THE COMPLEX ENTREPRENEUR

Before taking up the relation of complexity to success, it should prove helpful to understand how the various types combine to produce the multipattern, complex entrepreneur. What is the likelihood, based on the established entrepreneur sample for instance, that at least one other type will be present in the same person, if a particular type exists.

For those who exhibit the personal achiever pattern, there is a very high probability that some other pattern—at least one—will be present; this occurs 86 percent of the time. This propensity for multiple patterns represents a major added strength for these personal achievers.

Since the personal achiever and real manager types often appear together, it is not surprising that the latter carries with it a high incidence of complexity also. In fact, the real managers have at least one additional strong pattern 82 percent of the time. Thus many real managers appear to have another source of entrepreneurial strength that can serve to get them through the early growth period until the venture is large enough to be actually managed.

The next most frequent bond to complexity exists for the expert idea generators. Here, in 67 percent of the instances there is at least one other strong pattern above and beyond that of expert idea generator. This additional pattern is most likely to be the real manager. Thus there is a good chance that sequencing can occur—to the benefit of the venture.

Table 6.8
Success Subsequent to Testing Obtained by Empathic Supersalespeople in Comparison with Entrepreneurs Possessing No Strong Pattern

Evidence of Entrepreneurial Success	No Strong Pattern Present		Empathic Supersalesperson Pattern Present	
	N	%	N	%
Substantial	0	0	8	33
Some	10	48	15	63
Little	11	52	1	4
N*	21(6)	100	24(3)	100
$x^2 (df=2)$	$17.12, p<.01$			

*Numbers in parentheses indicate additional cases with no follow-up evidence.

Table 6.9
Intercorrelations of Raw Scores for Empathic Supersalesperson Measures

Characteristics	1a	1b	2	(3)	4	(5)
1. Empathic						
1a. Behavioral	—					
1b. Feeling	.14	—				
2. Help	.15	.24*	—			
(3) Social	-.28**	-.30**	-.02	—		
4. Harmonious	.01	.05	.19	.12	—	
(5) Sales Force	-.15	-.11	-.05	-.02	-.25*	—
Mean	60.5	3.5	3.4	10.1	58.5	4.4
Standard Deviation	21.4	1.9	2.1	2.9	18.8	6.2

*$p<.05$
**$p<.01$
( ) Low scores contribute to empathic supersalesperson score.

Finally, the empathic supersalespeople have the least likelihood of achieving complexity. In only 48 percent of the cases is another strong pattern present as well. Thus a majority who should follow the selling route appear to have only that route to follow. Without judicious staffing of the venture, major growth seems unlikely under these circumstances.

There is only one four-pattern entrepreneur in the established entrepreneur sample. Of the 10 three-pattern entrepreneurs, 5 combine the personal achiever, real manager, and expert idea generator types. Next most frequent is the combination of real manager, expert idea generator, and empathic supersalesperson with 3 instances. Among the 27 two-pattern complex entrepreneurs the most frequent combination is personal achiever and real manager; next most frequent is real manager and expert idea generator.

These relationships underlie the correlations of Table 6.10. Note that the real manager score is positively correlated with the personal achiever score, and to a somewhat lesser extent with that for expert idea generator. Yet the scores for personal achiever and expert idea generator are unrelated. The correlations involving the empathic supersalesperson score are all negative, and significantly so in two instances.

Comparisons in terms of success levels attained subsequent to testing were made using complex entrepreneurs and those having no strong pattern within the established entrepreneur sample, just as they were for the individual types. The results are given in Table 6.11. Complexity is defined both in terms of multiple types (2, 3, or 4) and in terms of the composite score obtained by adding the scores for the four types. Either way, the evidence that complexity predicts subsequent success is very strong, although the figures are somewhat better for the composite score.

The performance record of the complex entrepreneurs outdistances that of the empathic supersalespeople and expert idea generators as set forth in Tables 6.6 and 6.8. It is not as distinctive, however, when compared to the figures for the personal achievers and real managers set forth in Tables 6.2 and 6.4. The reason for this becomes apparent when we compare the incidence of very successful ventures under entrepreneurs of different types with the degree to which these entrepreneurs are in fact complex and thus possess multiple patterns:

Type	Substantial Evidence of Success	More Than One Type
Personal achiever	58%	86%
Real manager	52%	82%
Expert idea generator	45%	67%
Empathic supersalesperson	33%	48%

It is apparent that a major factor in the outstanding performance of the personal achiever firms and to a slightly lesser extent the real manager firms, is the fact that these companies are more likely to be influenced by a person who

Table 6.10
Intercorrelations of Type Scores

Score	Personal Achiever	Real Manager	Expert Idea Generator	Empathic Supersalesperson	Composite Score
Personal Achiever	—	.35**	.02	-.30**	.70**
Real Manager		—	.22*	-.24*	.74**
Expert Idea Generator			—	-.14	.47**
Empathic Supersalesperson				—	.00

*$p<.05$
**$p<.01$

Table 6.11

Success Subsequent to Testing Obtained by Complex Entrepreneurs in Comparison with Entrepreneurs Possessing No Strong Pattern

Evidence of Entrepreneurial Success	No Strong Pattern Present		Complex Entrepreneurs			
			Multiple Types		High Composite Score	
	N	%	N	%	N	%
Substantial	0	0	17	53	17	68
Some	10	48	13	41	7	28
Little	11	52	2	6	1	4
N*	21(6)	100	32(6)	100	25(6)	100
$x^2(df=2)$			21.99, $p<.01$		25.82, $p<.01$	

*Numbers in parentheses indicate additional cases with no follow-up evidence.

can bring multiple talents to bear. These numbers once again indicate that possessing multiple patterns is a major asset to an entrepreneur.

When one looks only at the people with three or four strong patterns, almost all of them are in the "firm has grown a lot" category. When there are two strong patterns, there is still a heavy concentration in the top category, but the "firm has grown some" category begins to fill up as well. The other four categories have only a scattering of firms. When there is only one strong pattern present, the most frequent single category is "firm has grown some," now replacing "firm has grown a lot" in that regard. There are many more instances where damage was done by recession and many more cases where the entrepreneur and firm parted ways. The few examples of bare survival among entrepreneurs with at least one strong pattern occur here. The evidence is pronounced that the more strong patterns a person has, the better the prospects for entrepreneurial success in the future.

This is brought out in a somewhat different way in Table 6.12. Note that the substantial evidence of entrepreneurial success category shows a steady increase in the number of firms present as the number of strong patterns increases. The percentages rise from 0 to 25, to 43, and finally to 78.

With this information in hand, we now turn to the data on venture origins. The distinctive features that emerge are the fact that complex entrepreneurs with multiple routes available to them are particularly likely to do start-ups alone and they are unlikely to be involved in a low-growth professional or sales practice. Both make sense. With multiple patterns a person can cover more of the business, perhaps including sequencing, without going outside oneself. Partners are simply less necessary. Also with multiple patterns, there is more reason to want to grow an organization. Private practices are not fully satisfying.

If one compares these conclusions with those for the four individual types, the professional and sales practice numbers look much the same. Entrepreneurs of all four types and with varying degrees of complexity all seem predisposed toward growth, not the restrictive size of a practice. However, the predisposition of complex entrepreneurs for start-ups without partners stands out as more pronounced. It is definitely more frequent than among the personal achievers, empathic supersalespeople, and real managers. The expert idea generators are much closer, but this might be expected given the desire these people have to implement their own personal visions. Successful complex entrepreneurs are drawn to the independent initiation of their ventures in disproportionate numbers, and the nature of their talents suggests that that is as it should be.

CONCLUSION

This test of the typology provides consistent empirical support for it. All four types yield significant results, but those for the empathic supersalespeople are in certain respects the most interesting. Here, where the confounding with complexity is minimized, significant findings are still obtained. Also note that the

Table 6.12
Success Subsequent to Testing Obtained by Entrepreneurs with Varying Numbers of Strong Patterns

	Number of Strong Patterns Possessed							
	0		1		2		3 or 4	
Evidence of Entrepreneurial Success	N	%	N	%	N	%	N	%
Substantial	0	0	8	25	10	43	7	78
Some	10	48	20	65	11	48	2	22
Little	11	52	3	10	2	9	0	0
N*	21(6)	100	31(4)	100	23(4)	100	9(2)	100
$x^2(df=6)$				34.14, $p<.01$				

*Numbers in parentheses indicate additional cases with no follow-up evidence.

existence of more types in a person leads to more success, irrespective of which types are involved. This too supports the basic typology.

The evidence insofar as complexity is concerned is strong, too. The hypothesized relationships are obtained consistently.

The fit concept involving types and the career routes each type should follow was not empirically tested in this study. Evidence on this point was derived from the subjects, but it is entirely clinical in nature. A number of instances were noted where for varying periods of time entrepreneurs fell prey to various traps and pitfalls, and did not follow the appropriate route. It was quite apparent that when this happened firm performance suffered. However, because of the nature of the sample, there were few instances where this lack of fit moved through to total business failure. Cases of that kind were unlikely to make their way into the sample in the first place. Furthermore, there were not a great many situations involving a temporary lack of fit. All in all the available data were not suitable for quantitative analysis.

Finally, this study says little about how the existence of a type relates to the founding of a business. The findings on venture origins bear on this matter, but the time perspective is one that extends backward from testing to firm formation or acquisition. We need a study that extends forward from testing to venture creation. Chapter 7 describes such a study.

NOTE

1. I am indebted to John O'del, Eric Williams, and Juan Carlos Pastor for conducting these interviews.

Testing the Typology: Relation to Entrepreneurial Criteria among Graduate Students in Business Management

The objective of this research is to test the typology and certain of its extensions using a sample which differs substantially from the established entrepreneur sample considered in the previous chapter. In addition, the criteria utilized, the dependent variables, are considerably different, extending from a predisposition to enter upon entrepreneurship, to skill in preparing a business plan, to the actual founding of a business. The study design remains longitudinal, however, with psychological measures obtained at an early point serving to establish types which are then related to entrepreneurial criteria usually obtained subsequently.

Before taking up the research methodology in detail, it seems appropriate to preface the discussion with a treatment of the state of entrepreneurship education in business schools. This should be of help in understanding the nature of the specific sample used in the research. For some readers this information will provide nothing that they do not already know, but for others it should serve to make the research more meaningful by placing it in context.

ENTREPRENEURSHIP IN THE BUSINESS SCHOOLS

Historically, there can be little doubt that entrepreneurship has not been the primary focus of teaching and research in the business schools. The most important book on the subject of business education published in recent years says very little about entrepreneurship, while giving substantial attention to corporate management. This is the volume by Porter and McKibbin (1988) which had strong backing from the American Assembly of Collegiate Schools of Business. One clearly comes away from this book with the view that MBA education is intended primarily to prepare students for careers in large companies.

Similarly, a major study of MBAs which focuses on graduates of the Massachusetts Institute of Technology (MIT) gives only passing attention to careers in entrepreneurship (Wallace, 1989). Yet MIT as a university has been a major source of high-technology entrepreneurs (Roberts, 1991b).

This emphasis on the corporate character of graduate business education is not new. Going back some 35 years, one finds a similar thrust in a book out of Carnegie Institute of Technology (now Carnegie-Mellon) written by Dill, Hilton, and Reitman (1962).

Yet many entrepreneurship courses are taught at both the undergraduate and graduate levels in schools of business administration and management, and these courses are increasing in both number and numbers of students served (Gartner and Vesper, 1994; Solomon and Fernald, 1991; Vesper and McMullan, 1988). These courses are discussed in an edited volume by Sexton and Kasarda (1992) and examples are provided in Vesper (1993) and in Center for Entrepreneurial Leadership Inc. (1993, 1994, 1995). A few universities are beginning to offer comprehensive programs and even degrees in the area; these universities make a wide portfolio of courses available.

The following quotation is instructive regarding this situation:

Results from Canada and Australia show that entrepreneurship education at the program level can result in the development of new businesses. In the Australian Swinburne case, 87% of graduates compared to 16% of traditional MBA's are involved in new wealth creating activities. A similar trend is reported for the Canadian case [University of Calgary]. . . . From the experience at Calgary it would appear that a halfway entrepreneurial MBA degree can produce relatively quick results whereas one or two courses in entrepreneurship has a negligible effect; suggesting that a lot more is required than a few courses to induce enhanced levels of entrepreneurial activity. The greater level of commitment to entrepreneurial education at Swinburne through fully integrated courses and involvement of pracademics (with entrepreneurial experience) apparently produces even better results (Gillin, Powe, Dews, and McMullan, 1996, pp. 1, 10–11).

It is interesting that the Swinburne and Calgary examples both come from outside the United States. My impression is that most U.S. MBA programs are indeed oriented to the preparation of students for corporate careers. Where entrepreneurship is taught, and this is certainly increasing, it often tends to be peripheral. This is true in the sense that courses are frequently given by individuals with entrepreneurial experience but who are not writing and doing research in the field, and who are therefore not part of the established university power base and culture (Ivancevich, 1991). It is also true in that many universities have a very small, although often enthusiastic, faculty in the area. They are therefore vulnerable to rapid staffing changes. When a professor who has been promoting entrepreneurship leaves, there may be little left behind, and courses and programs suffer. All in all, entrepreneurship in most U.S. universities still appears to be a highly popular, volatile, and not fully integrated field,

which is decidedly secondary to the corporate thrust that permeates the majority
of courses and is the subject of most faculty writing and research.

Taking a long-term view of the situation at the State University of New York
at Buffalo, from which our data stem, this description appears reasonably ac-
curate. The school is indeed quite typical of graduate schools of business administration in the United States, although more entrepreneurial exceptions are
clearly on the increase. This, then, is the context in which the research sample
of this chapter was obtained and the data collected.

THE SAMPLE OF GRADUATE STUDENTS IN BUSINESS MANAGEMENT

The 159 subjects were accumulated over a five-year period among partici-
pating MBA and Ph.D. students in a graduate entrepreneurship course at the
State University of New York at Buffalo. The course was offered six times in
this period, with the following additions to the sample:

Year 1	26
Year 2	22
Year 3	30
Year 4–1	29
Year 4–2	22
Year 5	30

Although there were occasional differences on individual measures, none of
the independent or dependent variables exhibited any significant differences
across these six classes. Thus, combining the data over the five years is justified.

The following characteristics of the course, which the author taught throughout, will help to define the subject sample.

Description

This is a semester-long MBA elective of three credits offered either once or
twice a year, always by the same faculty member. Enrollments run close to the
limit of 30 since student demand is substantial. There are no specific prerequi-
sites, but most students take the course toward the end of their program.

Two texts are used: Vesper's *New Venture Strategies* (1980, 1990) and Timmons's *New Venture Creation* (1990a). These serve primarily as reference
sources and although specific assignments are given, there is insufficient time
to cover much of the material in class. The course begins with administration
of various instruments measuring locus of control, type A behavior, intelligence,
risk taking, cognitive style, achievement motivation, managerial motivation, and
professional motivation. These are scored by the instructor, and serve as a basis
for discussion of personal factors in entrepreneurial success, as well as to assist

the students in determining whether they should or should not aspire to entrepreneurial careers.

In the second phase of the course students hear visiting speakers who have started a business they are currently running. These speakers are all graduates of a year-long non-degree program for established entrepreneurs conducted under the Center for Entrepreneurial Leadership at SUNY/Buffalo. In this program participants make similar presentations on their businesses and those that are particularly interesting and effective are selected for presentation to the classes.

Finally, each student presents a business plan for a start-up he or she has been involved in or would like to undertake. This oral presentation (given as if it was a pitch for funding) is critiqued by the other students and instructor. Subsequently, students prepare a written version of the plan, limited to 10 pages plus appendices. This paper is the major determinant of the grade received in the course.

History

Although there have been sporadic offerings in the entrepreneurship area at the undergraduate level, no such courses at the graduate level were offered at SUNY/Buffalo until the fall of 1988. Initially, the course was taught under a special topics title simply to see if it would attract students. It did, and consequently there was little difficulty in obtaining formal endorsement of a regular course from the appropriate faculty bodies. The first offering as a regular course was in the spring of 1991. A doctoral seminar on Strategy and Entrepreneurship was also given in the spring of 1992 under a special topics listing.

Experimentation

There has been little time to test varying instructional approaches. Students react very favorably to the class and seem to learn a lot. They like the practical, hands-on emphasis and the opportunity to deal with embryonic organizations outside the corporate sphere. Follow-up research is currently under way to relate the psychological instruments to subsequent entrepreneurial activities (Vesper, 1993, pp. 154–155).

As a group these students may be designated as potential entrepreneurs because they chose the course, presumably out of some interest in the subject with which it dealt. None were required to take it as a part of a major or program of study, and in fact no entrepreneurship major was available to them. It was apparent that the primary source of attraction was the opportunity to learn more about entrepreneurship so as to evaluate it as a career alternative.

Of the 159 subjects, 108 (68%) were males and 51 were females. The mean age was 27.4 and the standard deviation 5.7. However, the third class was a night class (the only one) and there the age level was 32.0. Interestingly, this class also had a higher level of type A behavior. Given that these students were all working and taking courses at the same time, while the other students were less likely to be so overextended, this makes considerable theoretical sense. Also, the 18 Ph.D. students (11% of the sample) were older, at 31.8 years. Many of these students had already completed an MBA, and as might be expected their grades in the course and overall were significantly higher.

The largest number of students in the course were marketing majors—22 percent. This was followed by finance (20%), human resources and organizational behavior (18%), and a general MBA which predominated among night students (15%). The only other sizable group was systems majors, which included manufacturing, at 11 percent. Such areas as accounting, business law, health administration, and international business were not much in evidence in the entrepreneurship course.

THE TEST BATTERY USED WITH THE STUDENTS

Chapter 5 sets forth the measures originally used to determine the levels of characteristics inherent in the various types. Because class time was used to administer the battery, not all of these measures were employed with the students.

The student battery and the types involved included the following (with the numbering being that of Chapter 5):

Personal Achiever Type—

 1. Strong Motivation for Self-Achievement
    (b) *Miner Sentence Completion Scale—Form T: Self Achievement Subscale*

 2. Type A Personality
    (a) *Individual Behavior Activity Profile*

 3. Desire for Feedback on Achievements
    Miner Sentence Completion Scale—Form T: Feedback of Results Subscale

 4. Desire to Plan and Set Goals for Future Achievements
    Miner Sentence Completion Scale—Form T: Planning for the Future Subscale

 6. Strong Personal Commitment to the Venture
    Miner Sentence Completion Scale—Form P: Professional Commitment Subscale

 7. Desire to Obtain Information and Learn
    Miner Sentence Completion Scale—Form P: Acquiring Knowledge Subscale

 8. Internal Locus of Control
    (b) *Levenson Internal-External Instrument: Internal Control Scale*
    (c) *Levenson Internal-External Instrument: Powerful Others External Control Scale*
    (d) *Levenson Internal-External Instrument: Chance External Control Scale*

Real Manager Type—

 7. Positive Attitudes toward Authority
    Miner Sentence Completion Scale—Form H: Authority Figures Subscale

 8. Desire to Compete with Others
    (a) *Miner Sentence Completion Scale—Form H: Competitive Situations Subscale*
    (b) *Miner Sentence Completion Scale—Form H: Competitive Games Subscale*

9. Desire to Assert Oneself
   Miner Sentence Completion Scale—Form H: Assertive Role Subscale

10. Desire to Exercise Power
    Miner Sentence Completion Scale—Form H: Imposing Wishes Subscale

11. Directive in Cognitive Style
    Decision Style Inventory: Directive

12. Desire to Stand Out from the Crowd
    Miner Sentence Completion Scale—Form H: Standing Out from Group Subscale

13. Desire to Perform Managerial Tasks
    Miner Sentence Completion Scale—Form H: Routine Administrative Functions Subscale

Expert Idea Generator Type—

1. Desire to Personally Innovate
   Miner Sentence Completion Scale—Form T: Personal Innovation Subscale

2. Conceptual in Cognitive Style
   (a) *Decision Style Inventory: Conceptual*
   (b) *Problem Solving Questionnaire: Intuition*

4. High Intelligence
   (b) *Vocabulary Test G-T: Forms A and B*

5. Desire to Avoid Taking Risks
   (a) *Miner Sentence Completion Scale—Form T: Avoiding Risks Subscale*
   (b) *Shure and Meeker Risk Avoidance Scale*

Empathic Supersalesperson Type—

1. Empathic in Cognitive Style
   (a) *Decision Style Inventory: Behavioral*
   (b) *Problem Solving Questionnaire: Feeling*

2. Desire to Help Others
   Miner Sentence Completion Scale—Form P: Providing Help Subscale

The tests were administered to the students during the first two class sessions. Because even entrepreneurship courses experience the dropping and adding of students at the beginning of the semester that is typical of most courses, there were a few students who did not complete the test battery and a few also that did not complete the course subsequent to taking the tests. Occasionally, a student would enter the course late, and in these cases the testing was done outside the classroom.

Scores were developed from the student battery using the same conversion process employed in Chapter 6. Thus, we had the following:

Personal achiever score—range 0 to 18
Real manager score—range 0 to 16
Expert idea generator score—range 0 to 12
Empathic supersalesperson score—range 0 to 6

Complex entrepreneurs
    Number of types present from 2 to 4
    Composite score—range 0 to 52

The four type scores are based on 79, 55, 101, and 36 items respectively.

- The mean personal achiever score among the students was 5.3, the standard deviation 3.1, and the actual score range 0 to 15.
- The mean real manager score was 2.4, the standard deviation 1.8, and the actual range 0 to 9.
- The mean expert idea generator score was 3.2, the standard deviation 1.7, and the actual range 0 to 8.
- The mean empathic supersalesperson score was 2.1, the standard deviation 1.7, and the actual range the full 0 to 6.
- The mean composite score for complex entrepreneurs was 12.9, the standard deviation 4.7, and the actual range 4 to 28.
- Multiple types were present in 25 students (21 with two, 3 with three, and 1 with four). The 25 represent 17 percent of the usable base N.

This latter result raises the question of how the types were actually defined using the student battery. The procedure involved going back to the established entrepreneur sample and obtaining scores from that group using only the test measures of the student battery. To establish the points on the personal achiever, real manager, expert idea generator, empathic supersalesperson, and composite score distributions where a type was identified, we moved down from the top by the same percentage of the established entrepreneur sample as had been employed previously in the Chapter 6 analysis with the larger test battery. Because the frequencies in the score distribution were not the same for the student and established entrepreneur batteries, this process did not yield exactly the same result as previously, but the cutting score was established so as to produce the closest possible percentage to that obtained with the full battery.

The results within the established entrepreneur sample look as follows:

	Score to Define Type	Percent in Type
Personal achiever	10 or above	28
Real manager	5 or above	28
Expert idea generator	5 or above	44
Empathic supersalesperson	3 or above	33
Composite score	20 or above	34

These percentages are very close to those for the full battery in the case of the personal achiever score and the composite score; they are only five or six percentage points off for the real manager score (low) and the empathic supersalesperson score (high). However, the expert idea generator score yields an 11 percent difference (high).

When this same definition of a type is applied using the student battery in the student sample, the following results are obtained:

	Percent in Type
Personal achiever	10
Real manager	10
Expert idea generator	25
Empathic supersalesperson	38
Composite score	9

The students have distinctly fewer individuals of the personal achiever, real manager, and expert idea generator types, and accordingly there are many fewer complex entrepreneurs. However, there are actually somewhat more empathic supersalespeople in the student sample than among the established entrepreneurs. These empathic supersalespeople are concentrated among the marketing and human resource management majors—not an unexpected finding.

Does the student test battery yield a score that is comparable to the full test battery? The correlations between the two scores in the established entrepreneur sample are as follows:

Personal achiever	.89
Real manager	.72
Expert idea generator	.94
Empathic supersalesperson	.81
Composite	.82

In addition, the intercorrelations among these scores obtained with the student battery follow essentially the same pattern as with the full battery (see Table 6.10). If there is any meaningful deviation from the full battery results it occurs when the real manager score is used, but even then the difference is not large.

A higher personal achiever score among the established entrepreneurs is due to statistically significant differences in self-achievement motivation, type A personality, desire for feedback, personal commitment, and on all three locus of control measures. Desire to plan and set goals and desire to obtain information and learn produce no significant findings.

The real manager score also differs between the two samples, and this occurs due to significant results favoring the established entrepreneurs in positive attitudes to authority, desire to exercise power, directive cognitive style, and desire to perform managerial tasks. There are no significant differences in terms of either index of the desire to compete, the desire to assert oneself, or the desire to stand out from the crowd.

On the expert idea generator score the difference is again significant, with the entrepreneurs having higher scores as a result of a greater desire to personally innovate, and also to avoid taking risks (as measured by the MSCS—T scale). This latter difference is very large, with the students scoring strongly in the risk taking direction. The age difference of 15 years between the two samples is clearly a factor here. No significant differences were found in conceptual cognitive style, intelligence, or risk taking as measured by the Shure and Meeker instrument.

The two groups do not differ significantly insofar as the empathic super-salesperson score is concerned, or on any of its component measures.

The composite score for measuring complexity yields means of 17.3 in the established entrepreneur sample and of 12.9 for the students ($t=7.61$, $p<.01$). This is consistent with what is obtained with the multiple-types measure.

Adding up all these figures leaves one with the distinct impression that the actual entrepreneurial potential in the student group is limited. It seems likely that many who might enter upon an MBA program such as this, and who possess entrepreneurial potential, are dissuaded by the strong corporate, although not necessarily managerial, emphasis of the program. At a time when corporate employment overall is declining in the United States, this decline resulted in the MBA degree becoming less attractive, and a decrease in enrollments as a consequence. A greater focus on the needs of potential entrepreneurs can change this pattern, and attract students who currently view the MBA as irrelevant. This, however, would require a major reimaging process for many business schools, a transfusion in terms of faculty expertise, and a substantial change in curriculum. Doctoral training programs would have to be altered dramatically to produce professors prepared to teach a more entrepreneur-oriented MBA curriculum. Things are moving in this direction, to be sure, but much more slowly than the need.

THE ENTREPRENEURIAL CRITERIA

In order to gain an understanding of how the psychological types relate to entrepreneurial endeavors among business graduate students, we took readings of the students as they began the entrepreneurship course, as they completed it, and subsequently after they had left school and been working for a while. The types were established on the basis of the tests administered at the very beginning of the course.

The reading of entrepreneurial propensity taken as the course began was based on information provided by the students. It dealt with their past, current, and intended future entrepreneurial activity. This approach has a solid grounding in research among student populations. The most frequent procedure is to use a question regarding the probability of starting a business in the near future or at some point later on (Crant, 1996; Koh, 1996; Matthews and Moser, 1995) as a criterion of entrepreneurial activity. Other approaches utilize an expanded concept of entrepreneurial career preference (Scherer, Brodzinski, and Wiebe, 1991).

On the other hand, the following statement, based on research among students, gives some pause:

Student entrepreneurs, while entrepreneurs in their own right, are different from nonstudent entrepreneurs. Because of this, using student entrepreneurs in research that is intended to be descriptive of and generalize to the entrepreneurial population as a whole is a questionable practice (Robinson, Huefner, and Hunt, 1991).

Accordingly, our entrepreneurial propensity score must be viewed with some trepidation. Nevertheless, on the evidence overall it seems indicative of activity in the entrepreneurship area, especially since it includes past or current activity as an entrepreneur in addition to future activity.

This propensity measure contains five free-response questions scored on a scale from 0 to 2, to yield an overall measure with a possible range from 0 to 10. The questions and the scoring of responses were as follows:

1. Are you working at present and, if so, what are you doing?

Not working or not self-employed	0
Partly self-employed and/or in what appears to be a professional or sales practice	1
Fully self-employed in a business	2

2. What is your immediate career objective after you leave school?

No mention of starting or buying a business	0
Mention of starting or buying a business, but with some uncertainty, or of starting what appears to be a professional or sales practice	1
Starting or buying a business	2

3. What is your long-range career objective?

No mention of starting or buying a business	0
Mention of starting or buying a business, but with some uncertainty, or of starting what appears to be a professional or sales practice	1
Starting or buying a business	2

4. Have you ever been involved in founding a business? If so, please describe it.

Never founded a business	0
Founded a business, but it was either very small or a franchise, or failed	1
Founded a business that did not fail	2

5. What are your reasons for taking this course?

No reason related to starting up a business	0
Reason stated related to entrepreneurship, but not fully involving a personal commitment to entrepreneurial activity	1
Reason stated as learning how to start a business	2

This measure was administered at the same time as the student test battery. The mean score was 2.9 and the standard deviation 2.1. Only 16 students (10% of the sample) were above the mid-point score of 5. Again, we find evidence that this is not a highly entrepreneurial group.

The next reading of the students' proclivity for entrepreneurship came as they left the course and submitted a business plan for a new venture. The assumption was that the students who wanted most to be entrepreneurs and were most likely to start new ventures would work hardest at their business plans and produce plans of the highest quality. Those who were simply trying to fulfill course requirements would do less well. These plans were a major factor in the course grades and in most cases largely determined them. Guides to preparing these plans came from Timmons (1990a) and later from Timmons (1990b). Thus, the students had a very comprehensive model to work from, and they were encouraged to go out and interview established entrepreneurs in the industry as well to get help developing their plans. To the extent they worked hard, and were original, their grades were likely to manifest that fact.

The planning guides from which the students worked covered the following:

Executive Summary (Summary Description of the Business; Opportunity and Strategy; Target Market and Projections; Competitive Advantages; Economics, Profitability and Harvest Potential; Team; and Offering).

Industry, the Company, and its Products or Services (Industry; Company; Products or Services; and Entry and Growth Strategy).

Market Research and Analysis (Customers; Market Size and Trends; Competition and Competitive Edges; Estimated Market Share and Sales; and On-going Market Evaluation).

Economics of the Business (Gross and Operating Margins; Profit Potential and Durability; Fixed and Variable Costs; Months to Break-even; and Months to Reach Positive Cash Flow).

Marketing Plan (Overall Marketing Strategy; Pricing; Sales Tactics; Service and Warranty Policies; Advertising and Promotion; and Distribution).

Design and Development Plans (Development Status and Tasks; Difficulties and Risks; Product Improvement and New Products; Costs; and Proprietary Issues).

Manufacturing and Operations Plans (Geographical Location; Facilities and Capacity Improvements; Strategy and Plans; and Regulatory, Other Compliance, Approvals, and Environmental Issues).

Management Team (Organization; Key Management Personnel; Management Compensation and Ownership; Other Investors; Incentives, Vesting, Employment Agreements; Board of Directors; Other Shareholders, Rights and Restrictions; and Supporting Professional Advisors and Services).

Overall Schedule

Critical Risks and Problems

Financial Plans (Profit and Loss Forecasts; Pro Forma Cash Flow Analysis; Pro Forma Balance Sheets; and Break-even Chart and Calculation).

Proposed Company Offering (Desired Financing; Securities Offering; Capitalization; and Use of Funds).

Financial Exhibits (Pro Forma Income Statement; Pro Forma Cash Flows; Pro Forma Balance Sheets; and Break-even Chart and Calculation).

Appendices which might include such items as (Lists, specs, pictures of products, systems, software; list of customers, suppliers, references; appropriate location factors, facilities, or technical analyses; independent reports by technical experts, consultants; detailed résumés of founders, key managers; and any critical regulatory, environmental, or other compliances, licenses, or approvals).

The plans were to be reasonably short (in the vicinity of 10 pages) and were written after an oral presentation critiqued by the class and the instructor. The objective was to obtain funding for the venture described. Research indicates that success in obtaining funding is in fact related to psychological factors of the kind utilized in the present study (Pandey and Tewary, 1979). The plans were graded by the author with the values assigned ranging from A to C$^+$; the mean grade was in the B$^+$ range. In 16 of the 159 cases no business plan grade was available because the student left the course subsequent to testing without preparing a plan.

The final, and most significant, entrepreneurial criterion was evidence of entrepreneurial activity, or the lack of such activity, subsequent to graduation. Did these people go out and found a business when they first had an opportunity to do so? Or, in a few cases, were they continuing in a venture that they had started prior to or during the time they were attending classes? To answer this question we waited until we knew the student had left the university (in almost all cases with a degree) and then attempted to contact the individual first via letters and if that failed, with telephone calls.[1] On the average, contact, if made, occurred a year after leaving the university.

Of the 159 students, 8 could not be used in the study because they were still in students status as the research ended. Another 36 students simply were lost. We tried to locate them and to find out about their employment status, but it proved impossible to do so. Thus, the follow-up sample actually numbered 115. In 85 of these cases (74%) we could find no evidence of entrepreneurial activity. The remainder were engaged in entrepreneurship as follows:

Part-time participation in a business start-up (usually in conjunction with some other job)—17 (15%)

Full-time participation in a business start-up—8 (7%)

Engaged in teaching and/or research in the entrepreneurship area—5 (4%)

The latter category was included to accommodate those among the Ph.D. students who were in fact engaged in a type of entrepreneurial activity. A sizable proportion of professors in the entrepreneurship field participate in entrepreneurial ventures at various points in their careers; this category was included to recognize that fact. We have found that university faculty in the entrepreneurship area often do have personality profiles consistent with actual entrepreneurial performance. It is consistent with this fact that many have started businesses. I remember attending one conference of teachers of entrepreneurship where this matter came up. A show of hands indicated that a great majority had at one time or another started a business.

Several aspects of this criterion should be noted. For one thing, we know little about the success of these ventures, only that they had been created, and as of a short time later in most cases, had not failed. How many were in fact professional or sales practices we could not determine, but it seems apparent that some would have been placed in that category had sufficient information been available. Most of the ventures were quite small at the time we contacted the student-turned-entrepreneur. Also, we could find little evidence of corporate venturing. There was a small amount of this kind of activity, as well as of purchased businesses and family business participation, in the entrepreneurship group, but not on any substantial scale. It is conceivable that we missed some corporate venture activity in the "no evidence of entrepreneurial activity" group; that errors of this kind occurred often is very unlikely.

Overall it seems apparent that this is not a highly entrepreneurial group. However, the follow-up was only short term, and the students may well become more entrepreneurially active later. On the other hand, the lack of strong patterns and the primarily corporate rather than entrepreneurial nature of their education would have to raise questions in this regard.

Table 7.1 contains data on the relationships among the three entrepreneurial criteria—the two proximate measures involving early entrepreneurial propensity and skill in business plan preparation, and the ultimate index of actual entrepreneurial activity. The categories employed in Table 7.1 are those used in the validation analyses. As anticipated, the three criteria are all significantly related.

RESULTS—THE PERSONAL ACHIEVER TYPE

Table 7.2 gives the relation of the personal achievers among the students to the three criteria in comparison with the 56 students who had no strong patterns at all. The propensity score finding is pronounced; 75 percent of these students were in the highest category on propensity. On the business plan the results do not quite reach significance, but they are close, and 69 percent of the personal achievers on whom data are available obtained A^- or A grades. Also, 69 percent of the personal achievers on whom we had information gave evidence of entrepreneurial activity, as against only 5 percent of those with no strong pattern. This result, on the criterion that is most relevant, is striking.

Table 7.1
Relationships among Entrepreneurial Criteria Using Categories Employed in Validation Analysis

| | Entrepreneurial Propensity Score | | | | | | | |
| | 0-1 | | 2-3 | | 4-10 | | Totals | |
Business Plan Grade	N	%	N	%	N	%	N	%
A⁻ or A	17	22	25	33	34	45	76	100
B⁺	6	24	12	48	7	28	25	100
B or less	14	33	21	50	7	17	42	100

$x^2(df=4)$ 10.33, $p<.05$ (missing data=16)

| | Evidence of Entrepreneurial Activity Post-graduation | | | | | |
| | None | | Present | | Totals | |
Entrepreneurial Propensity Score	N	%	N	%	N	%
4-10	20	56	16	44	36	100
2-3	37	84	7	16	44	100
0-1	28	80	7	20	35	100

$x^2(df=2)$ 9.30, $p<.01$ (missing data=44)

| | Business Plan Grade | | | | | | | |
| Evidence of Entrepreneurial | B or less | | B⁺ | | A⁻ or A | | Totals | |
Activity Post-graduation	N	%	N	%	N	%	N	%
Present	2	7	3	11	22	82	27	100
None	26	32	15	18	41	50	82	100

$x^2(df=2)$ 8.78, $p<.02$ (missing data=50)

Table 7.2

Performance on Entrepreneurial Criteria of Personal Achiever Types in Comparison with Students Possessing No Strong Pattern

	No Strong Pattern Present		Personal Achiever Pattern Present	
Entrepreneurial Propensity Score	N	%	N	%
4-10	13	23	12	75
2-3	23	41	3	19
0-1	20	36	1	6
N	56	100	16	100
$x^2(df=2)$	15.34, p<.01			
Business Plan Grade				
A⁻ or A	20	36	9	69
B⁺	15	28	3	23
B or less	20	36	1	8
N*	55(1)	100	13(3)	100
$x^2(df=2)$	5.72, p<.10			
Evidence of Entrepreneurial Activity Post-graduation				
Present	2	5	9	69
None	36	95	4	31
N*	38(18)	100	13(3)	100
$x^2(df=1)$	23.48, p<.01			

*Numbers in parentheses indicate additional cases with missing data.

All in all, the personal achievers in the student sample are not a very large group, but the evidence for a strong tie to entrepreneurship is substantial. These people get into entrepreneurial activities just as soon as they possibly can.

RESULTS—THE REAL MANAGER TYPE

Table 7.3 sets forth the results for the real managers, who, like the personal achievers, are few in number among the students. With 60 percent of these real managers in the top propensity category the findings on this criterion are significant. However, the business plan results do not reach significance, primarily because a sizable proportion of the real managers did not do particularly well in this regard. Yet real managers do get into entrepreneurship in sizable numbers, 64 percent of those on whom information could be obtained.

The overall picture for the real managers yields somewhat less support for the two proximate criteria than with the personal achievers. Yet evidence of entrepreneurial activity post-graduation is at roughly the same level in the two groups. A number of real managers do become entrepreneurially active, many more than among those who have no strong pattern.

RESULTS—THE EXPERT IDEA GENERATOR TYPE

The expert idea generators (see Table 7.4) in the student sample do not appear to be as motivated to jump quickly into entrepreneurship as the personal achievers and real managers. This is manifest in the lack of a significant finding on the entrepreneurial propensity criterion. The data are in the right direction, but they are not strong. Also, on the entrepreneurial activity criterion, the proportion of active expert idea generators is clearly down from the results of Tables 7.2 and 7.3—39 percent versus 69 percent and 64 percent. Yet these findings remain highly significant, as are those on the business plan criterion. In fact, the expert idea generators have the highest percentage of A⁻ and A grades of any of the four types.

This pattern of findings suggests that the expert idea generators are planning to get into entrepreneurship, but in a number of cases need time to acquire and consolidate their expert status. These are people who require more time to learn and who thus tend to be older when they enter entrepreneurship. Our net, cast at an early point in their careers, may very well not have been positioned to catch them.

RESULTS—THE EMPATHIC SUPERSALESPERSON TYPE

The data of Table 7.5 for empathic supersalespeople are very much like those for the expert idea generators. Significance is found in the same places—with the business plan criterion and post-graduation entrepreneurial activity. Yet the 32 percent in the top propensity category and the 62 percent with A⁻ or A

Table 7.3

Performance on Entrepreneurial Criteria of Real Manager Types in Comparison with Students Possessing No Strong Pattern

	No Strong Pattern Present		Real Manager Pattern Present	
Entrepreneurial Propensity Score	N	%	N	%
4-10	13	23	9	60
2-3	23	41	3	20
0-1	20	36	3	20
N	56	100	15	100
$x^2(df=2)$		7.70, $p<.05$		
Business Plan Grade				
A- or A	20	36	7	54
B+	15	28	1	8
B or less	20	36	5	38
$N*$	55(1)	100	13(2)	100
$x^2(df=2)$		2.64 NS		
Evidence of Entrepreneurial Activity Post-graduation				
Present	2	5	7	64
None	36	95	4	36
$N*$	38(18)	100	11(4)	100
$x^2(df=1)$		19.66 $p<.01$		

*Numbers in parentheses indicate additional cases with missing data.

144

Table 7.4

Performance on Entrepreneurial Criteria of Expert Idea Generator Types in Comparison with Students Possessing No Strong Pattern

	No Strong Pattern Present		Expert Idea Generator Pattern Present	
	N	%	N	%
Entrepreneurial Propensity Score				
4-10	13	23	15	38
2-3	23	41	14	35
0-1	20	36	11	27
N	56	100	40	100
$x^2(df=2)$			2.30 NS	
Business Plan Grade				
A⁻ or A	20	36	24	71
B⁺	15	28	3	9
B or less	20	36	7	20
N^*	55(1)	100	34(6)	100
$x^2(df=2)$			10.28, $p<.01$	
Evidence of Entrepreneurial Activity Post-graduation				
Present	2	5	12	39
None	36	95	19	61
N^*	38(18)	100	31(9)	100
$x^2(df=1)$			11.77 $p<.01$	

*Numbers in parentheses indicate additional cases with missing data.

145

grades on the business plan are below the expert idea generators, and the 37 percent figure for entrepreneurial activity is the lowest obtained by any of the types. Also, remember that this is the only type that contains roughly the same numbers of people among the students as among the established entrepreneurs.

In this instance it appears that many of these empathic supersalespeople are taking their marketing degrees and heading off to the large corporations for which they have been trained. A likely hypothesis is that they are entering on sales and marketing careers which will occupy them for many years; many may never enter into entrepreneurship.

RESULTS—THE COMPLEX ENTREPRENEUR

To get an understanding of how complexity operates among the students, let us start with the question of how likely it is that at least one other type will be present in the same person, if a particular type exists.

Among the personal achievers this figure is 50 percent—down from 86 percent among the established entrepreneurs. Thus, the students do not bring nearly the same added strength from complexity to their personal achiever type that established entrepreneurs do.

Real managers from the student sample, however, have essentially the same proportion of complex entrepreneurs with multiple types as the established entrepreneurs do—80 percent, as against 82 percent for the latter group. Many of these real managers have an added strength that will take them through the early period of a growing business up to the time when their managerial capabilities can be brought to bear.

The student expert idea generators possess another strong pattern above and beyond that of expert idea generators 45 percent of the time. This figure is down considerably from the 67 percent among the established entrepreneurs.

Finally, among the empathic supersalespeople in the student sample, complexity is present in only 30 percent of the cases. As with the established entrepreneurs this is the lowest complexity rate of any of the types. However, the drop from the established entrepreneur percentage of 48 is not as pronounced as with some of the other types.

There is only one four-pattern person in the student sample, and only three individuals with three strong patterns. Consequently, little can be said about complexity levels above two types; there simply are not enough instances to consider separately. At the level of two types the most frequent combination is expert idea generator and empathic supersalesperson. This result appears to reflect the severely depressed proportions of personal achievers and real managers in the student sample.

Table 7.6 compares the students without a strong pattern with those who exhibit complexity, either through multiple types or a high composite score, using the three entrepreneurial criteria. The findings are statistically significant in all but one instance, and even there the chi-square value is at $p<.10$. Being

Table 7.5

Performance on Entrepreneurial Criteria of Empathic Supersalesperson Types in Comparison with Students Possessing No Strong Pattern

Entrepreneurial Propensity Score	No Strong Pattern Present		Empathic Supersalesperson Pattern Present	
	N	%	N	%
4-10	13	23	18	32
2-3	23	41	22	39
0-1	20	36	16	29
N	56	100	56	100
$x^2(df=2)$		1.26 NS		
Business Plan Grade				
A⁻ or A	20	36	32	62
B⁺	15	28	7	13
B or less	20	36	13	25
$N*$	55(1)	100	52(4)	100
$x^2(df=2)$		7.03, $p<.05$		
Evidence of Entrepreneurial Activity Post-graduation				
Present	2	5	15	37
None	36	95	26	63
$N*$	38(18)	100	41(15)	100
$x^2(df=1)$		13.05, $p<.01$		

*Numbers in parentheses indicate additional cases with missing data.

a complex entrepreneur clearly contributes to subsequent entrepreneurial activity. The two proximate criteria produce less striking results, but even on these, support for the complexity hypothesis is obtained, especially when the composite score is used to establish complexity.

When comparisons are made between the presence of subsequent entrepreneurial activity, which appears to be the most appropriate criterion, and the incidence of multiple types, the results are as follows:

Type	Entrepreneurial Activity	More Than One Type
Personal achiever	69%	50%
Real manager	64%	80%
Expert idea generator	39%	45%
Empathic supersalesperson	37%	30%

As with the established entrepreneurs and a firm growth criterion, there is reason to believe that complexity influences the level of subsequent entrepreneurial activity of the students. However, there is one substantial departure from the previous pattern. A number of personal achievers enter into entrepreneurship without being complex entrepreneurs. It is tempting to predict that there will be a somewhat higher incidence of business failure later on in this group, or at least a failure to become established entrepreneurs, but the data are not actually available to say one way or the other.

This evidence for the value of complexity is reinforced in another way by the data of Table 7.7. Unfortunately, the lack of three- and four-pattern individuals restricts the usefulness of these findings for testing the hypothesis that increasing numbers of strong patterns result in increasing performance on entrepreneurial criteria. However, as far as it goes, the information in Table 7.7 does support that hypothesis. Entrepreneurial activity increases from 5 percent with no strong pattern, to 28 percent with one, to 68 percent with two or more. This is the most pronounced finding, and the most convincing. Yet the percentage with elevated propensity scores, even though not quite significant at $p<.05$, rises in the same manner (from 23% to 48%), as does the proportion with A$^-$ or A grades on the business plan (from 36% to 68%). All in all, none of the evidence contradicts the multiple types hypothesis and a considerable amount supports it.

ILLUSTRATIONS OF ENTREPRENEURIAL ACTIVITY AMONG THE STUDENTS

The brief case histories which follow are intended to make the statistics of this chapter somewhat more meaningful. These are the kinds of things that students of various types actually did.

A Personal Achiever: John Jaski. Mr. Jaski pursued a degree program which gave him both a law degree and an MBA. His undergraduate degree was in

Table 7.6

Performance on Entrepreneurial Criteria of Complex Entrepreneurs in Comparison with Students Possessing No Strong Pattern

	No Strong Pattern Present		Complex Entrepreneurs — Multiple Types		High Composite Score	
	N	%	N	%	N	%
Entrepreneurial Propensity Score						
4-10	13	23	12	48	9	69
2-3	23	41	6	24	1	8
0-1	20	36	7	28	3	23
N	56	100	25	100	13	100
$x^2(df=2)$			5.21, $p<.10$		11.10, $p<.01$	
Business Plan Grade						
A⁻ or A	20	36	15	68	10	84
B⁺	15	28	2	9	1	8
B or less	20	36	5	23	1	8
N^*	55(1)	100	22(3)	100	12(1)	100
$x^2(df=2)$			6.79, $p<.05$		8.69, $p<.02$	
Evidence of Entrepreneurial Activity Post-graduation						
Present	2	5	13	68	10	91
None	36	95	6	32	1	9
N^*	38(18)	100	19(6)	100	11(2)	100
$x^2(df=1)$			26.06, $p<.01$		33.75, $p<.01$	

*Numbers in parentheses indicate additional cases with missing data.

Table 7.7

Performance on Entrepreneurial Criteria of Students with Varying Numbers of Strong Patterns

	Number of Strong Patterns Possessed					
	0		1		2-4	
	N	%	N	%	N	%
Entrepreneurial Propensity Score						
4-10	13	23	26	37	12	48
2-3	23	41	30	43	6	24
0-1	20	36	14	20	7	28
N	56	100	70	100	25	100
$x^2(df=4)$			8.19, $p<.10$			
Business Plan Grade						
A⁻ or A	20	36	40	62	15	68
B⁺	15	28	8	13	2	9
B or less	20	36	16	25	5	23
N*	55(1)	100	64(6)	100	22(3)	100
$x^2(df=4)$			11.17, $p<.05$			
Evidence of Entrepreneurial Activity Post-graduation						
Present	2	5	15	28	13	68
None	36	95	39	72	6	32
N*	38(18)	100	54(16)	100	19(6)	100
$x^2(df=2)$			25.92, $p<.01$			

*Numbers in parentheses indicate additional cases with missing data.

political science, and he operated a small business in the construction industry during this period.

As a personal achiever, Jaski is characterized by a very strong achievement motivation, a desire to plan and set goals for future achievements, an especially pronounced internal locus of control which is tied to a belief that external chance events will not exert influence, and a strong type A personality. Although the personal achiever pattern is clearly dominant, all three other patterns are above the average for entrepreneurs.

Jaski has opened a solo law practice, having been admitted to the bar prior to completing the MBA. Although on the surface this might appear to represent a professional private practice, there are several factors that dispel this impression. For one thing the practice operates in tandem with another solo practice in another city. Second, Jaski has every intention of growing the practice through the addition of both support staff and other lawyers. Finally, he has opened a retail book store not far from his law office. Clearly, this is a professional who is expanding into entrepreneurship. In the process he is making effective use of both his legal and his business education. Certainly, in the short term the legal education is more relevant. However, as he diversifies into other businesses beyond his profession, the MBA can add increasing value. Personal achievers often have as one of their characteristics a desire to find out information and learn, and to the extent this is true—the MBA can be very attractive to them.

On the business plan Jaski received a grade of B$^+$ and his entrepreneurial propensity score was in the highest category.

A Real Manager: Norma Uleman. Ms. Uleman is a marketing MBA with a good background in accounting and computers as well. She is predominantly a real manager who tends to have a strong directive cognitive style, a liking for competition, a pronounced desire to exercise power, and a desire to differentiate herself from others around her. She is well above the entrepreneur average on all three other patterns as well, with the result that her combined entrepreneur score is quite high. By this criterion she would have to be considered a complex entrepreneur, even though only the one pattern really stands out.

Uleman started a business providing bookkeeping services on a mobile basis to small and mid-sized companies. It was a highly computerized operation. The business continued for some time subsequent to the award of her MBA, but finally she moved to another city with her husband and was forced to terminate it. She now has entered the corporate world, first in sales and then in an administrative capacity. This close tie to corporate management is characteristic of real managers, and certainly the sales orientation fits with what can be expected prior to entering upon a full-scale managerial position. It is hard to say where Uleman will go from here, but certainly a return to entrepreneurship cannot be ruled out. Her MBA is neutral in this respect; it can help her in either type of career. Having passed through one entrepreneurial venture, she is moving toward a corporate career where the MBA experience should be immediately applicable. Yet there remains the possibility that all of this will ultimately be put to an entrepreneurial end. It is still early and difficult to tell.

Insofar as her entrepreneurial propensity score is concerned, Uleman was at a very high level; her business plan grade was an A.

An Expert Idea Generator: Costas Pappas. Mr. Pappas was reared in Greece. His MBA is in marketing and international business. As an undergraduate in the United States he obtained a degree in business administration, but with a strong orientation to liberal studies.

He is, to an extent far above what is indicated by the other pattern scores, an expert idea generator. This involves a strong desire to introduce innovative solutions, a major commitment to both intuitive and conceptual cognitive styles, and a compensating desire to avoid taking risks. This is the essence of an expert idea generator pattern, and the only other pattern even approximating it is that of a personal achiever, still well behind.

Pappas returned to Greece after his MBA and worked for a large corporation there in the treasury management area for several years. More recently he has gone on his own, leasing out yachts to the tourist trade for vacations in the surrounding waters. He has been able to locate a niche in this industry whereby he can borrow money to finance yacht purchases and still make a substantial profit. His skill is clearly in niche identification, and this skill was enhanced through what he learned during his MBA training. He has learned the skills of business administration to a point of expertise, then worked in finance to perfect this expertise, and only then started a venture which depends on financial know-how.

Although his entrepreneurial propensity score was at about the average for the students, Pappas obtained an A⁻ grade on his business plan.

An Empathic Supersalesperson: Gloria Sosa. Ms. Sosa has earned an MBA in marketing. Her undergraduate degree is in accounting, and she is a CPA. Although consistent with her accounting background Sosa possesses strong professional motivation, she has the empathic supersaleswoman pattern of an entrepreneur. She is behavioral in her cognitive style with a highly positive orientation to people, and she also has a very strong desire to help others. She has a concern for the sales force as an instrument of company strategy, ranking that factor number one in her company among various competitive strategic thrusts. No other entrepreneurial pattern is particularly significant.

Sosa operates her business while continuing to work as a CPA in an accounting firm and to teach accounting at a community college. Thus her entrepreneurial activity is part-time and it is with a partner. The business, which involves real estate development, started up while she was in graduate school. Originally, it had an equity interest in apartment complexes which it also managed. More recently it has moved into home construction. Sosa handles financial matters for the firm, but she is also increasingly involved in marketing and customer relations. Her graduate education has contributed in these latter areas. Movement from accounting to the sales and marketing thrust that characterized the MBA is of recent origin, but continuing. If this route is followed consistently the results should be favorable and the MBA education should be useful. At this point it is a bit early, however, to determine whether the psychological pattern and career route as reflected in the MBA will gel completely.

Sosa's entrepreneurial propensity score is high, placing her well up in the top category. She received an A on her business plan.

A Complex Entrepreneur: Louis Alba. Mr. Alba has an MBA with a finance major. He is very strong on three of the four patterns—empathic supersalesperson, real manager, and expert idea generator—and comes very close to being equally strong on the personal achiever pattern as well. He is a complex entrepreneur because he possesses these multiple patterns and also because he has a very high combined entrepreneur score.

As an empathic supersalesman he is characterized by a feeling cognitive style and a very strong desire to help others. As a true manager he possesses a directive cognitive style, a strong desire to exercise power, and a desire to differentiate himself so as to stand out from the crowd. As an expert idea generator he is a person who has the desire to introduce innovative solution, a very distinctly intuitive cognitive style, and yet a substantial desire to avoid taking risks.

Alba, along with several partners, formed a firm to provide floral designs and horticultural displays while he was still an undergraduate. The venture has been sufficiently successful so that he has been able to support his MBA work from its earnings. His long-term objective is to form a company to engage in international trade with the Eastern European countries. At present he is exploring opportunities and developing ideas with this objective in mind. His MBA education has proven valuable as he looks at various methods of financing this type of venture, although he also feels he needs a stronger background in international law.

In this instance the student has already achieved success in one venture prior to starting the MBA. He is young, however, and reaching out for new opportunities. He is not fully convinced at this point that his MBA provides all the expertise he needs for this purpose, although it certainly has provided him with new avenues.

On the business plan Alba obtained an A grade, and his entrepreneurial propensity score was in the highest category.

Another Complex Entrepreneur: Michael Tyler. Mr. Tyler has an MBA degree with specialization in finance. His undergraduate work was of a scientific nature. He is a complex entrepreneur in that he possesses multiple patterns consisting of both the personal achiever and expert idea generator types. This has not proved to be a frequent combination in any of the groups studied. The personal achiever pattern is reflected in a strong achievement motivation, a very pronounced desire for feedback on achievement, a desire to plan and set goals for future achievements, an internal locus of control which is added to a belief that chance factors have little influence, a type A personality, and a very strong desire to find out information and learn.

As an expert idea generator Tyler has a strong desire to introduce innovative solutions, an intuitive and conceptual cognitive style, and the desire to avoid risks needed to keep his enthusiasm for his ideas under control. He is indeed a very creative person.

For some time Tyler has been engaged in inventing products for inclusion in weapons systems. Some of his ideas have been good, some he has ended by rejecting. He now has taken one such idea to the point of a patent application and the establishment of a joint venture to manufacture the product. Clearly, the MBA has been of value as Tyler has negotiated with various firms to finance and produce what he has created. However, he is the kind of person who researches things and learns on his own also, quite independent of the formal educational process. Thus it is difficult to assess how much the MBA contributed.

Tyler came to the MBA with a strong entrepreneurial orientation. It looks as if the MBA has added value above and beyond what existed previously, but this is not entirely clear. Perhaps the inventions would have found their way in any event. Tyler is a self-learner who may not have needed business training to develop and implement his ideas.

On both of the proximate criteria Tyler emerges as highly entrepreneurial. His entrepreneurial propensity score is at a very high level and his business plan received an A.

CONCLUSION

Once again the findings of the study described in this chapter support the typology and its derivative hypotheses. All four types are validated. Furthermore, this occurs in a context where complexity is much less in evidence than among the established entrepreneurs and where consequently, confounding of this kind, if it can be called that, is less as well.

The types, and complex entrepreneurs also, show signs of entrepreneurial activity prior to graduation, and then go on to actually do what these signs suggest. The proximate criteria, consisting of a stated past and present proclivity for entrepreneurship and skills in devising a business plan, do not yield quite the consistent results that actual entrepreneurial activity post-graduation does, but one or the other of these proximate criteria produces significance in every single comparison. Thus, we feel justified in extending the conclusions regarding the validity of the typology and its extensions from the practicing entrepreneurs discussed in Chapter 6 to the actual initiation of a venture.

The matter of the fit between personality type and career route is addressed only minimally by this research. The data available, and this is evident in the cases discussed above, often indicate a very fragile relationship between a type and the appropriate route. But the ultimate success of these ventures is often fragile as well. This chapter's research is concerned with the process of getting started in entrepreneurship, and at this point everything seems to be in flux. As the tie between type and career route solidifies, a tie to growth and success should solidify as well.

Finally, the rather minimal entrepreneurial potential of these students should be reiterated. This is a graduate program with a primarily corporate emphasis. The course is the only one dealing with entrepreneurship available to these students, and taking it is entirely voluntary. Accordingly, the students involved in this study would be expected to be the most entrepreneurial of those in the graduate program as a whole. Yet even in such a self-selected sample there are repeated indications that this is not a high potential group insofar as entrepreneurial endeavor is concerned. In all likelihood this occurs due to the primarily corporate emphasis, and reputation, of the overall program. A graduate program devoted to entrepreneurship in all of its aspects should attract more entrepreneurial talent. However, we do not know that for certain. That is a research agenda for the future.

NOTE

1. I am indebted to Susan Stites-Doe, Eric Williams, and Juan Carlos Pastor for their work on this phase of the research.

Part III

Using the Typology to Study Certain Groups

Chapter 8

Women and Men in Entrepreneurship

Although for many years entrepreneurship, like managing, was considered the province of men, that is no longer true. In the past most businesses were started by men. However, the ratio has been shifting so that now women are starting new ventures at more than twice the rate of men (Buttner, 1993). Entrepreneurship is a major growth area for women.

This does not mean that the sales volume of women-owned businesses averages at the same level as for firms owned by men, however, although the figures are getting closer. One reason is that the women-owned businesses are newer and thus have not had time to grow as much. It is also true that a disproportionate number of the firms that women have started represent part-time or seasonal ventures. Finally, and this may prove most important in the long run, most women start service businesses, not manufacturing operations; the figure runs currently at 90 percent. Thus their firms are heavily concentrated in sales, consulting, design and architecture, public relations and advertising, and personnel and business services. Retail stores, travel agencies, real estate firms, and the like are most frequent. In many such cases the market served is localized, and the growth potential limited.

What does this say about the entrepreneurial talent of women? Two major works on the subject of women entrepreneurs point up certain differences between women and men which might be interpreted as indicating a somewhat lesser entrepreneurial potential among women, at least in the short term (Hisrich and Brush, 1986; Hagan, Rivchun, and Sexton, 1989). These books emphasize that women have had less business and technical education, may have interests that limit their entrepreneurial potential in certain respects, have not developed business networks as men have, and may be lacking in some personality characteristics making for entrepreneurial success. These books are not saying that women necessarily lack the talent for the long haul. They are suggesting that some of the present differences in entrepreneurial accomplishments between men and women can be explained on the basis of talent differentials.

Yet others view talent differences between men and women in the entrepreneurial arena as nothing more than a myth (Shefsky, 1994). They consider women and men to be equally capable of becoming successful entrepreneurs right now. Buttner (1993) contends that there are no meaningful personality differences between male and female entrepreneurs. Others take the position that the two are more similar than different in personality make-up, while noting that meaningful differentials have been found (Brush, 1992). Sexton and Bowman-Upton (1990) report a study which found women entrepreneurs to have a lower energy level, to be more risk avoidant, to possess a greater desire for autonomy, and to like change more. Based on the types and their inherent characteristics, all but the first of these differences would appear to give women entrepreneurs a leg up in reaching success.

There is considerable uncertainty here. Views are just as mixed regarding personality differences between male and female entrepreneurs as they are regarding the role of personality factors in entrepreneurial success (see Chapter 1). Part of the problem is that different literatures are considered, but also available data are interpreted in different ways. We need to know more. What follows is my attempt to bring new findings to the table, and thus to introduce a new perspective on the question of women and men as entrepreneurs.

WOMEN AND MEN AMONG THE ESTABLISHED ENTREPRENEURS

There are only 12 among the 100 successful entrepreneurs studied in the research reported in Chapter 6 who are women. This is at least in part because the firms included are well established, and thus the recent uptrend in women-owned businesses is only minimally reflected in the composition of this group. In a group of entrepreneurs with very young firms, constituted quite recently for somewhat similar educational purposes, a full 50 percent of the participants were women.

In any event comparisons of the 12 with the 88 men must be considered tentative at best. The findings from such a study cannot establish anything with certainty, but they can be instructive, and serve to refine hypotheses for further research.

The women are some three years older than the men and average a year less education. These differences are small and are unlikely to have an impact on the results. However, the firm-related differences are sizable. The women have firms with only 24 employees on the average, in contrast to 63 for the men. Annual sales for the women are just under $2 million; for the men they are $4.7 million. Profits do not appear to vary much, although the women's firms are lower. Income from the business for the women is only half that of the men.

Almost all of the businesses headed by women are in the service sector. In general these findings regarding our female sample would appear to be typical (Brush, 1992). Remember also that these comparisons are based on data obtained as the entrepreneurs entered the study.

Turning now to the personality variables and the types themselves, Table 8.1 compares the men and women. Looking first at the proportion of strong patterns, there is very little difference among the personal achievers and empathic super-salespeople, and none whatsoever among the real managers and expert idea generators. Complexity, which certainly is a measure of entrepreneurial talent, appears to be more frequent among the women, particularly when the combined entrepreneur score is used. This is the only statistically significant difference in the table. At least in this small group of established entrepreneurs, there is some reason to believe that the women may possess somewhat more talent in the sense that they are more complex personalities, having high scores on a majority of the types.

This greater complexity should translate into more success at follow-up. Unfortunately, our sample of women entrepreneurs shrank even further at this point. In fact, we lost four women, a third of the sample, in contrast to only 14 percent of the men. Consequently, it becomes meaningless to talk about statistical significance. Nevertheless, the women do concentrate in the "substantial evidence of entrepreneurial success" category with 50 percent located there, in contrast to 28 percent of the men. The "same" and "little" follow-up categories both have proportionately fewer women. There is some reason to believe that the talents of these women—all eight of them—are reflected in the success levels of their firms.

The data on the origins of these firms produce some interesting findings when women and men are compared. Certain of these fit well with past research. The most striking, and significant, finding is that women are much more likely to start a business with a partner (or several partners). In the great majority of these instances a husband was involved. This is consistent with the findings from other studies which indicate an increase in businesses of this kind (Frishkoff and Brown, 1993). In some cases the husband has remained involved, but there are other instances where because of death or divorce the woman came to take over the firm completely. More often than not the husband has been a positive force and a major source of support, but not always. We have cases where the husband contributed in one way or another to major problems that the business faced.

Partners can bring skills and expertise to a business that entrepreneurs lack. It is possible that the high frequency of partners is a transitional phenomenon and that, as more women now receive business and technical educations, the need for this sharing of the reins will drop off. Even today, many women go on to grow substantial firms on their own. I know of one woman who after her husband's death took their small publishing house to the very top of its field, doubling its sales many times over. The point is that family members, and

Table 8.1
Women and Men in the Sample of 100 Established Entrepreneurs Compared Using the Typology

Theoretical Variable	Women (N=12)		Men (N=88)	
	N	%	N	%
Personal Achiever Type	5	42	24	27
Real Manager Type	4	33	29	33
Expert Idea Generator Type	4	33	29	33
Empathic Supersalesperson Type	3	25	24	27
Multiple Types (2 or more)	5	42	33	38
High Combined Score	8	67	23	26*

* χ^2 (*df* = 1) = 8.21, *p*<.01

husbands, are just like any other partners—some help and some do not, some are needed in the business and some are not. Any partner should be evaluated for the potential contribution. Husbands are no different in this regard.

With partnership start-ups more frequent in our female sample, sole start-ups are down. This is to be expected. However, there are other forms of venture origin that are down as well. One is the family business situation. Ward (1987) indicates that only one-third of family firms continue to the second generation and less than 15 percent continue to the third. But even within this limited context, succession has involved male children, particularly the first born, much more frequently than female (Dumas, 1992; Gersick, Davis, Hampton, and Lansberg, 1997). The results obtained with our small group of women entrepreneurs substantiate this. There is only one female from a family business, while 25 percent of the males are in this category.

This statistic is likely to change shortly. For one thing, more women-owned businesses will create more opportunities for succession by daughters. We are seeing evidence of this already. But beyond this, as women more frequently obtain education and experience that can be utilized in a business, the whole context of succession decision making should change. The possession of entrepreneurial talent—the needed types and the fact of complexity—should come to guide parental decisions in this area.

In addition, the data indicate that women are unlikely to enter into a corporate venture and serve as a turnaround person. A major factor here would appear to be that few women possess the particular competence needed for this role at the present time. Also possible is that the expert idea generator pattern required may be less frequent among women entrepreneurs.

WOMEN AND MEN AMONG THE GRADUATE STUDENTS IN BUSINESS MANAGEMENT

What do the student potential entrepreneurs tell us about the entrepreneurial talent of women relative to men? There are more women in this group, roughly a third of the total, and a number of different indexes of entrepreneurial orientation and activity are available. Remember, however, that the information on strong patterns is based upon a shortened test battery.

The females are at the same average age as the males and they are equally likely to be Ph.D. as opposed to MBA students. There is no real difference between the sexes in major area of study, although the males weigh in most heavily in the marketing field and the women in human resource management.

Table 8.2 contains the data on how the women and men compare on the theoretical variables of the typology. There are no meaningful differences; the largest percentage difference is 6 points. These women are not more complex, as was the case with the established entrepreneurs.

Although the figures in Table 8.2 suggest very little difference between women and men insofar as types are concerned, a deeper look at specific char-

Table 8.2
Women and Men in a Sample of Graduate Business Students Compared Using the Typology

Theoretical Variable	Women (N=51)		Men (N=108)	
	N	%	N	%
Personal Achiever Type	3	6	13	12
Real Manager Type	6	13	9	9
Expert Idea Generator Type	15	29	25	23
Empathic Supersalesperson Type	16	36	40	39
Multiple Types (2 or more)	8	17	17	16
High Combined Score	3	7	10	10

Note: No significant differences (*p*<.05).

acteristics within the types is somewhat more revealing. Within the personal achiever score the men have a greater desire to plan and set goals for future achievements. They also have a more internal locus of control, thus believing that what they do makes a real difference and that chance events and luck do not determine the way things work out. These factors are interrelated. People who believe that the luck of the draw governs are unlikely to plan and set goals because they do not anticipate that their planning will affect what happens in any event. People who believe in the importance of their own efforts are more likely to plan because their plans are viewed as determining what actually happens. This set of characteristics contains all of the significant differences found within the personal achiever score.

Within the real manager score the women are characterized by a more directive cognitive style, but the men have a greater desire to compete (using the Competitive Situations subscale of the MSCS—H). The two factors offset each other and so, in an overall sense, the women and men are no different. Within the expert idea generator score the one significant difference is the greater desire to avoid taking risks (using the Shure and Meeker test) evinced by the women. In the absence of a greater desire to personally innovate, or a more conceptual cognitive style, this difference means little; there is no risk-creating characteristic that needs to be held in check. Within the empathic supersalesperson score there are again two offsetting factors. The women exhibit a more empathic cognitive style on the Problem Solving Questionnaire, but the men have a greater desire to help others.

The indication of differences on certain characteristics related to personal achieving is the only finding from this analysis that suggests any differences on the types. This tendency is reflected in the fact that in Table 8.2 the men are slightly, though not significantly, more likely to be personal achievers. Is there anything here of sufficient magnitude to affect the results obtained with the entrepreneurial criteria among the students? The data on this hypothesis are given in Table 8.3.

On the entrepreneurial propensity level reading taken from the students as the entrepreneurship course began, there is some evidence of the men concentrating more in the upper category and the women concentrating more on the low end of the scale. The difference is not sufficient to produce significance, however.

On the business plan reading taken at the end of the entrepreneurship course, the same type of trend is in evidence, although on the low grades there is no difference at all. There may be some support here for the idea that the men throw themselves into the development of a business plan with more energy and effort, but it is far from overwhelming, and not statistically significant.

The best evidence for a difference between the female and male students in terms of entrepreneurial talent comes from the follow-up figures. The men appear to be somewhat more engaged in enterpreneuring of either a full- or part-time nature, or in entrepreneurship teaching and research, although the level of entrepreneurial activity is not sufficient to produce clear evidence of signifi-

Table 8.3
Women and Men in the Sample of Graduate Business Students Compared Using Three Entrepreneurial Criteria

	Women		Men	
	N	%	N	%
Entrepreneurial Propensity Score				
4-10	13	26	41	38
2-3	22	43	39	36
0-1	16	31	28	26
N	51	100	108	100
$x^2(df=2)$		2.38 NS		
Business Plan Grade				
A⁻ or A	19	44	57	57
B⁺	11	26	14	14
B or less	13	30	29	29
N*	43(8)	100	100(8)	100
$x^2(df=2)$		3.30 NS		
Evidence of Entrepreneurial Activity Post-graduation				
Present	5	15	25	30
None	28	85	57	70
N*	33(18)	100	82(26)	100
$x^2(df=1)$		2.86, $p<.10$		

*Numbers in parentheses indicate additional cases with missing data.

cance. The interpretation of these figures becomes even more difficult when one considers the fact that most women enter upon their first entrepreneurial venture, only after prior employment in a related area (Brush, 1992). Thus the women may well have somewhat longer to go before becoming entrepreneurs. This may account for the follow-up results—more of the men than the women have reached the time for venture creation; more women will come along later. There are so many uncertainties here, and so little by way of statistical significance, that it is best to assume that we still do not have a clear-cut answer to our question.

WOMEN AND MEN AS VIEWED FROM THE BELLU STUDIES

Bellu (1992, 1993) compared 47 female entrepreneurs with an even larger group of female managers—all from the New York City area. All of the female entrepreneurs founded their firms, the firms had been in business for at least three years, and there were at a minimum 25 employees. These were, accordingly, reasonably successful businesses. Comparisons were made with managers at the middle level or higher and from companies of at least 250 employees. The entrepreneurs were somewhat older but that is not unexpected with women-owned businesses.

Table 8.4 contains not only the original entrepreneur-manager comparison for females, but additional comparison data involving the 100 established entrepreneurs of Chapter 6, and two other groups of entrepreneurs studied by Bellu. In the first instance these entrepreneurs came from the northeast (New York and Vermont), operated rather small firms, and were primarily in the service sector (Bellu, 1988). In the second instance, the firms had been in business for at least three years and had at least 10 employees (Bellu and Sherman, 1993, 1995). In all of these comparison groups the entrepreneurs had founded their firms and the proportion of women in the sample varied from 12 to 22 percent.

These findings are limited to two types—(1) personal achievers for whom we have information on strong motivation for self-achievement, desire for feedback on achievements, and desire to plan and set goals for future achievements; and (2) expert idea generators where we have figures on the desires to personally innovate and to avoid taking risks. In addition, the total scores from the MSCS—T which combine all five of its subscales are used as a proxy for the complex entrepreneur combined score. The analyses of Table 8.4 rely upon mean score data and then convert these to percentile equivalents using existing norms for entrepreneurs in general (Miner, 1986) (not necessarily those who survive and succeed). Percentages above 50 are on the upside, those below 50 are on the downside relative to the normative sample.

In this analysis we are using MSCS—T scores as proxies for the type scores. Data are not available that bear on the real manager type and the empathic supersalesperson. Furthermore, information to combine the test data into com-

Table 8.4

Percentile Equivalents for Mean Scores on *Miner Sentence Completion Scale—Form T*: Proxy Variables among Female Entrepreneurs (Bellu, 1993) and Various Comparison Groups

Types and Characteristics Measured	Female Entrepreneurs—Bellu, 1993 (N=47)	Comparison Groups			
		Female Managers—Bellu, 1993 (N=66)	Established Entrepreneurs (N=100)	Entrepreneurs	
				Bellu, 1988 (N=70)	Bellu and Sherman, 1995 (N=43)
Personal Achiever Type					
1. Strong Motivation for Self-Achievement	65	36	65	62	59
3. Desire for Feedback on Achievements	62	63	62	67	67
4. Desire to Plan and Set Goals for Future Achievements	47	32	41	58	44
Expert Idea Generator Type					
1. Desire to Personally Innovate	36	36	63	43	38
5. Desire to Avoid Taking Risks	49	40	63	49	71
Combined Complex Entrepreneur Score					
MSCS-T Total Score	55	37	64	60	59

prehensive type scores are not available either; thus, individual characteristics become the units of analysis. When compared with the full type scores in the established entrepreneur sample of Chapter 6 and the more limited scores used in the student analyses of Chapter 7, the correlations are as follows:

- Strong motivation for self-achievement versus personal achiever score (.47 to .49).
- Desire for feedback on achievements versus personal achiever score (.24 to .32).
- Desire to plan and set goals for future achievements versus personal achiever score (.31 to .38).
- Desire to personally innovate versus expert idea generator score (.46 to .53)
- Desire to avoid taking risks versus expert idea generator score (.17 to .25).
- MSCS—T total score versus combined complex entrepreneur score (.47 to .52).

These correlations are derived from the sample of 100 established entrepreneurs. All correlations, except that of .17, are statistically significant at $p<.05$ or better. The correlations appear to justify using the characteristics as proxies for the more comprehensive scores. Setting the mean scores equal to percentile equivalents in the normative sample is not the same as using cutting scores to establish types with high certainty at approximately the 70th percentile level (rather than near the 50th). Nevertheless, this is the best that can be done with the data available, since the full distributions are not in hand. In any event, the same criteria are applied to all samples so that comparisons can meaningfully be made across the groups in Table 8.4.

Turning now to the findings inherent in Table 8.4, the women entrepreneurs clearly have a strong self-achievement motivation by any standard. It is well above that of the comparison managers ($t=2.62$, $p<.01$). Their desire for feedback on achievements is not above the comparison managers, but it remains high and at the same level as other groups noted. The desire to plan and set goals for future achievements is more in the middle range, but still exceeds the comparison managers ($t=1.77$, $p<.05$) and is at least the equal of the other comparison, primarily male, entrepreneurs on average. All in all the figures for these rather successful women entrepreneurs appear to be at about the level one would expect. If this is a best test of the question regarding male-female differences, and we believe it is, the figures indicate that women are certainly not below men on the personal achiever type. The more likely conclusion is that they are about the same.

Table 8.4 also considers the expert idea generator findings. Here the figures for women entrepreneurs are less strong. They are not significantly below the women comparison managers but they are down from the 100 established entrepreneurs and the other groups as well. Thus on the innovation measure their percentile score of 36 compares with an average of 48 for the other, predominantly male, entrepreneurial groups. On the risk avoidance measure the women entrepreneurs are at 49, but the average for the other groups is at 61. Taken as a whole these data point to a somewhat, although not pronounced, decrease in the expert idea generator type among women entrepreneurs. This conclusion is based in part on the fact that, contrary to the findings for personal achiever characteristics, the female entrepreneurs do not score significantly above the female managers on either of the expert idea generator measures; this is not what would have been expected. In addition, when the female entrepreneurs are compared with the other, predominantly male, groups and effect sizes are calculated, these effect sizes exceed half a standard deviation on both measures.

Finally, we have used the total score from the MSCS—T as a proxy for being a complex entrepreneur, more specifically for the combined score measure. Contrary to the findings from the established entrepreneur sample, the women entrepreneurs are consistently below the other entrepreneurial groups. They exceed the female managers ($t=2.26$, $p<.05$), however; and on the average their mean score is only 6 percentage points below the three predominantly male comparison groups. This is not sufficient to establish any difference between women and men insofar as complexity is concerned.

CONCLUSION

What do these studies say about differences in talent between men and women entrepreneurs? The established entrepreneur sample yielded the conclusion that women are more likely to be complex entrepreneurs, and that this can contribute to greater success. However, the studies of business students and of female entrepreneurs in the New York City area did not support this finding. Given the sample size problem in the established entrepreneur research, it seems wise to defer to the conclusions derived from the larger groups.

Analysis of the business student data unearthed little evidence of differences between the men and women. The only possible finding to this effect involved a set of characteristics related to planning within the personal achiever score. In this specific regard the men were higher, even though no significant differences were found in the incidence of the personal achiever type. The marginal tendency for the men to engage in entrepreneurial activity after leaving the university more frequently than the women, however, could reflect the impact of this planning-related syndrome. Yet, in the established entrepreneur sample and among Bellu's (1993) female entrepreneurs, there is no support for a greater frequency of personal achievers among males. Thus, any widespread talent differential among personal achiever types seems unlikely.

The strongest evidence for a difference between women and men using the four-way typology comes from Bellu's (1993) female sample. There is reason to believe from this study that women entrepreneurs are somewhat below men in the extent to which they possess the expert idea generator pattern. The other two studies do not exhibit this same differential, but clearly the Bellu data are the best available insofar as successful, practicing women entrepreneurs are concerned.

Furthermore, as noted at the beginning of this chapter, women entrepreneurs are most likely to be in a service business. Men have a greater presence in manufacturing, in high technology, as well as in turnaround ventures. These are all areas where the expert idea generator is likely to find a career route that fits the type. Thus there is a certain logic to the finding that men are somewhat more frequent among expert idea generators and that women as a group are less frequent. However, it should be apparent that any individual woman can be an expert idea generator and be just as innovative and visionary and successful as any individual man.

Do women or men possess more entrepreneurial talent? Overall, one would have to consider it a draw, given that women pursue a route appropriate to their talents. Most are indeed in the service sector and that is clearly where, as a group, their strengths are most likely to be fully utilized.

What our findings say is that women have as good a chance for entrepreneurial success as men. There may be remaining problems insofar as business networks, obtaining financing, and the like are concerned (Buttner, 1993), but from a talent perspective, to the extent appropriate routes are followed, women and men are equally capable of achieving success. Women need to assess their own personality patterns and structure their plans for success, and thus the routes they follow, in exactly the same way men do. The outcomes may be slightly different because the personality patterns are not identical, but the process required is the same.

Chapter 9

High-Technology
Entrepreneurs

For some years we have been conducting a program of research utilizing Form T of the *Miner Sentence Completion Scale*, primarily, and focused on entrepreneurs in high technology. As it progressed this research was published in a variety of sources with different combinations of authors—Smith and Miner (1983, 1984, 1985), Smith, Bracker, and Miner (1987), Miner, Smith, and Bracker (1989, 1992a, 1992b, 1994), and Miner (1990).

As a prelude to this discussion it should prove helpful to review the conclusions from a prior research program dealing with high-technology entrepreneurs. Publications from this program chronicle the growth of firms in the greater Boston area, many of which had strong links to MIT (Roberts, 1989, 1991a, 1991b).

CONCLUSIONS FROM THE ROBERTS RESEARCH

To my knowledge the program of research conducted by Roberts out of the MIT context is the most comprehensive and penetrating of any in the high-technology area, and probably in the entrepreneurship field as a whole to this date. The conclusions he noted are as follows:

1. Entrepreneurs are very likely to have had self-employed fathers. But first-born sons are not more likely than their siblings to become high-technology entrepreneurs.

2. Technical entrepreneurs come far more frequently from development work than from research, where they excelled as high performers.

3. Entrepreneurs are not all alike; they display wide ranges of personalities, motivations, and goals for starting new enterprises.

4. The key initial technologies of the new firms were transferred primarily from development projects carried out by the entrepreneurs at their previous employers.

5. Initial capitalization is typically very small and provided from the entrepreneurs' personal savings. Multiple co-founders raise larger amounts of initial capital.

6. Specific plans and an initial product help generate greater initial capital.

7. Widespread deficiencies in business plans and in team composition hurt the new enterprise's ability to raise "outside" capital.

8. Companies that go public later in their corporate lives undergo far easier and less expensive financing.

9. Family background has no impact on entrepreneurial success. Successful entrepreneurs are made, not born!

10. Prior supervisory, managerial, and especially sales experience by founders contributes to successful enterprises.

11. Entrepreneurs with a high need for achievement are more likely to succeed.

12. Multifounder teams generally perform far better than single founders, and the greater their number the more likely is their success.

13. Firms that start with products significantly outperform those that begin as consultants or R&D contractors.

14. The more technology transferred initially from the entrepreneurs' "source" organization, the greater the eventual company success.

15. Firms that begin with a marketing orientation, and/or evolve one early in their development, are more likely to succeed.

16. Companies that focus on core technologies and markets do much better than those that diversify into multiple technologies and markets.

17. "Founder's diseases" are widespread, but not universal, with two-thirds of the founders of successful technological enterprises being displaced before their companies achieve "super-success" (Roberts, 1991b, pp. 27–28).

The ensuing comments on these points will tie them more closely to our typology, and provide a backdrop to what follows.

1. This suggests that family businesses as they have existed in the past are not a major factor in high technology.

2. It may well be that those who come from research, rather than development, are more likely to establish a professional practice.

3. This conclusion fits well with the conclusion that there are four personality types, and four different routes to entrepreneurial success.

4. To the extent expert idea generators are involved, they need to take time to develop expertise; this fits with the process of transferring development projects, and a more advanced age at venture founding.

5. Whether partners are involved and how long they last are likely to be directly dependent on the types involved.

6. Real managers and empathic supersalespeople would appear to be at somewhat of a disadvantage here.

7. Real managers and expert idea generators would appear to be at somewhat of a disadvantage here.

8. Real managers should manage the IPO process more effectively.

9. Again, the argument against a family business background is upheld.

10. Real managers and especially empathic supersalespeople have a pronounced leg up.

11. This argues for the importance of the personal achiever type.

12. Multiple founders are more likely to incorporate various types among the multiple types available, thus filling out the business.

13. This is because many consultants and R&D contractors are engaged in professional practices and have no commitment to growth.

14. Expert idea generators are more likely to do this; this is one of the ideal routes for them.

15. As we will see, empathic supersalespeople tend to be lacking among the founders of high-technology firms; anything that can be done to deal with this problem early on needs to be done.

16. This would seem to argue for the power of the founding ideas of expert idea generators.

17. The need for real managers following the managing route is just as great in high technology as elsewhere; yet a sizable number of these entrepreneurs are complex entrepreneurs with the real manager pattern, and thus able to make it through the "founder's disease" barrier.

It appears that there are many parallels between the MIT findings and what our typology implies. As we pursue the results of our research, cast in typology terms, this compatibility between the two research programs becomes even more evident.

Roberts (1991b) argues for a highly promising future for high-technology entrepreneurs. I would agree, but only if some really pronounced, self-imposed obstacles can be overcome.

THE SAMPLES USED TO STUDY HIGH-TECHNOLOGY ENTREPRENEURS

The National Science Foundation, and a number of other federal government agencies as well, provide financial support to smaller firms to help them develop and bring to market various technological innovations. This program has consistently attracted a considerably larger number of grant applications than can be funded. Funding, when it does occur, initially takes the form of a modest seed-money grant and then subsequently in a much smaller number of cases, a more substantial financial commitment. Fostering technological advances in this way has been a feature of government policy for some time. That policy and its implementation are discussed in detail in an article by Hetzner, Tornatzky, and Klein (1983). Although, as indicated in a book by Tornatzky and Fleischer (1990), the National Science Foundation program has not been shown to yield substantial firm success in the marketplace, it can provide a useful source of high-technology entrepreneurs for study.

We were able to obtain information from 118 individuals, who indicated they were founders of their firms, in this way. Their mean age was 47 years. Almost all were men (112). Most had obtained advanced degrees of some kind and 60 percent held doctorates. Some 33 states were represented, with the largest numbers coming from California and Massachusetts. The roles that the Silicon Valley, south of San Francisco, and the Route 128 area near Boston have played in high-technology entrepreneurship were clearly manifest in our data.

These firms were not always very large. The mean number of employees was 21.7 (standard deviation 31.1), the dollar volume of annual sales $0.9 million (standard deviation $1.2 million), and the entrepreneur's yearly income from this position $38 thousand (standard deviation $29,400).

In addition to the entrepreneurs themselves, we were also able to obtain information from a group of managers and scientists, who submitted grant applications but were not involved in the founding of their firms. These people provide a valuable means of comparison. They are involved with high-technology organizations, but not as actual entrepreneurs. These individuals numbered 41, with three being women. Their mean age was 46, and 36 percent held doctorates, but only 10 percent did not have advanced training beyond the bachelor's degree. These people come from larger firms than the entrepreneurs. They held a wide range of titles, but almost universally they had the technical expertise to qualify as experts in the area of the grant application. In many cases the grant application process appears to have been delegated to them as part of their research and development responsibilities.

Finally, the 100 established entrepreneurs of Chapter 6 served as a comparison group. Thus, a highly diversified and quite successful sample of entrepreneurs was utilized. The high-technology entrepreneurs were not at nearly this same level. When we first made contact with the latter, their firms averaged less than $1 million in annual sales, in contrast to well over $4 million. A number were quite small, and in retrospect appear to fit the professional practice model more closely than that of true entrepreneurship. In a limited number of cases we suspect a firm was actually created to provide a base from which to submit the National Science Foundation grant proposal. Also, these are not all necessarily inventor entrepreneurs either. Only about half had ever patented an invention and in many cases the patents obtained had little if anything to do with the grant proposal, or the present company product line in any form, for that matter. In short, we appear to be dealing with a reasonably typical group of small, high-technology firms in all stages of both growth and decline, but that does not mean that the founder himself (or in a few cases herself) is necessarily a real inventor as well. Others in the firm may be doing this, or it may be that the project submission involves mostly development work on an idea created elsewhere.

THE TESTS USED IN THE HIGH-TECHNOLOGY ANALYSES

Since the high-technology entrepreneurs were studied via a mail survey, it was not possible to obtain many measures. Thus proxies had to be used in place of the full battery described in Chapter 5. These were as follows:

Personal Achiever Type—

1. Strong Motivation for Self-Achievement.
   (b) *Miner Sentence Completion Scale—Form T: Self Achievement Subscale*

3. Desire for Feedback on Achievement.
   Miner Sentence Completion Scale—Form T: Feedback of Results Subscale

4. Desire to Plan and Set Goals for Future Achievements.
   Miner Sentence Completion Scale—Form T: Planning for the Future Subscale

Expert Idea Generator Type—

1. Desire to Personally Innovate.
   Miner Sentence Completion Scale—Form T: Personal Innovation Subscale

3. Belief in New Product Development as a Key Element of Company Strategy.
   Company Survey: Ranking of Competitive Strategies

5. Desire to Avoid Taking Risks.
   Miner Sentence Completion Scale—Form T: Avoiding Risks Subscale

Empathic Supersalesperson Type—

5. Belief in the Sales Force as a Key Element of Company Strategy.
   Company Survey: Ranking of Competitive Strategies

Scores were developed from these measures using the same conversion process as used previously. Since we had no measures for the real manager type, there was no score of this kind. Accordingly we had:

Personal achiever score—range 0 to 6
Expert idea generator score—range 0 to 6
Empathic supersalesperson score—range 0 to 2
Complex entrepreneurs
    Number of types present from 2 to 3
    Composite score—range 0 to 14

The three types are based on 24, 17, and 1 item, respectively.

Among the high-technology entrepreneurs the mean personal achiever score was 2.4 and the full 0 to 6 range was utilized. The mean expert idea generator score was 2.8, again spread across the full range. The mean empathic super-salesperson score was .3 covering all three component score levels. The mean composite score was 5.5 with an actual range from 0 to 12. Multiple types were present in 22 cases (with only one person having all three types). The 22 represent 19 percent of the total. The scores for the high-technology entrepreneurs were consistently below those of the 100 established entrepreneurs, except in the case of the expert idea generators where the means were identical. The manager/scientists were substantially below the high-technology entrepreneurs except for the empathic supersalesperson score; there the entrepreneurs were the ones with low scores.

Types were defined using the score distributions from the established entrepreneur sample and to the extent possible maintaining essentially the same percentage for the abbreviated proxy measures as existed with the full battery. This is the procedure described for the student battery in Chapter 7. In the established entrepreneur sample the results of this process were as follows:

	Score to Define Type	Percent in Type
Personal achiever	4 or above	31
Expert idea generator	4 or above	34
Empathic supersalesperson	2	28
Composite score	8 or above	33

These percentages are very good approximations of those obtained with the full battery with the established entrepreneurs.

When the same definition of a type is applied using the abbreviated set of measures in the high-technology sample, the results are:

	Percent in Type
Personal achiever	27
Expert idea generator	34
Empathic supersalesperson	6
Composite score	27

The empathic supersalespeople are clearly down among the high-technology entrepreneurs, and that pulls the composite score down as well.

How good as proxies are the abbreviated scores when compared with the full battery in the established entrepreneur sample? The correlation involving the three personal achiever scores is .55, the expert idea generator scores .73, and the empathic supersalesperson scores .48. All are significant at $p<.01$. None of the three abbreviated scores are significantly intercorrelated. All in all, it appears that the proxies are doing much the same thing as the scores they represent. They are certainly not perfect representations, but they are acceptable.

THE FOLLOW-UP CRITERIA OF SUCCESS

There is ample evidence that the MSCS—T components of the various scores are related to criterion measures such as annual growth in number of employees and growth in sales. Furthermore, the high-technology entrepreneurs are consistently above the manager/scientists on the MSCS—T at the time of initial measurement (Miner, Smith, and Bracker, 1989). However, the key consideration is what happened subsequently. Did those with high type scores grow their firms more?

To get at this crucial factor we carried out a follow-up an average of 5 years and 7 months after the initial testing. From the original 118 cases adequate data were obtained at follow-up on 59. Among the remaining instances the most pronounced problem was that the entrepreneurs could not be located at the address we had, nor could our correspondence be forwarded. There were a few instances of simple non-response, and a few more where the data were inadequate (Miner, Smith, and Bracker, 1994). The evidence suggests that many of the individuals who could not be included in the follow-up analysis were business failures (Miner, Smith, and Bracker, 1992b). However, data to show this with certainty are not available. Thus, we rely on the 59 cases where we are certain of what happened. These were allocated as follows:

To categorize the 59 entrepreneurs in terms of the growth of their firms over the five-plus years, we classified high-growth and low-growth samples. The high-growth sample contained 21 people whose firms had increased their sales by $1 million a year or more over the interim. In addition, there were two instances in which the necessary sales figures were not available, but either an increase in number of employees of 50 or more had occurred or the entrepreneur's income from the business had increased by $75,000 or more. Finally, there was one case in which the original firm had been sold, but was known to be prospering at the time of sale. This high-growth sample of 24 entrepreneurs was contrasted with a low-growth sample of 35 individuals who did not meet the above criteria. In 26 of these cases, available measures of firm growth did not reach the specified levels. There were seven instances in which the company was quite small, having less than five employees, and was simply discontinued at some point. The remaining two companies were doing poorly, and in each case the entrepreneur was forced to sell out. To our knowledge, there were no actual bankruptcies involved (Miner, Smith, and Bracker, 1994, pp. 627–628).

RESULTS—SAMPLE COMPARISONS

Table 9.1 compares the high-technology entrepreneurs with the 100 established group and with the manager/scientists in high-technology firms. In general, strong patterns and indicators of multiple patterns are more frequent in the two entrepreneur groups than among the manager/scientists. This is as it should

Table 9.1

Incidence of Various Types and Complex Entrepreneurs in High-Technology Entrepreneur, High-Technology Manager/Scientist, and Established Entrepreneur Samples

| | High-Technology Entrepreneurs (N=118) | | Comparison Groups | | | | Chi-square (df=2) |
| | | | High-Technology Manager/Scientists (N=41) | | Established Entrepreneurs (N=100) | | |
Components of the Typology*	N	%	N	%	N	%	
Personal Achiever Type	32	27	3	7	31	31	8.82 p<.02
Expert Idea Generator Type	40	34	10	24	34	34	1.45 NS
Empathic Supersalesperson Type	7	6	9	22	28	28	19.44 p<.01
Multiple Types (2 or more)	22	19	4	10	21	21	2.45 NS
High Combined Score	32	27	4	10	33	33	8.06 p<.02

*Real manager type not included due to lack of any measure in the high-technology sample.

be. The only exception is the lack of empathic supersalespeople among the high-technology entrepreneurs. Selling appears not to be something that comes naturally here. It is not just that a mere 6 percent are strong as empathic supersalespeople, in actual fact, most of the high-technology entrepreneurs give little evidence of possessing this characteristic at all. This finding requires some discussion.

Roberts (1991b), in his Boston-area study, reports much the same thing. His technical entrepreneurs evinced a pronounced lack of market orientation, with the result that formal marketing and sales organizations were nowhere to be found in the early period as these firms were getting started. Although this situation often corrected itself later in the successful companies, marketing and sales continued to be reported as a major problem. Typically, much of the selling was done by the lead entrepreneur. On both our evidence and the information Roberts obtained, following the selling route in this way is not an appropriate utilization of the technical entrepreneur's time and does not work well. In most cases it appears to be a natural outgrowth of not paying much attention to how the sales function should be structured and then letting customers make the determination as to whom to contact.

Among the types, being an expert idea generator is most frequent with high-technology entrepreneurs, personal achievers come next, and empathic super-salespeople are almost nonexistent. We do not have direct information regarding the real manager pattern, but Roberts (1991b) indicates that, to be successful, technological firms need to bring in managerial talent from the outside, suggesting that this talent may well be lacking among the founders.

The problem is that these firms are engaged in bringing new products to the marketplace, and that marketplace typically does not know yet that it needs the product. Just when the selling job is most difficult, the potential for failure in this respect is greatest. Not surprisingly, a large percentage of high-technology firms change their identity or disappear over time (Bird, 1989). As Roberts (1991b, p. 269) notes—''A wide array of founder and company characteristics and activities testify to the critical role of marketing in generating success of the technology-based enterprise. These evidences are in sharp contrast to the technologically arrogant assertion, 'If you build a better mousetrap, the world will beat a path to your door.' ''

These firms have to pay attention to the selling process from the very beginning if they are to grow. The best way to do this is to include at least one person with extensive, successful sales experience in the original founder group. Ideally, this individual would be an empathic supersalesperson, although some real managers can perform this function well also. Usually, this will not be the lead entrepreneur, who is much more likely to be an expert idea generator or a personal achiever. The individual with sales experience must then be allowed to follow the selling route. Problems can arise if the lead entrepreneur usurps the selling route, believing that is what he or she should do, and then fails out of being unsuited to the demands of that role. This appears to happen quite often.

If the introduction of a selling partner seems infeasible, then someone should be hired at the outset who has the experience to handle this activity. The key point is that there needs to be a self-conscious effort to deal with the selling issue from the very beginning. Better mousetraps do not sell themselves. They simply sit in the closet. This does not mean that those who are not so disposed should become salespeople. It does mean that they should give thought to sales and marketing and make provisions for them. For personal achievers, or real managers, this should not be difficult. For many expert idea generators it may require some corrections to normal ways of thinking.

This problem at the interface between the scientists who produce the high technology and the sales and marketing people who bring it to customers appears to extend into corporate venturing as well. Burgelman and Sayles (1986) found major communication breakdowns at this interface. They note three theoretical forms of relationship:

1. Marketing-oriented managers can direct scientists into what appear to be exciting markets with assured high demand. (This is often called, in fact, "demand pull.") Here innovation, the need, is father to (or mother to) the new "invention."

2. Scientists, attuned to the realities of the corporation's interests, look for new technologies and scientific breakthroughs with good commercialization potential. (This is called "technology push.")

3. Marketing and scientific specialists work together, bringing their own skills to a joint endeavor to develop new technology with sound market possibilities (Burgelman and Sayles, 1986, p. 33).

Although all three of these alternatives are possible, what was actually found was a poorly working version of the second form—technology push. Conflict between R&D and marketing was endemic. R&D scientists claimed the marketing people did not know enough to provide useful guidance about the marketplace. Consequently, the sales and marketing function was often ignored. Marketing people for their part viewed the R&D scientists as egocentric, stubborn, and non-responsive to the real needs of customers. The net result was that technological innovations typically occurred without benefit of a market orientation and consequently failed to meet sales goals. Because of internal conflicts, exactly the same deficiency in the sales and marketing area that we found in entrepreneurial ventures appeared to be present in the corporate version as well. The scientists, presumably many with an expert idea generator pattern, were not suited to follow the selling route, but they devalued those who might be so suited, and thus thwarted their pursuit of that route.

A solution to problems of this kind has been to bring scientists and sales personnel together in entrepreneurial teams housed within a new venture division. The objective is to break down unit boundaries and create a venture closely approximating those of a free-standing nature we have studied. Companies like Minnesota Mining and Manufacturing (3M), Owens-Illinois, and DuPont used this approach at an early point. Yet as Fast (1978) has demonstrated, the consequence has often been no better. The basic problem of a lack of market orientation among the high-technology scientists who provide the reason to be for these organizations remains, whether one is dealing with a free-standing entrepreneurial venture, a corporate R&D project, or a company new venture division.

Among the findings presented in Table 9.1, the one indicating a lack of empathic supersalespeople among high-technology entrepreneurs is by far the most significant. Although based on rather sparse data, it receives some support from other research studies as well.

However, Table 9.1 also contains two non-significant results where the theory might seem to predict significant findings. The most striking of these is the failure to establish any differences between samples on the expert idea generator type. This appears to occur because the non-entrepreneur sample has a relatively large number of expert idea generators. It also contains a large number of scientists, many of whom would be expected to be expert idea generators. The results obtained with the multiple types measure of complexity are clearly influenced by this lack of difference on the expert idea generator type. But without the real manager being represented, this measure is rather constrained in any event. Note that the combined score measure of complexity, which has more variability, does produce a significant finding.

RESULTS—SUBSEQUENT SUCCESS

Table 9.2 presents what happened to firms whose founders exhibited the various psychological types. After five and a half years obtaining follow-up information proved difficult, a number of cases were lost. However, this result was particularly frequent among those who did not give evidence of possessing any strong pattern. The likelihood of business failure here seems very high.

The distinction between high-growth firms and the others was made based on where the company was five and a half years before and where it was at follow-up. There are some real success stories in the high-growth group. One company went from just over $4 million in annual sales to $42 million; another went from $2.7 million to $17 million. There were some sizable increases in employment, although no company increased to over 500 employees and jumps to over 100 occurred in only 30 percent of the firms. The low-growth firms were in the majority of cases very small, with five or less employees, and they had not expanded over the years. There were a number of these that we know had been discontinued, but the more typical picture was simply continuation with a small group of people and sales well under half a million dollars a year. This fits well with the concept of a professional practice, in this case devoted either

Table 9.2
Success Subsequent to Testing for High-Technology Entrepreneurs Categorized by Position on the Typology

Components of the Typology*	Low Level of Growth (N=35)		High Level of Growth (N=24)		Totals (N=59)		Chi-square Vs. No Strong Pattern
	N	%	N	%	N**	%	
No Strong Pattern in Evidence	26	87	4	13	30(32)	100	—
Personal Achiever Type	5	22	18	78	23(9)	100	22.87 p<.01
Expert Idea Generator Type	6	26	17	74	23(17)	100	20.04 p<.01
Empathic Supersalesperson Type	2	50	2	50	4(3)	100	3.29 p<.10
Multiple Types (2 or more)	2	15	11	85	13(9)	100	20.55 p<.01
High Combined Score	2	11	17	89	19(13)	100	27.81 p<.01

*Real manager type not included due to lack of any measure.
**Numbers in parentheses indicate additional cases with no follow-up evidence.

to technical consulting or to the pursuit of personal interests doing contract research.

In Table 9.2 the figures for the various personality types are compared with those for the entrepreneurs lacking any strong pattern. The differences are striking. Without a strong pattern, it is rare to have a high-growth firm. With one, the numbers are sharply reversed. The personal achievers seem to perform the best, even slightly outdistancing the expert idea generators. The classic entrepreneur clearly is not absent from high technology. The area not only attracts such people, but they do well there. Roberts (1991b) also found that success in high-technology entrepreneurship is related to achievement motivation; it is not merely for the expert idea generators. The figures for the empathic supersalespeople do not appear as pronounced as for the other two patterns. However, they exceed those for the people with no strong pattern. The problem is that they are based on only a very limited number of cases. In fact, there are only two firms that grew, and two more that did not, included in the empathic supersalesperson numbers. The real finding is that there are very few such people in high technology, not that they are less likely to be successful.

It is evident that having a complex personality with multiple patterns, however that is defined, remains a major plus in the high-technology domain. What is more distinctive is that entrepreneurs with multiple types have a very low likelihood of failure (or of low growth in the professional practice mode). The numbers for the complex entrepreneurs run at about half of those for personal achievers and expert idea generators. Conversely, if one is blessed with multiple patterns the likelihood of success is very high. In considering the data of Table 9.2, it is important to note that there are not large imbalances among the individual types in the extent to which each incorporates multiple patterns. This is least frequent for the expert idea generators, but the range is only from 53 percent to 62 percent for the three individual types. Also, in interpreting the table, remember that the real manager type is an unknown entity. Some of those with no strong pattern in evidence may in fact be real managers, and there may be a considerably greater amount of complexity present than the figures indicate.

CONCLUSION

Technology and technological change are a major factor in entrepreneurship (Shane, 1996). When there are periods of time with high rates of technological innovation, entrepreneurship increases. Furthermore, strategy as articulated by the lead entrepreneur is a major factor in the growth rate of high-technology firms (Feeser and Willard, 1990). Thus the type of person that a high-technology entrepreneur is and the kind of strategy with which that person feels comfortable and pursues have a great deal to do with economic growth.

We tend to think of the high-technology world as dominated by scientists who are expert idea generators following an idea generating route and inventing new products. There is considerable truth to this view. Some of these individuals find the freedom to innovate by founding new companies. However, others appear to achieve the same freedom within companies which they do not own and did not start. There are a goodly number of expert idea generators among our high-technology managers and scientists, for example. Yet it is also true that expert idea generators may opt for a professional practice doing consulting and research on projects that they find particularly attractive personally. Practices of this kind by definition do not grow in terms of number of employees or beyond a certain point in dollar volume of sales either.

Largely for this reason it is the personal achievers and, of course, the complex, multiroute entrepreneurs who are most likely to found and grow successful high-technology firms. Thus in many respects the world of high-technology entrepreneuring is much like entrepreneuring elsewhere. The achievement-oriented, high-activity person can well take a firm into aggrandizement here. The ideas may come from somewhere else, but the process remains much the same, even to the point of "hitting the wall" and the requirement for managerial skills as a firm grows. Thus high-technology entrepreneuring is not just for the expert idea generator; it is also an arena populated with a large number of successful entrepreneurs of any type.

Finally, although it needs them badly, high-technology entrepreneurship does not seem to attract many empathic supersalespeople. Perhaps these people are more drawn to products and services that do not require substantial technical knowledge as a prologue to the process of actually selling. In any event it is essential that a company find some solution to the problem created by this often unfulfilled need. There is the suggestion in the manager/scientist figures in Table 9.1 that some firms deal with this issue by hiring empathic supersalespeople to spearhead their sales efforts. This can work, but including a person following the selling route in the original partnership would seem to provide for a more stable solution and probably at an earlier point.

Chapter 10

Entrepreneuring Beyond U.S. Borders

A study of entrepreneurship in 13 countries around the world yields the following conclusion:

The central thrust of this study has been to determine whether or not there are underlying patterns shared by entrepreneurs despite the cultural diversity of their origins. The findings reviewed here suggest that such an underlying pattern, not only exists, but that it can be identified and replicated using split-sample statistical techniques. . . . The results suggest that entrepreneurs have a persistent and characteristic value orientation, irrespective of the values of their base culture. Furthermore, these values appear to be aligned along four dimensions first identified by Hofstede (1980). . . . The dimensions are: (1) individualism; (2) power distance; (3) uncertainty avoidance; and (4) masculinity. We found that in a number of quite different societies, entrepreneurship is associated with high individualism, high power distance, low uncertainty avoidance, and high masculinity scores (McGrath, MacMillan, and Scheinberg, 1992, pp. 125, 133).

Yet there is also evidence that the entrepreneurial propensities of people from specific countries are important when these people come to the United States as immigrants. To the extent a particular country produces individuals with entrepreneurial talent, it is also likely to send this talent to the United States (Waldinger, Aldrich, and Ward, 1990). We know that immigrants are particularly inclined to found new businesses on their arrival, often because other opportunities are closed to them, but there is more to it than that. Certain countries are much more disposed to be a source of new business start-ups than others, when their nationals come to the United States. Who, then, are these people and from what countries do they come?

The Waldinger, Aldrich, and Ward (1990) volume notes an extraordinary variation in business start-ups among various ethnic groups in the United States. The groups that are more inclined to entrepreneurship come from many parts of the world, but without exception the tendency to start a new business is most pronounced in the first generation and thus those immigrants who are closest to the home country culture. In later generations this propensity tends to taper off.

Examples of high entrepreneurial intensity groups are the Cubans in South Florida, particularly in Miami, and the Koreans in New York City, and to a somewhat lesser extent in other large cities such as Los Angeles. It is noteworthy that other Hispanic groups have not matched the Cubans in this regard, nor have other oriental groups matched the Koreans. The one exception to the latter statement is the Chinese, many of whom have been very entrepreneurially active not only in the United States, but in many Asian countries (Weidenbaum, 1996), and in the recent period in Paris.

Other ethnic groups that should be noted are the Jews, Italians, Greeks, and Indians. All have been disproportionately active in starting and operating new businesses in the United States. These businesses have been concentrated in industries such as clothing, restaurants, construction, and retailing, but a large number of other industries are represented as well.

Information is available on the entrepreneurial types of those who have started businesses in the home countries of several of these ethnic groups, these include Italy and Israel. Here the types would be expected to be at high levels based on immigrant behavior in the United States. We also have test data from entrepreneurs in Sweden and Poland, where the U.S. experience would suggest a lower level of entrepreneurial talent might exist. The Polish findings may also provide some insight into the situation in Eastern Europe generally. With regard to the other high-intensity ethnic groups in this country, we lack information from Cuba, Korea, China, Greece, and India, although in the latter instance data are available from another source. McClelland and Winter (1969) document a close tie between strong achievement motivation and entrepreneurship in India.

Although immigrant potentials are significant, there are other ways in which the entrepreneurial talents inherent in other countries become important. Countries with an entrepreneurial bent represent better investment opportunities in certain respects. Furthermore, companies that seek to extend their corporate venturing operations on an international level would do well to move into those particular countries where they are most likely to attract people with proven entrepreneurial talent. In short, countries that are major sources of entrepreneurial personalities offer many business opportunities that other countries do not.

TYPES AND TALENTS IN ITALY

The situation with regard to the measurement of types in other countries is much the same as with Bellu's analysis of female entrepreneurs, discussed in Chapter 8. Again, the findings are limited to two patterns—personal achievers, for whom information is available on strong motivation for self-achievement, desire for feedback on achievements, and desire to plan and set goals for future achievements, and expert idea generators, for whom there are figures on a desire to personally innovate and to avoid taking risks. As before, the analyses utilize average scores and convert these to percentage equivalents using the norms for entrepreneurs in general (from the United States). Percentages above 50 should be considered increasingly high as the value becomes larger.

Figures for Italy are reported in publications by Bellu, Davidsson, and Gold-farb (1989, 1990). Within Italy, groups of entrepreneurs were studied from the northern part of the country in Lombardy, and from the south in Sicily. In the north the mean age was 40, and in the south 48. All were males. In the north the firms were primarily in manufacturing, while in the south most were construction companies. The northern entrepreneurs were largely college graduates; in the south the educational level was considerably lower. Both groups had companies with less than 50 employees.

The figures given in Table 10.1 for these Italian entrepreneurs are compared with those for two groups of *managers* from the same two regions who work in firms of similar size, but do not own them. In the north the matching on demographics was very close. In the south the managers were younger, with a mean age of 33, and better educated (college graduates); their firms were primarily in manufacturing and wholesale, not construction. The established entrepreneurs of Chapter 6 were used as a U.S. comparison group.

From Table 10.1 it is apparent that on the three personal achiever characteristics both groups of Italian entrepreneurs are high. The northern Italy entrepreneurs do not reach significance in the comparisons with managers from that region on the feedback and planning measures, but their scores are still high. The southern Italy entrepreneurs differ significantly from their control managers on all three measures. Relative to the established entrepreneurs from the United States, the Italian figures are high also. The mean personal achiever percentile value across the three measures is 68 in the north of Italy and 71 in the south. The U.S. value is 56.

Much the same picture emerges for the expert idea generator measures. All of the entrepreneur-manager comparisons are significant, with the Italian managers consistently having high scores. As compared to the U.S. entrepreneurs, who have percentile equivalents on both measures of 63, the two Italian samples average 69 and 70, respectively.

On the index of complexity both Italian samples are not only significantly above the managers from that country, but they exceed the U.S. entrepreneurs by a goodly margin as well. All this is what would be expected from the entrepreneurial behavior of Italian immigrants in the United States. At least on two types, Italian entrepreneurs are just as high as we expected them to be, and this is just as true for the southern part of the country as for the north.

Table 10.1

Percentile Equivalents for Mean Scores on *Miner Sentence Completion Scale—Form T:* Proxy Variables among Italian Entrepreneurs (Bellu, Davidsson, and Goldfarb, 1990) and Various Comparison Groups

Types and Characteristics Measured	Northern Italian (Lombardy) Entrepreneurs (N=31)	Southern Italian (Sicily) Entrepreneurs (N=34)	Comparison Groups		
			Northern Italian (Lombardy) Managers (N=33)	Southern Italian (Sicily) Managers (N=33)	U.S. (Buffalo) Established Entrepreneurs (N=100)
Personal Achiever Type					
1. Strong Motivation for Self-Achievement	76	65	44	26	65
3. Desire for Feedback on Achievements	71	86	56	59	62
4. Desire to Plan and Set Goals for Future Achievements	57	63	39	39	41
Expert Idea Generator Type					
1. Desire to Personally Innovate	62	62	22	10	63
5. Desire to Avoid Taking Risks	75	77	36	25	63
Combined Complex Entrepreneur Score					
MSCS-T Total Score	78	81	35	23	64

TYPES AND TALENTS IN ISRAEL

Bellu, Davidsson, and Goldfarb (1989, 1990) also provide information on Israeli entrepreneurs drawn from the region around Tel-Aviv. The firms are concentrated in manufacturing and wholesale/retail, and have less than 50 employees. Roughly a third of the entrepreneurs are females and the mean age is 44.

The comparison *managers* are younger—mean age 30—and have a higher level of education. Again the sample is about one-third female. The companies are concentrated in manufacturing and service, and have less than 50 employees. Once more the established U.S. entrepreneurs are used to provide a U.S. comparison.

With regard to the personal achiever type there is no question that strong self-achievement motivation characterizes the Jewish entrepreneurs. The figures in Table 10.2 are very convincing on this score, and the manager comparison is significant. The numbers on the desire for feedback on achievements are strong as well, although the Israeli entrepreneurs and managers do not differ. It appears that this is a characteristic that typifies Israeli managers, as well as entrepreneurs. Insofar as the desire to plan and set goals for future achievements is concerned, there is very little differentiation among the groups at all. The entrepreneurs are not particularly high, but they are not really low either. A look at the average percentile equivalent across the three measures puts the Israeli entrepreneurs highest at 61, certainly a very positive figure, and above the 56 in the U.S. sample. The comparison managers are down at 47. On balance one has to conclude that entrepreneurs in Israel are characterized by a goodly amount of the personal achiever pattern.

The expert idea generator pattern is also at a high level. There is a marked desire to introduce innovative solutions among the Israeli entrepreneurs, which is well above the level exhibited by any other group and is significant. The desire to avoid taking risks is not elevated to nearly the same extent, but nevertheless the Israeli managers are significantly more prone to take risks. Averaging across the two measures, the Israeli entrepreneurs come out at 62, at essentially the same level as the U.S. entrepreneurs, and well above the average percentile of 41 for the Israeli managers.

The data for complex entrepreneurs place the Israeli entrepreneurs at a very high level, although not quite up to the Italians, and significantly above the comparison Israeli managers.

This picture of high levels of entrepreneurial talent in Israel, at least insofar as two of the four patterns are concerned, provides additional insight into the dynamics of Jewish entrepreneurship in the United States. Korman (1988) has this to say on that subject:

The entrepreneurial role became a success story for Jewish Americans because of the confluence of three factors. First, the American economy needed entrepreneurs to help

Table 10.2

Percentile Equivalents for Mean Scores on *Miner Sentence Completion Scale—Form T*: Proxy Variables among Israeli Entrepreneurs (Bellu, Davidsson, and Goldfarb, 1990) and Various Comparison Groups

Types and Characteristics Measured	Israeli (Tel-Aviv) Entrepreneurs (N=35)	Comparison Groups	
		Israeli (Tel-Aviv) Managers (N=36)	U.S. (Buffalo) Established Entrepreneurs (N=100)
Personal Achiever Type			
1. Strong Motivation for Self-Achievement	71	29	65
3. Desire for Feedback on Achievements	63	61	62
4. Desire to Plan and Set Goals for Future Achievements	49	52	41
Expert Idea Generator Type			
1. Desire to Personally Innovate	75	49	63
5. Desire to Avoid Taking Risks	49	32	63
Combined Complex Entrepreneur Score			
MSCS-T Total Score	70	43	64

it grow. Second, the childhood socialization patterns of Jews tended to encourage the traits and ways of looking at the world that lead one to look on entrepreneurial activities favorably. Third, the self-controlled nature of the entrepreneurial role made it particularly appealing to people who felt themselves to be outsiders and who therefore had to be wary about putting themselves under the influence and control of others (p. 20).

Yet the information now available regarding Jewish entrepreneurs in Israel suggests that being an outsider may be of somewhat lesser significance in this mix. In Israel, Jews are the insiders and still the picture looks much the same. As in the United States, Jewish entrepreneurship is abundant, and it is supported by the personal achiever and expert idea generator personality patterns at the very minimum. Certainly, being an outsider may contribute to the entrepreneurial success of Jews in the United States that Korman (1988) chronicles, but it appears that ethnic culture and the personality patterns it produces play a key role.

TYPES AND TALENTS IN SWEDEN

Evidence from research conducted by Davidsson (1989a, 1989b) indicates that entrepreneurship is far from dormant in Sweden and that it tends to be fueled by a strong achievement motivation just as in other countries. Yet we do not find Swedes at the forefront of entrepreneurial activity in the United States in the same way that Italians and Jews are. On this basis we would conclude that the entrepreneurial talent stream from Sweden to the United States is something less than that from some other countries.

To test this conclusion we used information provided by the research of Bellu, Davidsson, and Goldfarb (1989, 1990). The Swedish entrepreneurs were all located in the greater Stockholm area and were engaged primarily in service activities. Their firms, like those of the comparison managers, were of varied size but all were under 300 employees. The managers had much less education, they all were involved in sales and marketing, and a few had had some prior entrepreneurial experience.

Table 10.3 provides the comparisons. On the personal achiever characteristics the entrepreneurs exceed the managers in only one instance—the motivation for self-achievement that Davidsson (1989a, 1989b) noted. This difference is significant, however, and the other two, favoring the managers, are not. The self-achievement mean still is well below that for the established entrepreneurs in the United States. On the average the Swedish entrepreneurs score 49 on the three personal achiever characteristics, in contrast to 50 for the Swedish managers, and 56 for the U.S. entrepreneurs. The manager sample may be lacking to some extent as a comparison group, with the result that its scores may be inflated. This may compromise the comparisons within Sweden to a degree. Yet the Swedish entrepreneurs remain at roughly an average level as established by the normative sample, and they are not the equal of the established entrepre-

Table 10.3

Percentile Equivalents for Mean Scores on *Miner Sentence Completion Scale—Form T*: Proxy Variables among Swedish Entrepreneurs (Bellu, Davidsson, and Goldfarb, 1990) and Various Comparison Groups

	Swedish (Stockholm) Entrepreneurs (N=31)	Comparison Groups	
Types and Characteristics Measured		Swedish (Stockholm) Managers (N=26)	U.S. (Buffalo) Established Entrepreneurs (N=100)
Personal Achiever Type			
1. Strong Motivation for Self-Achievement	47	27	65
3. Desire for Feedback on Achievements	62	75	62
4. Desire to Plan and Set Goals for Future Achievements	38	48	41
Expert Idea Generator Type			
1. Desire to Personally Innovate	34	40	63
5. Desire to Avoid Taking Risks	53	51	63
Combined Complex Entrepreneur Score			
MSCS-T Total Score	45	48	64

neurs. These are not the kind of personal achiever scores that we found in Tables 10.1 and 10.2 for entrepreneurs from Italy and Israel.

Insofar as the expert idea generator type is concerned, the picture is much the same, but without any significant entrepreneur-manager differences at all. On average, however, the managers score higher—46, to the entrepreneurs' 44. Both are below the average for the normative sample, and well below the established entrepreneurs. The desire to personally innovate is at the lowest level of any group, and well below the average for entrepreneurs in the United States. The desire to avoid taking risks is up at the average, but still basically equal to the managerial percentage figure. Furthermore, risk avoidance is needed to counteract the enthusiasm for ideas inherent in the expert idea generator. If there are few ideas, there is little to counteract. From the data available to us it appears that the expert idea generator personality is not characteristic of Swedish entrepreneurs.

The combined complex entrepreneur score findings fit with what has been said previously. They do not contain real manager and empathic supersalesperson components, and those could change the picture. But a change that would bring this score up to the Italian or Israeli, or even the established U.S. levels seems unlikely.

Overall it appears that Sweden does not generate a particularly large amount of entrepreneurial talent, and that except for achievement motivation, those who do possess such talent are as likely, or even more likely, to serve as managers as to become entrepreneurs. The general picture produced by this analysis is consistent with the view that Sweden is not a country that has fed substantial entrepreneurial talent to the United States.

The data do not say why these findings are obtained. However, Begin (1991) offers some insights that are worth considering. Sweden does not provide many of the joys of entrepreneurship that exist elsewhere. Tax rates can rise to as high as 80 percent of earnings. The labor force is almost totally unionized, and the unions have substantial influence over managerial decisions as a consequence of the fact that the government is controlled by a party that is union dominated. The strong values of the Swedish culture in support of social democracy and egalitarianism give little support to managerial authority, including entrepreneurial management. Participative management is widely endorsed and employee-dominated committee structures are extensive. The net effect of all this is that government, unions, employees, and the total culture combine to place substantial restrictions on entrepreneurial freedom. It is not surprising that this would create a dearth of expert idea generator entrepreneurs with a desire to introduce innovative solutions. But there also appears to be an impact on the personal achiever type as well. The political context in Sweden gives more control to the government and to strong unions, much less to the individual, as in the case of the entrepreneur. This is not an environment in which you can do things on your own easily. One can only hypothesize regarding what would happen to the empathic supersalesperson and real manager under these circumstances, but it appears likely that they would be stifled to some degree as well in the entrepreneurial context.

TYPES AND TALENTS IN POST-COMMUNIST POLAND

Up until quite recently, Poland, like most other Eastern European countries, has been dominated by communism and the Soviet Union. Freedoms of many kinds have been limited, especially the economic freedom on which entrepreneurship thrives. This negative environment for entrepreneurship is eroding as communism has lost its hold. Yet many uncertainties remain, ranging from the possibility that Western-style capitalism will take full hold to the prospect that communism will reestablish itself. In the interim there is considerable moving back and forth with little evidence as yet of the benefits that capitalism can yield in areas such as full employment, economic growth, and stable profits. Prediction is difficult, and forecasting must occur within very wide margins, if it is to succeed at all (Arendarski, Mroczkowski, and Sood, 1994).

It was within this context that O'del (1997) carried out a study of Polish entrepreneurs in the Krakow region of southern Poland (the area known as Malopolska). The enterprises varied widely, ranging from computer sales and grocery stores to car repair services and construction firms. However, they had one thing in common—they were small. The average firm had only three employees, although in a few instances employment rose above 20, to as high as 60. This appears to be typical (Paradiso, 1990). Just under 30 percent of the entrepreneurs were female, as a group they were young, averaging 35 and with only 6 percent over 50.

An ideal study comparing the United States with another country would compare U.S. entrepreneurs, U.S. managers, entrepreneurs from the other country, and managers from the same other country. Rarely has it been possible to utilize this four-way design to the fullest. In the studies that Bellu and his colleagues conducted, only the other country's entrepreneurs and managers were studied, although some comparisons to U.S. entrepreneurs were possible as well. In contrast, in the Polish study U.S. and other country entrepreneurs only were involved. The U.S. group was deliberately selected to match the small size of the Polish firms. Accordingly, this was a selected group within the U.S. context. The companies concentrated around three employees, with a few rising into the 30s to 50. This U.S. sample derived from the Eastern Seaboard and included a range of businesses, many of which were of the same types as the Polish firms. The mean age was 42, with 19 percent over 50; 42 percent were female.

Table 10.4 contains the results for the Polish and American entrepreneurs, as well as for the 100 established entrepreneurs from the United States. The personal achiever numbers indicate some difference between the two countries. Most pronounced is the significantly higher desire to plan and set goals for future achievements in Poland. This is apparent using both U.S. samples. However, the Polish entrepreneurs have a personal achiever score across the three measures

Table 10.4
Percentile Equivalents for Mean Scores on *Miner Sentence Completion Scale—Form T*: Proxy Variables among Polish Entrepreneurs (O'del, 1997) and Various Comparison Groups

| | | Comparison Groups | |
| | Polish (Krakow) Entrepreneurs (N=83) | U.S. (East Coast) Entrepreneurs (N=83) | U.S. (Buffalo) Established Entrepreneurs (N=100) |
Types and Characteristics Measured			
Personal Achiever Type			
1. Strong Motivation for Self-Achievement	43	51	65
3. Desire for Feedback on Achievements	52	48	62
4. Desire to Plan and Set Goals for Future Achievements	56	41	41
Expert Idea Generator Type			
1. Desire to Personally Innovate	38	54	63
5. Desire to Avoid Taking Risks	33	55	63
Combined Complex Entrepreneur Score			
MSCS-T Total Score	43	51	64

of only 50—right at the average based on U.S. norms. The small U.S. firms score 47 and the larger established firms are at 56.

There are additional findings, however, that need to be taken into account. These stem from the locus of control index that O'del (1997) used. This is the Levenson instrument (numbers 8b, 8c, and 8d for the personal achiever type). U.S. entrepreneurs tend to be slightly more internal, but in particular they lack the strong belief in the impact of luck and chance on their outcomes that characterizes the Polish entrepreneurs. In this respect the Polish entrepreneurs emerge as significantly less likely to be personal achievers. The uncertainties that characterize their external environment appear to leave them feeling at the mercy of fate. They do not know what will happen next, and accordingly a strong feeling that chance governs characterizes the Polish entrepreneurial community. This belief is substantial, producing an effect size of 1.5 against the matched U.S. sample, and an even larger effect versus the established sample. Because we do not have good norms for the Levenson instrument it is not possible to cast this result in terms that would permit placing it in Table 10.4. However, this result clearly counteracts the difference in favor of the Polish entrepreneurs produced by their superior desire to plan and set goals for future achievements. On balance the personal achiever score in Poland is certainly not high.

The numbers as regards the expert idea generator type are even less positive. The desire to personally innovate is at a significantly low level relative to the U.S. groups. This is definitely not a strong characteristic among Polish entrepreneurs, presumably in part because the freedom to develop it has not been available. Also, however, entrepreneurship in Poland has attracted those who are prone to risk-taking, not those who desire to avoid it. It looks to be the case that entrepreneurship right now is much like a gambling hall, with high uncertainty and considerable risk. And like gambling halls it attracts gamblers. If you are lucky you will win for a while. But in the long run most will lose if they keep betting. This is because the government take in the form of taxes is substantial. Averaging this risk-taking propensity with the desire to personally innovate, the Polish entrepreneurs have an expert idea generator score of 36. In the United States the matched sample value is 55 and the established entrepreneur value 63. The disparity here is very large.

Overall, the complex entrepreneur measure reflects a somewhat lower level of entrepreneurial talent in Poland with results much like those found in Sweden. Again the data support the hypotheses derived from ethnic differences in U.S. entrepreneurial activity. The existing talent problems appear to have been influenced to a large extent by the post-communist environment, but the behavior of Polish immigrants in the United States suggests that more long-standing influences of Polish culture are also involved. Over the years immigrants from Poland have not exhibited strong entrepreneurial propensities, but the personality patterns back in Poland are not particularly entrepreneurial either.

The picture of the post-communist entrepreneur in Poland that emerges is that of a person faced with great uncertainty and instability who wants to plan and set goals, but is unable to do so successfully. As a result the entrepreneur feels at the mercy of fate; real personal control of events and innovation seem difficult, if not impossible. In this context risk takers and gamblers are attracted to the entrepreneurial arena because of the high stakes involved. These are often young people who have little to lose. They will give entrepreneurship a try and if luck is not on their side, they will try something else. There is little ego deflation involved in any event—it is not their fault if the business fails, they simply were unlucky. This is a clinical interpretation from the data and certainly requires more study. Yet it hits the high (and low) points of the test scores well. If further research supports it, and the situation does not change, entrepreneurship in Poland would appear to be in for a difficult future.

A question arises regarding the extent to which this picture may generalize to other post-communist countries, especially Russia. There is little research evidence on this score. Hisrich and Grachev (1995) report on a study of 32 Russian entrepreneurs, which included a measure of personality characteristics, and conclude that "the overall traits exhibited by the Russian entrepreneurs were similar to those of entrepreneurs in the U.S." (p. 6) Yet this may be due to a mixing of types so that no characteristics emerge as particularly strong.

A study by Kaufmann, Welsh, and Bushmarin (1995) avoids this confounding by utilizing the Levenson measure of locus of control only, and thus focusing on characteristics within the personal achiever type. Their data for 174 Russian entrepreneurs indicate a considerably lower internal control score in Russia than in the United States and a much higher chance external control score. This latter result fits with what O'del (1997) found among Polish entrepreneurs. Thus, some basis for hypothesizing similar entrepreneurial types and talents in Poland and Russia exists. This should be a fruitful area for research which could produce useful information regarding the future of entrepreneurship in the post-communist world.

CONCLUSION

It is apparent that major ethnic variations in the personality patterns associated with entrepreneurial endeavor exist. Some ethnic groups exhibit much entrepreneurial talent, and some exhibit much less. Furthermore, these talent differentials appear to be mirrored in the immigrant population of the United States and other countries. All of the findings considered in this chapter are consistent with that interpretation. Italy and Israel are high-talent countries, and Italian and Jewish immigrants tend to be successful entrepreneurs in large numbers in this country. Sweden and Poland are not high-talent countries, and Swedish and Polish immigrants tend not to be major sources of entrepreneurial endeavors here.

Given the fact that Sweden has had a socialist government for many years and Poland is just emerging from a long period of communist domination, it is tempting to conclude that these governmental structures account for the lack of an entrepreneurial bent in the populace. There may indeed be some truth in that view, especially under a communist regime, which proscribes all trappings of capitalism, including entrepreneurship. However, it is also true that in countries where entrepreneurial talent is limited, entrepreneurship is valued less and the potential for a socialist or communist form of government is therefore greater. In short, the underlying ethnic culture may predispose people to be less entrepreneurial and also to adopt governmental forms that are antithetical to entrepreneurship.

In any event ethnic variations exist, and they appear to exert sufficient influence so that they should be considered when drawing conclusions about entrepreneurial talent and the incidence of types. If a person is an Italian or Jewish immigrant to this country, or presumably a Chinese or Greek or Indian immigrant also, there is a better chance that one or more of the types associated with entrepreneurial success will be present. This high probability context tends to decline in successive generations as American culture exerts an equalizing influence, but it takes a considerable time for it to disappear completely. Thus various ethnic origins can provide added impetus to entrepreneurship and added likelihood of entrepreneurial success. That entrepreneurship has prospered in the United States is in large part due to immigration policies that fostered bringing a large number of people from many countries to "the new world." We should recognize, however, that insofar as entrepreneurship is concerned, a more focused policy, concerned with fewer nationalities, could have produced the same result.

Part IV

Entrepreneurship Development

Chapter 11

Using the Typology to Create Tailor-Made Development Activities

Programs of many kinds may be grouped under the entrepreneurship development umbrella. They may serve to help a prospective entrepreneur to start a business, or a corporate manager to initiate a venture. They may have the objective of teaching established entrepreneurs how to grow their businesses. They may operate to facilitate the succession process in family businesses, so that the hurdles this process often faces are minimized. They may simply intend to provide the knowledge needed so that a particular venture can survive. They may relate to special concerns such as going public, selling a business, or obtaining financing from venture capitalists. In many cases these are non-degree programs offered by colleges and universities, although there are many other providers as well. A good source of information is the volume edited by Hoy, Monroy, and Reichert (1993, 1994).

The approach to the subject of entrepreneurship development taken here is in many respects unique. Working with entrepreneurs over the years, it has become increasingly apparent that those with different personality patterns seek different things from development programs, are attentive to different aspects, and benefit from different types of programs, or features of programs. Thus the four-way typology of patterns and routes provides a useful way of approaching entrepreneurship development. This chapter discusses the kinds of training and development most likely to be beneficial to personal achievers, real managers, expert idea generators, and empathic supersalespeople. They are not necessarily at all the same.

Chapter 12 takes up a specific program as it was operated by the School of Management at the State University of New York at Buffalo for seven years. This program has a number of different components, and thus provides a useful vehicle for demonstrating how different features of a program can serve to help various types of participants. The program has its imperfections, and there are certain components which it now appears should have been incorporated that were not, and others that should have been deleted. Nevertheless, the program provides a useful vehicle for evaluating and discussing various aspects of entrepreneurship development.

ENTREPRENEURSHIP DEVELOPMENT FOR PERSONAL ACHIEVERS

In a recent book, Block and MacMillan (1993) do an excellent job of arguing the case for venture learning. Because they operate with a great deal of uncertainty in uncharted waters, ventures—whether corporate or independent—have a huge need to acquire information about themselves and the environment around them. As this learning occurs, uncertainty turns to certainty and many situations that were previously out of control come to be more manageable. Personal achievers seem to implicitly understand this, and accordingly they tend to strive to maximize venture learning.

This would seem to make personal achievers good candidates for development programs. In many respects they are. They are very receptive to learning that is factual and focused directly on the needs of their ventures. This means, however, that they are not very receptive to teaching that is abstract and lacking in clear implications for action, and which deals with contexts far removed from their firms, as large corporations often are. Information that is not apparently relevant simply tends to get tuned out, and programs that have too much of this information get tuned out completely. A good program for personal achievers thus needs to provide information that can be put directly to use in the venture. It does not have to be simple, or even beautifully packaged, but it does need to be practical. This means that instructors who can lay legitimate claim to being knowledgeable about entrepreneurship have a huge step up. Personal experience in the entrepreneurial world helps a lot.

A type of program that appears to have considerable appeal, and produces major benefits as well, is provided by achievement motivation training. An article by Timmons (1971) describes this approach as it is used in the development of minority entrepreneurs. The training has been used widely for this purpose—to stimulate the start of new ventures and also to bring about growth in existing enterprises.

As indicated, the training enables participants to develop achievement-motivated behavior patterns—problem solving, goal setting, business planning, risk handling—through specially designed business games. Participants experience both the anxieties and satisfactions of setting and achieving personal and business goals, with these experiences conceptualized to real-life situations through practice. Considerable emphasis is placed on examining and testing goals for specificity, realism, challenge, time-phasing, and personal commitment. Obstacles that might hinder attaining goals are closely evaluated. Sources of feedback on goal attainment are considered. Participants complete the TAT—or Thematic Apperception Test (where stories are told in response to various pictures)—and learn to interpret their stories so as to understand their own motives.

This kind of training does work to foster business initiation and business growth among minorities and to foster the same type of entrepreneurship development in other countries of the world as well. An article by Miron and McClelland (1979) and a book by McClelland and Winter (1969) document this point. The training works well with other groups too. Furthermore, it is apparent from these sources that those who benefit most are the personal achievers. Achievement motivation training helps people to follow the achieving route.

A second type of entrepreneurship development specifically focused on personal achievers is a program which results in the development of a business plan. This approach is widely used in formal college and university courses in entrepreneurship (Solomon, Weaver, and Fernald, 1994). However, it is often extended to free-standing entrepreneurship development efforts as well. In the university setting the assumption is that business plans will be used for the purpose of attracting start-up capital, and what is taught is planning for that purpose. These plans are inevitably formulated in a situation where, because the business has no history, forecasting is very difficult and often just plain wrong. Furthermore, the very fact that the goal is to influence others to put their money behind a business makes for a degree of optimism that may not always be realistic. Yet this type of business plan preparation, which is fine for its intended purpose, is often extended to entrepreneurship development programs which are directed not to potential entrepreneurs, but to those with an established track record. That can be a mistake.

The problem is that there are at least three types of business plans, and each needs to be taught differently. One is a quest for financing of a start-up. The second is a plan to operate and make decisions in the future based on strengths and weaknesses, opportunities and threats which are known because the business has operated long enough to establish them. Here forecasting may be difficult, but it is possible simply because there has been a degree of venture learning, and accordingly some degree of uncertainty reduction has occurred. The goal could be financing growth, in which case there is a mixture of the first and second types, but more frequently it is simply operating the business on a stable keel into the future.

Third, there is a business plan intended to facilitate the transition into a new ownership or source of control—a merger, succession in a family business, a personal achiever hitting the wall and yielding the reins to a real manager, or a buyout. Here the objective is to show the traditions and culture that have been generated and what they mean for the future of the business—the vision that is currently in place. Those who are taking over may not follow this plan, but they need to know what it is to benefit from past learning and to ensure an orderly transition which does not result in a waste of resources.

When developing a business plan one has to be very clear as to what the objective is. Programs that provide guidance in developing a plan should distinguish the three types and focus learning on the one that is most appropriate for the particular person. Almost always these programs result in a formal, written business plan as a product. Often there is an oral presentation to a group as well. A number of factors contribute to the quality of these plans, but personal achievers tend to be highly motivated in this respect and as a result they are unlikely to produce a low-quality plan.

Furthermore, there is evidence that planning works. This derives from a number of studies that have been carried out comparing the profitability and other indexes of success of firms that do not engage in formal planning, or do so at a less sophisticated level, with the success levels of the more sophisticated planners. It does not always work because there are situations where uncertainty is so pronounced that effective forecasting is not possible. However, on balance the comparisons provide considerable support for the use of formal planning processes of this kind taught in entrepreneurship development programs. An analysis of the various studies, using meta-analysis, by Boyd (1991) is quite clear on this point. It is also apparent from a study by Bracker, Pearson, Keats, and Miner (1992) discussed in Miner (1993) that entrepreneurs who plan well are particularly likely to possess the characteristics of personal achievers.

This strong support for planning, and for development programs that teach people how to do it, needs to be tempered somewhat because of questions raised recently by Mintzberg (1994). To the extent planning cannot be based on effective forecasting of what will happen in the future, it is less useful. Also, if one is not careful, planning can become rigid and work at cross purposes with innovation. This is a special problem for the expert idea generator. In short, planning has to be adapted to the situation in which it will be used and it has to be done carefully and comprehensively. This is what a good business plan development program tries to teach.

Although planning per se can be of value to any business, plan development training is of particular value to personal achievers because they are most likely to be highly motivated in this regard. When used prior to start-up or entry into a venture the training has the following advantages:

The process of developing the business plan allows the individual to experience the challenges and rewards of entrepreneurship with little risk and provides a realistic preview of the process. Many discover that the reality of starting and running a business is not as attractive as they thought. Critical to this process is that it allows the individual to make mistakes with limited liability and resource drain. Many potential disasters and fatal business mistakes can be identified before they are implemented. Thus, this approach has been shown to enhance the success of the individual, resulting in many viable new organizations for those that successfully complete these classes (Eggers, 1975, p. 181).

Many of these advantages accrue as a result of exposure to the training in contexts other than prestart-up as well.

Achievement motivation training and business plan development training are merely two examples of approaches that can serve to increase and perfect the talents of personal achievers. Other similar procedures that either increase the already existing characteristics of these people or help them to follow the achieving route more effectively are equally to be recommended.

ENTREPRENEURSHIP DEVELOPMENT FOR REAL MANAGERS

This is where entrepreneurship development and management development become one. Anything that would serve to assist managers to perform more effectively will help entrepreneurs follow the managing route also. A good, up-to-date source on management development approaches is an article by Baldwin and Padgett (1993).

An example discussed in the Baldwin and Padgett paper is the use of job rotation or special assignments for developmental purposes. Here placements are made primarily with the objective of facilitating learning by experience. A manager may be rotated through several jobs at regular intervals and assume full responsibility for each. The job changes may be lateral transfers or promotions. Alternatively, people may be rotated through a series of positions that exist almost entirely for training purposes, although they may carry out various special projects also. Usually, this is the procedure used with management trainees. Understudy assignments, working as an assistant to an experienced manager, and participation in a rotating set of projects are other approaches.

The objective in these situations is to expose the person to a predetermined group of learning experiences. Working with different people on different activities in different situations maximizes development as long as the person does not stay to the point of overlearning and is not assigned to a position for which he or she has no qualifications at all. It is important in using this procedure that normal operations not be sacrificed to the training objective, and that may require considerable preplanning. Generally, larger companies are in a better position to implement job rotation approaches, but opportunities can be found in smaller firms as well. This is a very effective way of assisting people to learn about managing. It is far superior to simply assigning people to one managerial job and leaving them there, because it develops a capacity to cope with a wide range of situations and problems and thus to manage better. A variant that is widely used in small firms, especially family businesses, is to swap heir-apparent managers with another related firm. Thus the job rotation process extends outside the business for a period of time. This can be very effective. In some instances arrangements are made so that a person puts in stints with several different firms.

Management development may also involve different types of classroom learning of a kind that takes participants into new areas and experiences, with results similar to those from job rotation. An example is managerial role motivation training. The primary method of instruction here is lecture and discussion.

Participants develop skills in decision making and controlling through the study of methods for diagnosing and correcting the ineffective performance of subordinates. In the process they come to hold new perspectives on the managerial job and often strengthen their managerial motivation as well.

On occasion, case analyses are also included. Detailed written cases dealing with instances of ineffective performance are provided to participants and they are to determine what factors combined to cause the performance difficulties, as well as what corrective actions might be taken. Individual participants present their own analyses of the cases orally. Other participants and the trainer then critique these presentations. In addition to this analysis of written cases, participants are also encouraged to discuss specific instances of performance failure from their own experience as the training progresses.

Real managers can benefit considerably from development programs of this kind. The programs tend to make them better managers, more dedicated to their work and more successful in it. Evidence on this point is discussed in detail in Miner (1993). The training content itself is detailed in Miner (1985).

The following outline provides an example of what is involved:

1. The nature of ineffective performance, performance criteria and standards, key factors in performance failure, learning about oneself as a manager, and screening and firing as methods of dealing with unsatisfactory work performance.

2. The verbal ability demand levels of occupations, special mental abilities, identifying intellectual factors in failure, intellectual overplacement, and the use of transfer and training.

3. The nature of emotional problems, the effects of emotions on performance, emotions and effectiveness at different job levels, managerial action in dealing with emotional problems, alcoholism and drug problems.

4. The individual's motivational hierarchy, general and specific work motivation, methods of dealing with motivational problems, and the appropriate use of threat and discipline.

5. Physical illness and job performance, physical disorders of emotional origin, the performance consequences of aging, and the role of the manager in dealing with physical problems.

6. Performance effects of family crises, the nature of separation anxiety reactions, predominance of family over job considerations, and possible managerial actions in instances of family-based failure.

7. Group cohesiveness as a cause of failure, failure by managerial definition, including a positive group impact, sources of manager-induced performance problems, and dealing with oneself as a manager.

8. Ineffective performance and top-level policies, failures of implementation, inappropriate personnel placement, organizational over-permissiveness, excessive spans of control, and the use of inappropriate performance standards and criteria.

9. Job-value conflicts, alternatives for managerial action in dealing with cultural values, and the prospects for value change.

10. Subjective danger situations, dealing with economic and geographic causes of unsatisfactory performance, accident-proneness, danger in the work, and problems in the work itself.

11. The managerial job, aspects of motivation to manage, the managerial job as a subjective danger situation, avoidance motivation and managerial performance, and the difficulties of managerial self-control.

Approaches such as job rotation and managerial role motivation training or its variants serve to increase the managerial motivation of real managers and to assist them in pursuing the managing route more effectively. Thus they build upon the strengths of this entrepreneurial type. There are clearly other training and development activities of this kind that can be useful as well. The key is that, whatever approach is used, it serve to stretch the real manager abilities and competence of the person so as to produce a better manager.

ENTREPRENEURSHIP DEVELOPMENT FOR EXPERT IDEA GENERATORS

As previously noted, expert idea generators need a substantial amount of training for the purpose of bringing them to expert status. This may take a variety of forms. Formal training may extend from apprenticeships to a Ph.D. program. However, in many cases there is no formal training in the particular area of expertise, and learning occurs on various jobs or through personal study. More frequently a combination of approaches is used, with different types of development used for different purposes.

An example of how this works is provided by an expert idea generator who now owns a mini-conglomerate doing over $100 million in sales a year; the core business relates to security and the detection of crime. A college degree in criminal justice got him started. From there he went to a transport company where as director of security he learned the security business by doing. At the same time he attended polygraph school and learned how to become an examiner. Then he went to work for a company doing polygraph examinations. Gradually, he developed his own practice, and then hired other examiners to work for him. This was his first start-up. There have been many since, providing services such as guard and patrol, investigation, polygraph training, bus transportation, drug testing, honesty testing, and support to the security, law enforcement, and corrections communities. He owns a number of office buildings.

In the early period his ideas were for new businesses related to security concerns. As the number of these businesses grew, however, he became faced with the need to apply his skills to the business process in general. To assist him in this area he first took several non-degree courses at a local college and later completed the three-year Owner/President Management Program at Harvard Business School. He continues to think up, and start, new ventures. He is particularly interested in developing creative approaches to financing which do not dilute his ownership.

Clearly, this individual has drawn upon many sources for his learning. Expert idea generators tend to do this, and it is entirely consistent with the idea generating route to follow this type of approach.

An entirely different procedure that also helps expert idea generators traverse the idea generating route is some type of training in the skills and techniques of generating creative ideas, solving problems, and making decisions. This training can take a number of forms, but a common element is practice in looking at things and situations differently. Various problem-solving exercises may be used to do this. Originally, training of this kind focused on professionals involved in research and development activities. New-product identification was a major concern; however, the training has now spread more broadly with the objective of unearthing suggestions for quality improvement and more efficient operations generally. Frito-Lay, for instance, has trained more than 7,000 employees using a course that covers eight steps in problem solving: (1) problem finding, (2) fact finding, (3) problem definition, (4) idea finding, (5) evaluation and selection, (6) action planning, (7) selling or gaining acceptance, and (8) taking action. Texas Instruments has tied the training directly to its overall total quality improvement program (Solomon, 1990).

Another approach emphasizes creativity more and devotes considerable time to active practice and learning from experiences. Various tasks are used to encourage participants to discover concepts related to creative problem solving not considered previously. In one exercise participants each formulate a definition of a problem from a case and then compare all their definitions, thus learning that the same problem can be viewed in several fruitful ways. At another point each person generates an individual work problem and then develops a solution, and an implementation plan for the problem.

Studies conducted to evaluate the effectiveness of these kinds of programs indicate that there are improvements in cognitive processes, more favorable attitudes toward creative endeavor, and more creative problem-solving behavior. People do become more creative in their jobs (Basadur, Graen, and Green, 1982). This has direct implications for those attempting to follow the idea generating route to entrepreneurship. Training of this kind can sharpen the already existing talents of expert idea generators.

ENTREPRENEURSHIP DEVELOPMENT FOR EMPATHIC SUPERSALESPEOPLE

Development activities that involve considerable lecturing at the participants do not work very well with empathic supersalespeople. By nature they want to interact with other people and accordingly they tend to get restless when faced with a lengthy lecture situation. Group discussions, on the other hand, are attractive. They tend to participate actively, ask questions, and engage in the give and take. Considerable learning occurs in this manner. Furthermore, within the context of a total entrepreneurship development program they are very responsive to any opportunity for networking. Social activities are important in this regard. Empathic supersalespeople often engage in selling activities within a program, establish long-standing relationships, and learn from other participants. In fact, they probably learn more from interacting with other entrepreneurs than they do from expert instructors.

Formal attempts to teach selling in college courses have always faced the problem that so much that needs to be learned is product or service specific. You have to develop knowledge about what is being sold in order to sell it. But because products and services span such a wide range, it is difficult to create a program that is relevant for any given class. On the other hand, company-operated programs have no such problems. There homogeneity of participant needs is easily assured.

A useful example of such a program conducted for a multistore chain selling appliances, radios, and televisions in Florida is described by Meyer and Raich (1983). The training used behavior modeling and focused on specific aspects of the sales situation such as "approaching the customer," "explaining features, advantages, and benefits," "closing the sale," and the like. Guidelines or learning points for handling each aspect of a sales interaction were considered, followed by the presentation of a videotaped situation where a model sales person followed the guidelines in carrying out aspects of the sales interaction with a customer. The trainees then practice the same situation in role-playing rehearsals, reinforced and shaped by supervisors previously trained as instructors. This particular approach worked to yield a major change in commissions over a control group that did not receive training. It also served to reduce turnover and facilitate promotions. To the extent this type of training can be incorporated in entrepreneurship development programs for empathic supersalespeople, it can yield very good results.

A second type of program that can serve to help empathic supersalespeople follow the selling route is variously labeled as laboratory training, T-grouping, sensitivity training, human relations training, and team building; more broadly these programs can include organization development, quality of work life projects, quality circles, and autonomous—or leaderless—work groupings. These approaches, and a number of others considered in this chapter, are discussed in Miner (1992) and Miner and Crane (1995). Activities of this kind, when aimed at organizational change, can go well beyond training and development, but they typically include the latter in some form. Empathic supersalespeople are quite responsive to them. Without exception these efforts are intended to teach participative management and the moving of power and authority down in the business structure to lower levels. Thus the entrepreneur is expected to give up a degree of control. For many, such as the personal achiever, this presents a major problem; for empathic supersalespeople it is no problem at all.

Training of the kind I have in mind may include some lectures and experiential exercises or games, but at the core is the T (or training)—group. In these groups, members learn about group processes and interpersonal relations. Although there is a trainer, or sometimes more than one, he or she does not impose a structure on the group. There may even be no specified task to be performed; members often are initially frustrated and embarrassed. As the program continues, however, it becomes apparent that the task is to learn about groups and one's own relationships to them. The trainer encourages openness in expressing feelings. The group discusses topics such as the effects of authority, the motives of members, and the need to be understood. Members gradually open up, becoming more willing to reveal themselves and trust others. This process of self-revelation can make some members uneasy, some less emotionally stable individuals may even become extremely anxious. Yet in the end the group typically does tend to develop some structure that may prove beneficial.

Under the team-building label this process has tended to focus more on how a team can solve organizational problems, but team learning remains important. Empathic supersalespeople are very responsive to this type of developmental experience. Accordingly, positive effects can be anticipated. These effects seem most likely to the extent empathic supersalespeople are involved. Other types of successful entrepreneurs may not participate as well—expert idea generators and personal achievers in particular. As Tannenbaum and Yukl (1992) have shown, there clearly are positive effects to be anticipated from the kind of participative training involved here, if the right people participate.

Empathic supersalespeople are very likely to develop teams of various kinds—management teams, sales teams, production teams, advisory boards, engagement teams, network teams, and so on. They are also very likely to share power with these teams. Anything that will help them do these things better, thus creating more effective teams and working with them in an efficient manner, is to be desired. Training which accomplishes these ends can help to develop the already existing special capabilities of empathic supersalespeople.

ENTREPRENEURSHIP DEVELOPMENT AND THE
COMPLEX ENTREPRENEUR

At this point we have what amount to four separate development approaches for those following the achieving, managing, idea generating, and selling routes to entrepreneurial success. Each clearly utilizes different procedures, indicating that, at least from this perspective, a single program for entrepreneurship development is not warranted.

One alternative is to segment entrepreneurs according to personality patterns and expose them to appropriate but different development modules. An individual with multiple patterns would simply undertake more modules. In the case of Leon Smith (see Chapter 4) this could mean taking all four modules—and experiencing quite a sizable development effort.

Such an approach is possible, but appears overly burdensome. Complex entrepreneurs would have their personality patterns assessed before training, either through some kind of self-assessment or the test battery. Then they would undertake training to develop the multiple talents revealed. One possibility at this point is to select the particular psychological type present that appears most likely to benefit from training, and focus on that. Also, through sequencing, complex entrepreneurs often use one of their strong patterns early on, and bring another to bear much later. The empathic supersalesperson type is particularly useful early in the venture's history, for instance, and the real manager type at a point when considerable growth has occurred. Training efforts could be sequenced so as to build on these strengths at the times when they are most likely to be used.

The point is that complex entrepreneurs need not try to develop all of their strengths at once. They can prioritize and sequence training modules as their needs and the situation dictate.

OBTAINING NEEDED TRAINING WITHIN A BUSINESS DEGREE PROGRAM

An obvious question is—Why not undertake a formal program of business study at either the undergraduate or graduate level and in the process acquire the learning that we have been discussing? Degree programs have within them major areas of study suited to the needs of students with different interests and capabilities. Could not personal achievers, real managers, expert idea generators, and empathic supersalespeople similarly find areas of study or sets of courses appropriate to their entrepreneurial needs?

One answer is that although courses in entrepreneurship do spawn entrepreneurial activity, as the research reported in Chapter 7 and other studies such as those by Hornaday and Vesper (1982) indicate, there are not enough of these courses to encompass all of the kinds of training needed to develop the four types. What we have at present are a reasonably large number of entrepreneurship courses focused on business plan development, which are of particular value to personal achievers, and a wide range of courses scattered across the curriculum that should be useful to expert idea generators. Perhaps with more courses, and more programs in entrepreneurship, there would be more relevant training available, but that is not the case at present.

However, many of the training approaches noted previously are not unique to the entrepreneurship context. They should be of value to those with other career objectives also. Job rotation for management development purposes could be incorporated in internship programs, but it rarely is. Managerial role motivation training has been used in business management courses, but not with great frequency. Approaches akin to creativity training have never achieved much acceptance in the academic context. Sales training as it is conducted by companies has not been incorporated by colleges and universities, with the possible exception of a few programs devoted to retailing. Sensitivity training experienced something of a boom some years ago in the academic setting, but is now seen infrequently. Achievement motivation training is rarely incorporated in any kind of university course.

The point is that even where these approaches have much wider relevance beyond entrepreneurship, they do not show up with any great frequency in business school curricula. They are typically made available through consulting firms, large corporations, independent foundations, or almost any type of entity besides a formal college or university course.

Exactly why this is the case is not clearly evident. It is apparent, however, that business schools have failed to meet market needs sufficiently often that a very sizable competitive industry has developed beyond their boundaries (Elliott, Goodwin, and Goodwin, 1994). The entrepreneurship field is certainly no exception to this trend. Some will argue that these approaches operate outside the bounds of academic science and thus lack scholarly repute. Yet many such programs have been created by academics of considerable stature, and have been supported by more research than exists in the case of established academic courses. In any event it seems apparent that for a variety of reasons the entrepreneurship development needs considered in this chapter are only infrequently achieved through formal university courses.

This raises a broader question as to how effective business degree programs are, in general, in meeting the needs of the various types of entrepreneurs. Many programs require learning a great deal that is not needed by entrepreneurs, and at least some may provide little that is. The corporate, big business emphasis can be a problem. Furthermore, universities that are strong on entrepreneurship at one point in time may not be at another. An added concern is the recent emphasis on obtaining business experience after the undergraduate degree before entering on an MBA. This makes some sense for those who will embark upon careers in corporate management, because the MBA course work is taken closer to the time at which it will be used in a managerial position. For a number of actual or potential entrepreneurs, however, it does not make sense at all.

Given these considerations, the decision to pursue an MBA should be taken only after some study of both the program being considered and of oneself. Does the program match well with the person's best career route or not? The MBA can represent a major contribution to an entrepreneur's success, or a wasted several years, or something in between. In most instances it is the latter and the judgment call can be very difficult to make in advance. Generally, the status and prestige that go with having an MBA from a major university are less useful to entrepreneurs than to those who pursue careers in large corporations or in the elite management consulting firms. It is what actually is learned that matters most for entrepreneurs.

For personal achievers who aspire to careers where they utilize the achieving route to guide ventures into growth, and diversify into several enterprises, an MBA with an entrepreneurial emphasis can be quite valuable. It should be completed just as early as possible, because only part of the learning that needs to be done is available in school. What is available there provides a good under-pinning for sorting out what additional knowledge and experience should be acquired elsewhere.

For real managers the route to entrepreneurship often moves through corpo-rate management. Consequently, the typical MBA program is probably more useful to real managers than to any other entrepreneurial type. It can help them pursue the managing route.

For expert idea generators who want to become niche exploiters an MBA can be very useful in learning to identify niches and in figuring out how to develop them. No doubt the formal learning will need to be supplemented by solid experience, but it is a good beginning. This argues for acquiring the MBA as early as possible. The more entrepreneurially focused the program the better. For many inventor-entrepreneurs it may be more appropriate to stress one's area of expertise and pursue the idea generating route that way, while hiring or teaming with someone else (perhaps someone who already has an MBA) to handle what is outside one's technical specialty.

For empathic supersalespeople most graduate business programs are of limited value. There are exceptions, but overall it is more important to simply get out and learn how to sell. I know of no MBA program that teaches that. I also believe that marketing departments should devote more attention to this key activity.

Finally, there is the complex entrepreneur who has multiple routes that may be followed either at the same time or sequentially. Here a truly venture-oriented MBA can be helpful, although if one of the routes available is managing, even the typical program may yield value. Again, however, the earlier the MBA is earned, the longer time it has to work. Also, there is reason to believe that complex entrepreneurs can be very successful without the formal education; there is a question as to how much value is added by the typical MBA. That will vary with the individual.

CONCLUSION

The objective of entrepreneurship development as it is described here is to help people follow the career routes appropriate to their personality patterns as closely and effectively as possible. Used in this way, entrepreneurship devel-opment is a very powerful tool. I strongly recommend that those who are, or are about to become, entrepreneurs experience it in some measure.

For anyone contemplating a new venture, an appropriate approach is to set forth in writing the specific venture one would like to create, and then indicate the steps that need to be taken to get there. This is much like developing a business plan, but it is also career planning and goal setting as well. Obtaining the financing for a new venture is only one aspect of the total exercise. These visions of a future state are what entrepreneurs-to-be often create on their own, especially expert idea generators. What I am suggesting is that this vision be made explicit, and that others be told about it, so that a degree of commitment occurs. Part of this vision should be a statement of learning needs required to reach the visionary goal, and what specific training should be undertaken for this purpose. The objective of this chapter is to provide assistance in this latter respect. This whole planning process requires a great deal of imagination to complete effectively. It has been argued that the central role of business education should be to cultivate this type of entrepreneurial imagination (Chia, 1996). Certainly, most business schools are far from achieving this role at present. Yet a move to a more entrepreneurially centered curriculum would help a great deal in reaching this goal.

Chapter 12

A Comprehensive Entrepreneurship Development Program

The objective in this chapter is to take a detailed look at an academic year-long entrepreneurship development program created to appeal to and benefit a wide range of entrepreneurs. This is the Center for Entrepreneurial Leadership (CEL) program conducted by the State University of New York at Buffalo, from which the 100 established entrepreneur sample used in the Chapter 6 research derived. Chapter 6 provides considerable information regarding those 100 entrepreneurs and their firms; it remains to describe the content and operation of the program itself.

A number of purposes are served by describing this program. For those who are not familiar with these kinds of comprehensive development efforts, it provides an opportunity to indicate what they are like. For those who are interested in creating a program of this kind, it provides an opportunity to consider and evaluate various program components. Finally, it provides an opportunity to look at comprehensive programs of this type in the context of the four-way typology. How do these programs measure up in terms of offering the kinds of training activities described in Chapter 11?

It is important to understand that the CEL program was basically a regional development effort. The region involved is known as Western New York. It includes Erie and Niagara counties which border on Lakes Erie and Ontario, although additional adjacent counties are sometimes incorporated as well. The hub of economic activities in the area is Buffalo.

Western New York has a distinctive economic history which differs in many respects from the history of the rest of New York. To understand why and how the CEL program was constituted, it is important to know something of this history. This will provide a backdrop for the presentation of the program itself.

HISTORICAL BACKGROUND ON THE ECONOMY OF
WESTERN NEW YORK[1]

Prior to 1825, Buffalo was a frontier settlement. However, with the opening of the Erie Canal connecting Lake Erie and Buffalo with Albany and the Hudson River, a period of economic expansion began which extended for almost 100 years. With some ups and downs these so-called glory years reached to the end of the Korean War in 1953. Since then it has been largely downhill (Ticknor, 1985).

Nevertheless, the glory years were impressive in their stature. In the early period, growth was a function of Buffalo's central role as a transportation link between the agricultural and mining regions of the Midwest and the population centers of the Northeast. Initially, water transportation through the Great Lakes and the Erie Canal was crucial. Later, rail transportation took over a major segment of this route. As of 1900, the port of Buffalo was the third largest in the country, behind only New York City and Chicago; as a railroad center it was second only to Chicago.

Building partly on this role as a transportation hub, and partly on inexpensive electricity from Niagara Falls, Buffalo expanded rapidly in a number of manufacturing areas in the early 1900s. During this period the steel, automobile, chemical, and aircraft industries came to the area. World War I brought a substantial defense boom. In 1920, Buffalo was the eleventh largest city in the United States in terms of population, and it ranked eighth as a manufacturing center. The population of the city of Buffalo had risen steadily over a 100-year period to some 500,000 people. Throughout this period, certain industries showed continuous growth, particularly steel and automobile manufacture, but also food products, chemicals, aircraft, and electrical machinery.

Yet overall, after World War I the Buffalo economy went into decline. Particularly significant was the purchase of a number of smaller Buffalo-area firms by national corporations such as General Motors, Republic Steel, National Steel, and Bethlehem Steel. During this time Buffalo became increasingly a branch town, and thus bereft of control over its own economic destiny.

Although the effects of the Depression of the 1930s were greater in Buffalo than elsewhere, so too was the growth impact of World War II. Manufacturing employment more than tripled in Buffalo during the war; the glory years were back. The city did more business with the government in this period than all but four other U.S. cities. Aircraft in particular skyrocketed. By 1946, Westinghouse and Western Electric had established a presence in Buffalo, as had Ford several years before.

Again there was an economic drop-off after the war and a great deal of strike activity as well, but the Korean War put an end to that. During the 1950–1953 period the Buffalo manufacturing sector became the tenth largest in the United States, and the port of Buffalo the twelfth largest; the city's population reached almost 600,000. Bell Aircraft produced a large majority of the helicopters used in the war. At the same time the area became increasingly concentrated on absentee-owned heavy industry. As it turned out, this was the last hurrah.

A number of factors eroded the glory of the earlier period. Buffalo's role as a transportation hub was influenced by changing population distributions, as more and more people moved to the South and West. The opening of the St. Lawrence Seaway in 1958, and in particular the Welland Canal linking Lake Ontario to Lake Erie (and thus bypassing Buffalo), decimated the grain shipping industry and had a strong negative impact on the production of food products overall. The decline in the railroad industry was national in scope, but Buffalo suffered disproportionately because so much of its economy was focused there. Inexpensive power from the Niagara River no longer produced an economic advantage.

The decline in manufacturing was occasioned primarily by international competition but also by competition from other areas of the country. The Vietnam War had a modest positive impact, but not nearly to the extent of past wars. As Buffalo's manufacturing declined, its potential for any wartime economic boom declined also.

Since the early 1970s the clang of factory gate closings has been almost incessant. Bethlehem Steel probably had the biggest impact, but other large, absentee-owned companies contributed their share to the decline. These companies include General Motors, Republic Steel, Ford, Bell Aircraft, and Allied Chemical. The steel and transportation equipment industries were the hardest hit.

Employment has been rising since the 1950s, but not nearly at the rate of the rest of the country. From the mid-1980s, this increase was evident in all sectors of the local economy except manufacturing; it continued through to the recession of the early 1990s, when a considerable drop occurred (Merchant, 1992). However, manufacturing employment has shown a continuing decrease; the slack that was taken up and the growth that there was are a consequence of developments in the service-producing industries. High-paying, unionized jobs in heavy manufacturing were replaced by much lower-paying jobs in the service sector (Scrace, 1991).

Unemployment was greater than 12 percent in the early 1980s. It declined to below 5 percent by 1990. These, however, are misleading figures insofar as economic growth is concerned, because large numbers of people left the local labor force and the Buffalo area. Most were young, and many were well educated. Overall there has been a serious population decline, especially in the city of Buffalo itself. Growth in the future is expected to be minimal at best (New York State Department of Economic Development, 1990).

Yet this depressing picture could have several bright spots in the future should a way be found to turn the economy around. One is that the Western New York area has access to a labor force that has the potential to fuel major economic expansion. A number of people in the area are currently underemployed; they are earning less and contributing less than they could were the opportunities there. In addition, the area has the ability to reattract many of the young people who migrated originally because of a lack of opportunity in Western New York (Smyntek, Scrace, and Swinarski, 1990). Another plus has been termed the *Toronto spillover* (Smyntek, 1991). Buffalo anchors to the south a lengthy industrial corridor which extends north to beyond Toronto. In Canada this corridor becomes much more expensive as a place to do business. Apparently fostered by the free trade agreement, an out-migration of capital investments, and even firms from Canada has begun. This has the potential to stimulate economic expansion in Western New York.

We may summarize this historical review as follows:

1. The Buffalo area economy has experienced a long-term decline, especially in the manufacturing sector.

2. This decline appears to reflect a lack of local loyalty on the part of the absentee-owned corporations headquartered outside the area.

3. Certain pluses do exist that could prove valuable if the area economy began to get on track.

THE ROLE OF THE CEL PROGRAM

The CEL program was intended as a method of developing homegrown companies in the Buffalo area, headquartered locally and loyal to the local economy. Ultimately, the hope was that these companies might be helped to grow to a point where they would return Buffalo to its past economic stature (Miner and Stites-Doe, 1994). There appeared to be a good chance that, building on the pluses in the situation, this could be accomplished. The specific program conceived to contribute to this objective operated in essentially the same form over seven years, during which 94 entrepreneurs actually graduated. Recently, changes in the personnel and administration of the School of Management at the State University of New York at Buffalo have introduced major program shifts, whose effects are as yet unknown. Thus the description which follows deals only with the first seven years. There are a number of components that need to be considered.

The Center for Entrepreneurial Leadership, whose sole duty initially was to administer the entrepreneurship program, is a component of the Center for Management Development within the School of Management at SUNY/Buffalo. Administrators of various kinds handled the program throughout the seven-year period.[2] The person who holds this position needs to be informed regarding the local business community and to have earned a degree of respect within it. In addition, the internal administrative structure included the dean of the School of Management, a faculty director (myself), and various MBA and doctoral students who handled hands-on, day-to-day operations.

The faculty director had an initial job description as follows:

The faculty director would occupy a special Chair for Entrepreneurial Leadership that would also provide affiliation with an existing department within the school. The ultimate chairholder would have a commitment to furthering the educational research aims of the Center, should have actual experience as a manager engaged in entrepreneurial activities, and should be concerned with integrating Center activities into other activities of the school. The chairholder should also have a commitment to the dissemination of his/her concepts, theories, or observations about entrepreneurial activity through writing as well as teaching and lecturing.

Much of this is what actually occurred. The only major departure was the failure during the seven years to create a Chair for Entrepreneurial Leadership, perhaps reflecting the economic problems of the Western New York area. The key point, however is that during this period the program was closely integrated with the teaching and research goals of the School of Management. The risk that such programs may become peripheral and lose legitimacy in the eyes of the faculty did not become a problem in this instance. I believe it is important with programs of this kind that this not be allowed to occur; otherwise they are very likely to lose sight of their basic mission.

THE POLICY COUNCIL

The policy council consisted of 15 to 20 members drawn from the local business community primarily, but including a few administrators from the School of Management. Initially, all the business members had entrepreneurial experience in one form or another. In most cases they moved their firms to positions of considerable size and could legitimately be considered senior members of the local entrepreneurial community. Their original role was to provide overall guidance in developing the program, contribute to initial funding, assist in locating participants for the program, serve in various leadership and operating roles during the conduct of the program, and represent the program to the local business community.

A major consideration was that these people would be able to network the program participants into growth opportunities. Some have tried, some have succeeded, a few have not tried. Overall it has been a mixed bag on this score. Nevertheless, the policy council as a whole has contributed substantially to the success of the program.

The intent of the policy council was to utilize the services of people who were visible in the business community for their *entrepreneurial* achievements. The idea was to make it clear that this was not just another *management* development program. A quote from Hisrich and O'Cinneide (1996) gets at the essence of what was involved: ''Each institution needs to establish a cadre of successful entrepreneurs from all sizes and types of organizations. These individuals should visit the campus for presentations and serve as an advisory council to faculty and students alike'' (p. 57). As the program began, this was that cadre.

RECRUITING AND SELECTION

At the beginning of Chapter 6 a quote from the CEL brochure was used to explain the specific types of students which the program was intended to attract. Mention was made of classic entrepreneurs, intrapreneurs, and change agents. Furthermore, the selection criteria were said to include (1) being the operating head of a business unit, (2) demonstrated entrepreneurial talent, (3) a desire for assistance in meeting existing challenges, and (4) making a commitment to become an active participant in the program.

The wide distribution of the brochure throughout the Buffalo area served as an important recruiting tool. Various newspapers and magazines publicized the program. Yet by far the most effective recruitment sources were the policy council members and former participants in the program.

The decision as to who should attend was in the hands of the policy council. Initially, there was not much selection, although the stated goals of the program did result in some rejections. Later, some tough selection decisions were necessary. The major criterion was who was more likely in the long run to contribute to the economic growth of the Western New York area.

Over the seven years, recruiting became increasingly effective, the degree of selection increased, and the size of the program doubled, approaching its possible maximum of 20 participants. A particular effort was made to recruit female and minority participants, and financial incentives were available for this purpose. Nevertheless, operating within the established entrepreneur criterion, it was difficult to find candidates of this kind. We did locate some outstanding participants, but not to the extent we had originally hoped.

THE OVERALL PROGRAM

Table 12.1 sets forth the schedule of activities as it evolved to its seventh year. This structure remained largely intact over the years, although there were many changes in specifics. The essential components are the initial orientation session, the participant clinics, the mentor program, the content sessions or symposia, book reviews, social sessions of various kinds, the personal assessment process, and for a short period a computerized business game. Of the 41 sessions noted, 28 were handled by businesspeople (most of them entrepreneurs), and another 3 are joint products of a businessperson and a professor. Only 5 (12%) were handled entirely by professors. The remainder were either strictly social in nature or basically administrative.

The essential philosophy behind this program is that entrepreneurs learn best from those whom they trust and respect—other entrepreneurs. Those who have real-world experience are the ones qualified to teach because they know the problems. It may or may not be that academics can provide more potentially useful information. What is important in programs of this kind is that the entrepreneurs believe in the source of the information, and view it as focused on the day-to-day operations of their ventures. Many business school faculty members are concerned primarily with large corporations. These faculty members find it difficult to communicate with entrepreneurs, simply because they do not have the same conception of what constitutes a business. In particular they tend to make assumptions about staff resources, available capital, influences on other businesses, employee competence, and the like that do not appear realistic to entrepreneurs. Clearly, there are professors who do not face this problem, but they are relatively few in number, and otherwise entrepreneurs prefer the company and advice of their own.

In answer to a question whether the program was worth the tuition charge ($2,500 through most of the time), the positive response rate was 89 percent with a substantial majority being very favorable. As we will see, however, there were many pluses and minuses with regard to the various components of the program. Questions of this kind were asked throughout the seven years.

PROGRAM COMPONENTS—ORIENTATION SESSION

This was the first session. It ran, like practically all other sessions, for two hours in the late afternoon. Basically, it was devoted to providing the participants with some idea of what to expect. There was also a discussion of entrepreneurial characteristics, drawing on the various studies that have been done, and an introduction to various books on aspects of entrepreneurship that the participants might find useful. The favorability rating for the session was 96 percent (percent positive responses). This session fed into, and sometimes overlapped with, a second session concerned with what might be expected from the assessment process.

PROGRAM COMPONENTS—CLINIC SESSIONS

There are 18 clinics noted in Table 12.1. The actual number per class varied with the number of participants in the program that year. Each participant makes a detailed presentation on the status of his/her firm as well as the problems and opportunities confronting it. The presentation is made to the other participants in the program as well as to a set of three or four reactors specially selected to provide relevant consultation. A typical schedule looks as follows:

4:30–5:15	Clinic presentation
5:15–5:30	Questions from reactors
5:30–5:45	Questions from other participants
5:45–6:00	Comments from the reactors

Table 12.1
Schedule of Activities—CEL Program

September

1   Orientation Session, Entrepreneurial Characteristics and Assessment Exercises I (Businessperson and Professor)
8   Assessment Exercises II (Professor)
15 Symposium—Business Plan (Businessperson)
22 Administration of Assessment Instruments
29 Clinic Orientation

October

5   Class Welcome Reception (Center for Tomorrow on campus)
13 Symposium—University Services (Administrator and Librarian)
20 Symposium—Building a Team of External Professionals (Businessperson)
22 Overnight Retreat (Beaver Hollow Conference Center)
27 Clinic Session

November

3   Clinic Session
10 Clinic Session
17 Clinic Session

December

1   Book Review—*Thriving on Chaos* by Tom Peters (1987) (Businessperson and Professor)
13 Clinic Session
15 Clinic Session and Holiday Get Together (Center for Tomorrow on campus)

January

5   Clinic Session
10 Clinic Session
12 Clinic Session
19 Clinic Session
20 Clinic Session

26   Symposium—Leadership and Motivation (Professor)

February

2	Clinic Session
9	Clinic Session
14	Clinic Session
16	Symposium—Business Ownership (Businessperson)
23	Clinic Session

March

9	Clinic Session
16	Symposium—Capital Acquisition and Financing (Panel of Businesspeople)
17	Clinic Session
23	Clinic Session

April

6	Symposium—Human Resources Management (Professor)
13	Symposium—Marketing and Sales (Businessperson)
20	Symposium—Information for Strategic Advantage (Professor)
27	Clinic Follow-up Session
Throughout the month	Individual Assessment Feedback Sessions (Professor)

May

4	Clinic Follow-up Session
11	Clinic Follow-up Session
18	Clinic Follow-up Session
25	Clinic Follow-up Session
	Evaluation and Summary of Assessment Data for the Class (Professor)

June

8	Graduation (Hyatt Regency Hotel)

6:00–6:15   Comments from other participants

6:15–6:30   Final comments from the reactors

Usually, written materials are provided to supplement the verbal presentation. In one way or another the following points are covered:

1. *Background of the firm.* History, products or services, markets, size, and industry characteristics;

2. *Structure of the firm.* Organization, participant's role, physical plant, ownership, and accounting and legal support;

3. *Financial information.* Sales, balance sheet status, profit and loss, cash flow, and capital expenditures;

4. *Company goals.* Short- and long-term objectives, business plan, and priorities;

5. *Major problems.* Dimensions, origins, impacts, and possible resolutions for each; and

6. *Significant opportunities.* Nature, source, impacts, and resources needed for each.

The reactors are chosen with regard to their ability to say something about the problems and opportunities facing the firm. They may be policy council members, faculty members, previous participants in the program, or knowledgeable people from the business community. Typically, they meet as a group with the individual making the clinic presentation prior to the formal presentation, to learn more about the business. There is a dual purpose in using reactors. One is to obtain valuable consultation and advice. The other is to aid the participant in developing a network of people in the business community who could prove helpful in business development.

Before any of the participants present their firms, a clinic orientation session, usually including a mock clinic, is held to provide guidance on preparing for and making a clinic presentation. Also, after all the clinics have been held, during the last month of the program, the participants present an oral report on what they have accomplished during the time since their clinic. The objective with these sessions is to indicate to what extent previously stated goals are being accomplished. Each report runs about a half hour. All of these aspects of the participant clinics—the clinic orientation, the clinic itself, the reactors, and the clinic follow-up—received very high favorability ratings, ranging from 94 to 96 percent.

PROGRAM COMPONENTS—THE MENTOR FEATURE

As used in the CEL program, mentors are individuals with considerable stature in the local entrepreneurial community, often policy council members, who assist the participants in the preparation and presentation of their clinics. They are assigned at the beginning of each year. Their responsibilities are to function as an advisor and a coach, and to serve as a sounding board for the ideas and plans of the program participant assigned. Mentors must be willing to devote the time and energy necessary to familiarize themselves with the participant's business operation and with the participant as a human being. The mentor must also be able to serve as a meaningful role model, constituting a real-world example of successful, contributing, ethical conduct.

Sometimes these relationships blossom; sometimes they do not. Ideally, the mentor relationship opens doors for the participant, provides sound business (and perhaps personal) advice, and makes it possible for the clinic to be an experience of maximum value. It does not always work that way. We developed mentor training programs, utilized input from participants in assigning mentors, and did everything we could think of to facilitate these relationships. The fact is, however, there were failures. Problems extended from mentor unavailability to a lack of participant enthusiasm for the mentor program. There were cases where mentors tried to buy out the participant's business, and to sell their services to the participant. But also there were some very good relationships developed; the range of success was all the way from outstanding to terrible. Overall, the favorability rating was only 68 percent for this aspect of the program.

Much of the problem appears to be inherent in the assigned nature of the relationship. In the corporate setting, informal, spontaneous mentoring that arises to fulfill needs of those involved has been found to provide career advancement advantages to the protégé (Whitely, Dougherty, and Dreher, 1991). This would appear to be consistent with the goal of firm growth inherent in the CEL program. However, research on assigned mentorship indicates that this type of advantage is often lost (Noe, 1988). Assigned mentors do prove to be of value, but primarily in providing a sense of security and confidence in times of stress. When companies are downsizing, for instance, assigned mentors prove useful as buffers against the stress involved (Kram and Hall, 1989). The difficulty is that the CEL program is not oriented toward getting entrepreneurs through periods of failure, and stress, but toward helping them achieve success and firm growth. The goals of the program and the approach to mentoring do not match. Yet promoting spontaneous mentoring is difficult in this type of context.

PROGRAM COMPONENTS—CONTENT SESSIONS

These sessions, usually labeled as symposia, were of the lecture and discussion type, and were led either by faculty members or businesspeople. They dealt with a variety of topics considered to be of interest to entrepreneurs. For a number of reasons there was considerable coming and going both of topic areas and session leaders over the seven years. However, the positively viewed symposia tended to continue.

Those sessions with a favorability rating of 80 percent or more, in order of their ratings, were:

1. Marketing and sales (94%)
2. Leadership and motivation (91%)

3. Developing a business plan (89%)

4. Human resource management (87%)

5. Business ownership and succession (85%)

6. Creative problem solving (82%)

7. Strategic planning (82%)

After these seven the ratings fell off rather sharply, although none were below 50 percent, and thus actually negative. Among these latter sessions were capital acquisition and financing, computer applications, management information systems, university services (such as the library), and negotiating.

In general the sessions receiving a less favorable response were taught by people associated with the university. However, the well-received symposia were as likely to be taught by professors as by businesspeople.

PROGRAM COMPONENTS—BOOK REVIEW SESSIONS

These were sessions in which a book that the participants had read was discussed. The average favorability rating was 80 percent, but there was wide variation depending on the book. It is apparent that if the book is highly relevant for entrepreneurs, as is *Thriving on Chaos* by Tom Peters (1987), a well-led book review session can do well. On the other hand, several books dealing with negotiations, including *Getting to Yes* (Fisher and Ury, 1981), did not do nearly as well.

PROGRAM COMPONENTS—SOCIAL SESSIONS

The objective in arranging various social events is to facilitate networking among participants, alumni of the program, policy council members, faculty, and administration. A considerable amount of business is done among the members of each class and with alumni. Various events are noted in Table 12.1. Many, including the retreat, involve spouses. The retreat is held Friday evening and on Saturday; there are programs for participants and also for spouses. It has proven very successful as a means of getting a new class to gel as a cohesive unit.

The retreat has garnered a 100 percent favorability rating ever since its inception. The Christmas holiday get-together has a 97 percent figure and the welcome reception 89 percent. However, whenever formal hosted dinners with an invited speaker were tried, they did not do well (favorability rating of 64 percent). The difficulty appears to be that what people really want to do at the social events is network, and the speaker, plus dinner table seating, tend to inhibit that. Graduation is also a social session primarily, but we do not have specific participant reactions to it. Informal feedback, however, would suggest a favorabilty rating of over 90 percent.

PROGRAM COMPONENTS—BUSINESS GAME

At one point a computerized business game was introduced into the program. The objective was to develop a set of decisions in a group context with respect to production, pricing, promotion, and so on, as these are necessary to run a company for four simulated quarters. The reaction was mixed, and ultimately a decision was made not to include this feature in the program on a continuing basis. Some viewed the game as more corporate than entrepreneurial in nature; some found the group decision making rather distant from the realities of their situation. On one occasion a group decision was totally ignored by the group leader in submitting the final decision for computer ingestion. In his world the leader made the decision, not some group. As a consequence of problems of this kind, the favorability rating was only 67 percent.

We now believe that a business game focused directly on entrepreneurship would have been much more desirable. Unfortunately, there are not many such games available. A recent review found only three entrepreneurship games, and had this to say about those that were found:

Those teaching entrepreneurship have relatively barren computerized simulation available to them. Relatively few topics are covered; often they are covered simplistically and narrowly with few alternatives available to the decision maker. In addition, the unique business world of the entrepreneur has not been captured in either a strategic, operational, or personal sense (Wolfe and Bruton, 1994, p. 410).

Yet, working with an experimental game, Low, Venkataraman, and Srivatsan (1994) were able to obtain quite favorable reactions from students who utilized the game. Games clearly are a promising teaching device for the field of entrepreneurship. However, there is still a great deal to be learned on this score. Furthermore, based on our experience, we would not recommend any game that does not have an entrepreneurial focus.

PROGRAM COMPONENTS—THE ASSESSMENT ASPECT

This is an aspect that will be considered in much greater detail in the next chapter, because it has implications extending well beyond any single entrepreneurship development program. However, explaining how these assessment activities operate as a component of an entrepreneurship effort is important also. This is the concern in this chapter.

Initially, we had thought that the assessments should focus on knowledge, skills, and abilities, with the objective of identifying cognitive strengths and weaknesses. The idea was to carry out a training needs assessment, which would help to identify areas where learning was required. With experience, however, we concluded that this was not what was needed. Consequently, we shifted to a clinical approach to psychological assessment intended to identify characteristics of a motivational, emotional, and overall personality nature that could impede firm growth or foster growth initiatives.

The first step within the CEL program has been the conduct of various pedagogical assessment exercise sessions at the beginning of the program. These follow upon the discussion of entrepreneurial characteristics. As the discussion moves to personality factors the participants complete brief tests in each area, which they score themselves. The intent is to give a greater understanding of some characteristic that makes for entrepreneurial success, and to provide an introduction to the assessment instruments the participants will complete later. The personality characteristics and tests used are as follows:

- *Lynn Achievement Motivation Questionnaire*—number 1a among the measures for the personal achiever type.
- *Individual Behavior Activity Profile* (abbreviated)—number 2a among the measures for the personal achiever type.
- *Rose Tension Discharge Rate Scale*—number 2b among the measures for the personal achiever type.
- *Matteson and Ivancevich Internal-External Scale*—number 8a among the measures for the personal achiever type.
- *Shure and Meeker Risk Avoidance Scale*—number 5b among the measures for the expert idea generator type.

These five measures are short and they work well for illustrating the characteristics measured. However, the ideal would be to have measures showing all four types; this group is too heavy on the personal achievers. Unfortunately, at the time these tests were selected, we did not know what the four types were.

Shortly after these sessions are completed, the participants fill out a much more extensive battery of tests (see Chapter 5). Initially, they made appointments and came to the university individually for this purpose; some still do. However, more recently an effort has been made to collect as many participants as possible in one place for the test administrations. A packet of materials is given to each person. Completing the materials may take three hours or longer. The emphasis is on measures that relate directly to entrepreneurship rather than personality assessment generally, and also, to the extent possible, multiple measures of the same factor are included.

The next step in the assessment process involves the collection of data on the firms, their characteristics, and their performance. To do this I attended all clinic sessions, taking notes on the presentations and discussions, and obtaining copies of all written materials.

The feedback sessions themselves are scheduled for the month of April, as shown in Table 12.1. These sessions have always been concerned with the interaction between the firm and the entrepreneur, but they evolved to a quite specific approach over time. The first step is to analyze all the tests and relate the resulting data to what is known about the company. The objective is to identify and understand company strengths and weaknesses that might have their roots in the psychology of the entrepreneur. This analysis is then fed back to the entrepreneur, forming a basis for discussion of how the problems facing the firm might be overcome and how growth might be accentuated. These sessions last from 1½ hours to 3 hours. They tend to be very candid. Only the participant and myself are involved, one-on-one. The typology of four personality patterns and career routes has been utilized frequently during the later years.

As an addendum to the assessment process, an oral summary of the test data for each class is given at the final session. Average scores are compared to those of prior classes and to available normative information. Each class tends to have certain distinctive features, almost a character of its own. We talk about this, and typically the discussion then moves to a process of looking back over the previous nine months to evaluate the various aspects of the experience.

In general this assessment process has been well received. Some approach the lengthy battery of tests with considerable skepticism, but reactions tend to improve after the assessment feedback is completed. Only very occasionally does a participant leave the program with a negative feeling toward this component. The favorability rating for the initial assessment exercises is 80 percent. The rating of the individual feedback is 87 percent. However, the more extreme negative reactions have now been tempered somewhat, so that on the average the assessment feedback matches the clinics in the extent of positive reaction; there are now no really negative responses. Information on the final session (evaluation and summary of assessment data) has not been obtained consistently, but what we have suggests a favorability rate in the 80–90 percent range.

Some people clearly enter a psychological assessment situation with negative feelings, and perhaps a certain amount of anxiety. The initial discussion of personality factors and the exposure to the experiential test exercises can ameliorate this. Consequently, there is more receptivity to the test battery and the feedback sessions.

ALUMNI ACTIVITIES

These activities are not a component of the program, but an adjunct to it. A formal alumni group has been formed with bylaws, programs, social events, a newsletter, meetings, a directory, and a bank account. It serves both business and social functions. The impetus came from the alumni themselves, although the administrators of the program and the policy council offered encouragement. This type of activity is part of the networking function. The objective of the program is to foster business deal making and firm growth to the extent possible, and that seems more likely if the members of the program continue to interact.

Also, quite independent of the formal alumni activity, there have been a number of business deals consummated where participants in the program have combined on new business initiatives.

THE CEL PROGRAM AND THE PSYCHOLOGICAL TYPES

How does a comprehensive entrepreneurship development program such as the one offered through the Center for Entrepreneurial Leadership measure up in terms of providing training for the various types? The clinics, including the clinic orientation, the reactors, and the clinic follow-up, are very favorably received. Because the participants are spread across all four types and are following all four routes, there also is something for everyone here. It is essential that each class have a good representation of each type. However, with complex entrepreneurs having multiple patterns present this is not difficult to achieve. The clinics are in fact a very good way of learning about the four routes and the kinds of people who should follow them. The difficulty is that each participant is exposed to a number of clinics that are not personally relevant.

This is not the case with the assessment process, which tends to meet the needs of all participants, since it is individualized for just that purpose. Clearly, the assessment feedback is most important, but the assessment exercises help to prepare the way for the lengthy test battery. The final session dealing with average test scores would appear to be optional. There does need to be an orientation session at the beginning of the program, however. The assessment process does not provoke as favorable a reaction as the clinics, but it is close. The problem is that a relatively small number of entrepreneurs start out quite negative. By the time the process is completed these extreme negative reactions seem to have disappeared, but it takes a while and some work to get to that point.

The social sessions in particular, but the existence of the policy council and the use of reactors at the clinics as well, contribute to the networking goal. Empathic supersalespeople are most inclined to network and they are best at this kind of activity. However, the other three types tend to become involved as well for specific purposes. Thus the existence of social events, a policy council, and the reactor group (who should be tied into the entire program more than they are in the Western New York instance) recommend themselves strongly. The alumni activities fit here as well, although they are not components of the program per se. To the extent they foster networking, all of these activities elicit favorable reactions. It seems likely that these sessions could be overdone, but this was not the case within the CEL program. For the empathic supersalespeople it may be impossible to create too many networking opportunities.

As noted, the mentor program presents problems. Maintaining quality control has proven difficult. Also, many of the career advancement features of mentoring are lost when mentors are assigned. At least for personal achievers, formal mentoring appears to convey an image of large corporations and rigid structures that is unattractive. One solution is to abolish the assigned program and attempt to foster informal, spontaneous mentoring during the program wherever possible. An alternative, which has not been tried but appears promising, is to deliberately match up mentors and protégés who possess the same personality types, and thus need to follow the same career routes. This would require administering the test battery to mentors, and not initiating the mentor program until after all tests had been scored. Because the mentor feature is a one-on-one activity that can be directly responsive to the needs of entrepreneurs of various types, it seems unfortunate to eliminate it. Matching by type might serve to circumvent the disadvantages of assigned mentoring for established entrepreneurs.

The content sessions, and the book review sessions also, that receive strong support from the participants, are all components that have special appeal to entrepreneurs with one strong pattern or another. The business ownership and planning sessions fit the personal achievers, as does the book *Thriving on Chaos* (Peters, 1987) with its stress on the value of unstructured operations. The marketing and sales session appeals strongly to the empathic supersalespeople, and so do aspects of the human resource management session. The latter also has features that fit well with the route pursued by real managers. The leadership and motivation session is especially appropriate for that group. Creative problem solving is the essence of what expert idea generators do. We believe that these are the kinds of content sessions that are most useful. They can be utilized with everybody as long as no one type of content receives too much emphasis. It is possible that within the CEL program, symposia for personal achiever types may have been somewhat overdone, and other types short-changed as a result.

In any event it is evident that content sessions and book reviews which are not focused on one or more of the four types do not receive a favorable response and probably should be avoided. Furthermore, there appears to be a tendency to expand the number of symposia over time and thus to make the program more like university course work in general. There is a kind of ''creeping academia'' involved. This needs to be counteracted if the entrepreneurs are to continue to feel the program is their own, and thus believe in its relevancy.

The CEL program does not really include any of the activities considered in Chapter 11, except perhaps a small amount of the business planning envisioned for personal achievers. An ideal program would include a number of breakout activities. Everyone would participate in several of these, but which ones would depend on the types present. Decisions in this regard could be informed by the assessment process, but still remain voluntary with the individual. A major problem is that with 15 to 20 participants and four types, the breakout sessions could be so small as to be economically infeasible. A way to deal with this is to make the program two years, rather than one year in duration. That way it would be possible to admit up to 40 students and still include all of the clinics. Furthermore, there has always been pressure for some kind of continuation program after graduation. The formation of the alumni association reflects this. A two-year program should therefore be entirely viable. As indicated, it would also serve to increase class sizes for breakout sessions to a level where these sessions would be financially feasible.

Breakout sessions for personal achievers might include achievement motivation training and the actual development of a business plan of a type appropriate to the participant's particular situation. Considerable coaching and guidance would be incorporated here, going well beyond the content sessions on planning.

With real managers the idea is to provide something that facilitates broad managerial learning. Managerial role motivation training is one such activity. Obviously, breakout sessions cannot directly incorporate job rotation, but procedures can be established to facilitate rotation by finding appropriate temporary placements. This would have to depend on the particular situation, but I am reminded of the practice whereby owners of small businesses exchange temporary placement of those children who are slated to take over major responsibilities in the family business. This is a very useful experience for real managers. A program such as that of CEL could easily operate as a brokerage for temporary managerial placements of a variety of kinds, to the advantage of both the program participant and the firm involved.

Breakout sessions intended for expert idea generators ideally would incorporate some type of creativity or problem-solving training. Another approach that a university might use is to enter participants into specific classes that would serve to extend the amount of expertise possessed in a certain area. These could be of a non-degree nature or they could be part of some degree program. The key is to select the particular course that is most suited to the person's needs, and then get the person into it.

Sales training involving behavior modeling, role playing, and the like can be used in breakout sessions intended for empathic supersalespeople. It may be difficult to make these sessions product or service specific, but a certain degree of individualization in this regard is possible. Also, sensitivity training, training in participative management or empowerment, and similar organization-development related approaches are well suited to the needs of empathic super-salespeople.

With enough people available in the pool of available participants, breakout activities of this kind can work. The fewer the number of people of each type available, the smaller the range of breakout alternatives that can be made available. Yet the breakout concept, providing activities for each type, appears to offer considerable potential.

PROGRAM EFFECTIVENESS

Ideally, we would have had such things as random assignments, a matched control group that did not take the course, and highly standardized measures of economic activity. Initially, we had hopes of utilizing a control group design to determine the impact of the CEL program. However, the financing to do this never materialized, and carrying out such a study on the existing budget was out of the question. Nevertheless, some estimates of program effectiveness are possible. Although flawed in many respects, they are the best available.

One source of data comes from direct and immediate evaluations of the program by the participants and others. This is process, rather than end-result, evaluation. On this score the fact that the program has survived, and grown to double its original size based primarily on endorsements by participants and policy council members, is a positive sign. It does not say that the basic regional economic development goal was being achieved, but it does say that some goal was being achieved.

Evaluations, both informal and formal, were elicited from the participants from the beginning. The results of this process are sprinkled through prior sections of this chapter. In most instances the questionnaires used asked for ratings on a scale of 1 to 6, with 3, 2, and 1 being increasingly negative and 4, 5, and 6 increasingly positive. With only one or two exceptions the responses have averaged on the positive side. Of 31 questions used at one time or another, 11 yielded an average rating of 5.0 or higher, another 5 averaged in the 4.5 and 4.9 range, and 9 more in the 4.0 to 4.4 range. This looks to be a very good response, but again we have nothing with which to compare these figures.

The follow-up process described in Chapter 6 provides another source of information. Have the firms grown and the entrepreneurs prospered? We are unable to say, for lack of a control group, that any growth might not have occurred without the program; yet if there had been no growth, it seems unlikely that the program was achieving its objectives. In actual fact the success rate (substantial and some) was at 81 percent. A great deal of growth occurred, even though the seven years extended through a major recession which, as is typical for Western New York (Ticknor, 1985), hit the area hard. There was only one bankruptcy business failure in the group over a period when many Western New York firms were filing for bankruptcy. This, of course, could say more about the initial selection of participants than the effectiveness of the program itself.

Another point relates to migration from the area. Have the entrepreneurs taken their firms and gone elsewhere, following the out-migration of talent that has plagued Western New York? Given the business climate, with high taxes and costly environmental constraints, this is certainly something that many have considered. Yet, only three participants moved out of state, and we believe all of these have retained some business interests in the Buffalo area. Thus the objective of creating a homegrown industrial base seems to have received support. If there is anything about which we can be reasonably certain, it is that the networking, and alumni activities, and class cohesiveness have served to hold these entrepreneurs and their businesses in the area.

How effective has the program been in achieving economic development for Western New York? We really do not know; proof of any kind on this score is simply not available. My own personal guess is that the impact has been positive, but within the overall context of business activity in the area, to date at least, the scale involved has been small. It would take a much more extensive program, of at least two years' duration and enrolling many more participants, to have any sizable economic development effect. In this view the CEL program represents essentially a pilot effort, whose consequences appear to be primarily at the individual firm level.

CONCLUSION

From the CEL experience the conclusion that comprehensive programs can be developed to assist all four types seems fully warranted. Whether any individual program does this would have to be determined one at a time. The objective is to maximize the amount of one-on-one time where individuals of each type receive learning experiences focused on their specific career routes. Next most important are program components that are equally relevant for all four types, or at least have some relevance for all types. A program that is over-balanced in its emphasis on one or two types, and which is advertised as comprehensive, is likely to face problems. A program that possesses many components which are unlikely to create relevant learning opportunities for any type is dead in the water.

Because it met the needs of many entrepreneurs, according to these criteria, the CEL program over its first seven years appears to have yielded some positive consequences. Accordingly, encouraging other economic regions with similar problems to follow a similar path seems warranted. The CEL experience is not uniquely relevant to Western New York. Something similar probably could be applied to many other areas of the country.

If this is done in a university context, an issue exists with regard to control of the program. In a very real sense, control of the CEL program was turned over to the local entrepreneurial community. Universities do not do this easily, and there is some evidence that the CEL program is now having some difficulty on this score. Nevertheless, I am convinced that the usual academic approach will not work for entrepreneurship development. A program designed by entrepreneurs, taught to a substantial extent by entrepreneurs, with admissions controlled primarily by entrepreneurs, seems most likely to do well and achieve its goals.

NOTES

1. Susan Stites-Doe was instrumental in the preparation of this historical presentation. Many of the details were made available through her research efforts.

2. The primary administrator in this role was Carol Newcomb, who headed the Center for Management Development throughout the period.

Chapter 13

The Role of Psychological Assessment

The focus of this final chapter is on the use of psychological assessment primarily for entrepreneurial career development, but also as an aid in selecting entrepreneurs for various investment and employment purposes. Psychological assessment is not utilized widely in the world of entrepreneurship, in part at least because few psychologists with the necessary skills have been attracted to the area. Furthermore, a theoretical model on which the assessment process could be based has been lacking. I believe that, nevertheless, major opportunities exist to use assessment effectively as an aid in dealing with various problems and decisions within entrepreneurship. The four-way typology appears to offer a useful theoretical model. My objective here is to demonstrate what opportunities exist, and how the typology may contribute to the psychological assessment of entrepreneurs.

SELF-ASSESSMENT AND SELF-UNDERSTANDING

One approach to assessment involves using various questionnaires, tests, and forms to attempt to gain insight into personal characteristics and propensities that might help or hinder entrepreneurial accomplishment. Ehringer (1995) refers to this type of insight as "awareness of mind," defined for the purposes of entrepreneurs as understanding the process of their thinking, understanding the patterns of their decision making, and understanding their personal principles. She makes a very good case for the view that entrepreneurial success is predicated on this kind of self-awareness.

Although insight and self-awareness can be developed simply by thinking about oneself and the reasons behind various actions, there are certain aids available that may help to facilitate this process. One such approach consists of tests or questionnaires dealing with some facet of the person or the venture which, when completed, tell people where they stand on the particular factor measured. These are typically published in a book, although every now and then they appear in the popular press as well. A book that contains indexes of this kind is Hisrich and Brush (1986)—three 10-item measures dealing with locus of control, independence and risk-taking, as well as a 14-item questionnaire covering the qualities of the woman entrepreneur. Essentially, the same exercises are contained in Hisrich and Peters (1995). In this instance, however, the questionnaire on entrepreneurial qualities is stated so as to apply to both men and women. There is also a 20-item Entrepreneur Assessment Quiz intended to provide an index of the "drive to be an entrepreneur."

Another similar approach is that of Cornwall and Perlman (1990), who present a number of what they call diagnostic aids. These are checklists to establish the degree to which an organizational entity is entrepreneurial in nature. Measures are given for identifying external opportunities, identifying internal opportunities, establishing entrepreneurial organizational cultures, determining organizational empowerment, diagnosing entrepreneurial structure and communication, diagnosing reward systems in an entrepreneurial organization, and assessing the use of control and effectiveness measures in an entrepreneurial organization. These questionnaires contain from 6 to 28 items with most being relatively short.

What is characteristic of these types of measures is that once a person completes them and scores them, the instrument provides feedback regarding some factor related to entrepreneurial success. This simplicity makes them appealing. However, it is also true that these indexes may not always measure what they are supposed to measure. They possess face validity, and the factors considered appear to be important for a successful venture, but evidence to this effect usually is not presented. This lack of empirical study is a major handicap that makes these tests and questionnaires less than ideal. Some of the five measures used to introduce the CEL test battery (see Chapter 12), which also can be self-scored, suffer in this respect as well, but others have been well researched (see Chapter 5).

In contrast to these uses of tests and questionnaires, forms or lists of characteristics are sometimes provided to assist people in rating themselves, using whatever knowledge of their personality make-up they possess. An example of this approach is contained in Timmons (1989). There he lists "a number of attributes which researchers, venture capitalists, and practitioners believe to be important for entrepreneurial success" (p. 168). The person is asked to rate himself or herself on a 5-point scale, with 5 being the strongest and 1 the weakest. The attributes themselves are:

Total commitment, determination, and perseverance

Drive to achieve and grow

Opportunity and goal oriented

Taking initiative and personal responsibility

Persistent problem solving

Veridical awareness and a sense of humor

Seeking and using feedback

Internal locus of control

Tolerance for ambiguity, stress, and uncertainty

Calculated risk-taking and sharing

Low need for status and power

Integrity and reliability

Decisiveness, urgency, and patience

Dealing with failure

Team builder and hero maker (pp. 169–171)

In addition, the ability to handle certain entrepreneurial roles is rated. Those noted are as follows:

Accommodation to the venture

Stress generation

Economic and professional values

Ethics (p. 172)

Many of these attributes and role requirements are familiar from previous discussions. However, the problem that certain of the characteristics lack validation against criteria of entrepreneurial success remains.

Miner (1996a) contains a form for self-appraisal which follows the four-way psychological typology. The form uses 7 personal achiever characteristics (condensed from 10), 6 real manager characteristics (condensed from 13), the 5 expert idea generator characteristics, and the 5 empathic supersalesperson characteristics. The procedure through which the characteristics for the types were condensed and labeled is described in Chapter 5. Each characteristic is to be rated on a three-point scale comparable to the conversion scores—Very Much (2), Sizable (1), and Less (0)—which indicates the degree to which the personality factor is characteristic.

The 23 ratings required are as follows (with the numbers of the measures used to operationalize the construct in parentheses):

Personal Achiever

Need to achieve (1a, 1b, 2a, 2b)

Desire for feedback (3)

Desire to plan and set goals (4)

Strong personal initiative (5)

Strong personal commitment to the organization (6, 7)

Belief that one person can make a difference (8a, 8b, 8c, 8d)

Belief that work should be guided by personal goals, not those of others (9, 10)

Real Manager

Desire to be a corporate leader (1, 2, 3, 4, 5)

Decisiveness (6)

Positive attitudes to authority (7)

Desire to compete (8a, 8b, 9)

Desire for power (10, 11)

Desire to stand out from the crowd (12, 13)

Expert Idea Generator

Desire to innovate (1)

Love of ideas (2a, 2b)

Belief that new product development is crucial to carrying out company strategy (3)

Good intelligence (4a, 4b)

Desire to avoid taking risks (5a, 5b)

Empathic Supersalesperson

Capacity to understand and feel with another (1a, 1b)

Desire to help others (2)

Belief that social processes are very important (3)

Need to have strong positive relationships with others (4)

Belief that a sales force is crucial to carrying out company strategy (5)

This procedure utilizes the same components that the test battery measures, but relies on personal judgment and insight instead. When Very Much ratings are multiplied by 2 and Sizable ratings by 1, scores may be calculated as follows:

Personal achiever—0–14 range

Real manager—0–12 range

Expert idea generator—0–10 range

Empathic supersalesperson—0–10 range

Combined, complex entrepreneur—0–46 range

As noted in Chapter 5, using the test score data, types are defined as follows:

Personal achiever—8 or above

Real manager—4 or above

Expert idea generator—5 or above

Empathic supersalesperson—5 or above

Multiple type complex entrepreneur—2 or more of the above

Combined complex entrepreneur—18 or above

This approach has the advantage that it ties the ratings to the four-way typology, which has been validated, and provides numerical cutting scores derived from the test results. In Miner (1996a) the reader is provided with numerous examples of entrepreneurs characterized by the various types which can serve to anchor the ratings.

Yet there are pitfalls here, too. Approaches such as those of Timmons (1989) and Miner (1996a) suffer from a tendency, at least in the United States, for people to rate their own attributes in such a way as to present themselves more favorably. This tendency has been studied extensively in connection with performance appraisals, where self-appraisals can be compared with evaluations by others, such as superiors. The following quote from Miner and Crane (1995) explains the problem:

Of the various approaches to measuring performance . . . self-ratings are the most likely to produce divergent results. The relationships with superior and peer or subordinate ratings and with objective indexes tend to be modest, at best, and often non-existent (Harris and Schaubroeck, 1988; Hoffman, Nathan, and Holden, 1991). Self-appraisals are not of much use for evaluative purposes such as decisions on compensation and promotion. They tend to be highly inflated, with almost everyone speaking well of themselves. When used for developmental purposes to stimulate problem solving and receptivity to suggestions, in conjunction with other procedures, however, self-appraisals have been found to be useful (Campbell and Lee, 1988).

In addition to their developmental use, self-ratings may exhibit a degree of value under other circumstances. . . . A laboratory study of a kind frequently used in research on performance appraisal, . . . found that providing comparative information on the performance of others had some tendency to bring self-appraisals in line with supervisory appraisals (Farh and Dobbins, 1989). Generally, it can be said that the more self-ratings are informed by creditable data on performance standards and the performance of others, the more realistic they will become.

The major problem with self-ratings appears to relate to the strong propensity toward a leniency bias we have noted. People consistently rate themselves more favorably than their superiors do, and often their scores cluster in a very narrow range at the top of the scale. Whereas these results have been obtained in the United States, it is interesting to note that just the opposite outcome has been found in China (Farh, Dobbins, and Cheng, 1991). There what amounts to a modesty bias appears frequently (pp. 248–250).

What the self-assessment forms ask for is much like self-appraisal of performance. In fact, many performance appraisal forms include questions dealing with personal attributes of the same kind as the characteristics noted in the self-assessment forms. Is there reason to believe there is value in the self-assessment approach to identifying entrepreneurial talent? One possible reason is that the self-assessment forms are intended for developmental purposes, and that is where self-appraisal has been found to work best. What the forms attempt to do is help entrepreneurs and potential entrepreneurs engage in a career development process. Also, books containing the forms tend to provide "comparative information on the performance of others" and to inform the ratings with "creditable data on performance standards." This is the kind of process that has been found to make self-assessments more realistic.

A tendency surely exists for those who identify with the entrepreneurial occupations and who want to view themselves as entrepreneurs to inflate their own scores and thus emerge on the self-assessment forms as more entrepreneurial than they are. Yet, used in a developmental context and with substantial comparative information available, the forms would appear to elicit bias of this kind somewhat less frequently.

Timmons (1989) suggests that feedback from others be obtained in filling out self-assessments; he makes a number of suggestions in this regard. This seems desirable as long as the individual has no ax to grind and knows a person well enough to provide valid input. Ideally also, feedback of this kind would be sought from a number of sources.

PROFESSIONAL ASSESSMENT AND FEEDBACK AS USED IN THE CEL PROGRAM

In Chapter 12, the way the psychological assessment component fits into the total CEL program was discussed. This approach to assessment with feedback, intended for developmental purposes, is also described in various of its aspects in several other sources (Miner, 1991b, 1996a; Miner and Stites-Doe, 1994). For purposes of career development it appears superior to the self-assessment approaches considered in the prior section.

Professional assessment of this kind uses a measurement process that is relatively free of bias (and thus objective), and that can, if used well, provide comprehensive information based on full knowledge of the person, or at least regarding the characteristics of concern. Thus it serves to overcome the potential minuses inherent in self-assessment. Furthermore, it allows for two-way communication, thus permitting more comprehensive understanding and more informed decisions than are usually possible with self-assessment.

To conduct a feedback session it is necessary first to have extensive test data relevant to the four personality types. This aspect is considered in Chapters 5 and 12. Second, if there is a venture in existence that the individual is serving in an entrepreneurial capacity, as there was with the CEL program participants,

·information needs to be provided on that venture. In Chapter 12 we saw how the personal clinic served that purpose. It is also possible for the individual to write out this information or to orally record it in some manner. Table 13.1 provides an overview of what should be included. This is an expanded version of the clinic outline noted in Chapter 12. In what follows, I will consider the situation where a venture has been in existence for some time and the full range of information indicated in Table 13.1 is available.

The feedback session starts with a review of problems faced by the individual and the firm. The objective is to get agreement on a list of problems that need to be addressed. The initial list might be altered during this discussion. Next, I review the results from the test battery, dealing not with test scores, only the characteristics they measure. Thus, we talk about intellectual capabilities, locus of control, managerial motivation, and so on. The data from different measures of the same construct are pooled with emphasis on what seem to be the better measures. An effort is made to get agreement on interpretations at this point. Where the meaning of a given test result in the context of the other findings is not clear, that fact is openly discussed. Often the individual will come up with a reconciliation that was not previously evident. The general approach in presenting results is positive; strengths are played up, but weaknesses are not ignored.

After the test data have been reviewed and discussed in this manner they are then recast into the framework provided by the four personality types. Thus, the overall level on each type and the particular strengths and weaknesses within the pattern are considered. The implications for routes to follow, and not to follow, are spelled out.

The final part of the feedback session is an attempt to apply the findings from the tests and other sources to the problems originally considered. I try to understand how these problems could have arisen and what might be done about them. Often the test data are helpful in providing explanations. Yet there are also instances in which the individual starts to look at problems in new ways and actually creates new solutions on the spot. There have been instances in these sessions in which individuals have developed entirely new approaches to their careers, and even a new career. Insofar as possible, setting specific and difficult goals is encouraged. This problem-solving part of the feedback session can extend over considerable time. Once people get involved in ideas of this kind they want to continue, and it is productive for them to do so.

Although in the past conducting a feedback session has involved working from a set of rough notes dealing with problems, test data, and possible problem solutions, neither these notes nor any other written feedback has been provided. Yet people often do want written as well as oral feedback. If such a report is prepared this should be done after the feedback session has been conducted. This written report should set forth the problems discussed, any strong patterns and the career routes they mandate, and recommended problem solutions. Such a document can be used subsequently as a reference source and guideline to

Table 13.1
Outline of Venture Information Needed to Conduct a Feedback Session

Background Information
   History of the firm
      Company name
      Founding date
      Predecessors, if any; founders
   Products or services
      Paths of development
   Markets served
      Principal customers
      Principal competitors
   Size of firm (various measures, such as employment, sales, and capitalization)
   Nature of the industry; industry trends

Structure of Firm
   Organization table
      Management team
   Individual's role with the firm
      History of involvement
      Personal background of individual (résumé)
   Physical plants; locations
   Ownership structure
   Accounting and legal support

Financial Information (both historical and prospective)
   Sales
      By product or service line

Balance sheet status
    Capital base
Profit and loss experience
Cash flow performance
Capital expenditures

Company Goals
    Short run; long run
    Thrust of present business plan
    Present priorities

Identification of Major Problems
    Exploration of dimensions of each
    Origin of problems; reasons for them
    Present/probable impact on company
    Possible resolutions already explored
        Research done
        Assistance received
        Results
    Prioritization of problems

Identification of Significant Opportunities
    Nature of the opportunities
        Probability of profitable realization
    Source of opportunities
    Probable impacts of opportunity realization on the company's success
    Resources and circumstances needed for exploitation
    Prioritization of opportunities

245

keep a person on the course decided upon in the feedback session. It can also serve to guide subsequent follow-up sessions, should these sessions prove desirable.

EXAMPLE OF A FEEDBACK SESSION USING THE CEL MODEL

An entrepreneur, Stanley Suberoff, had an existing business which he had founded some years before with three partners. His major concern at present, however, was a spin-off he was contemplating to manufacture and market a new product that he had invented. From the clinic session the following list of problems emerged:

- How should Suberoff go about pricing and manufacturing the new product?
- Should Suberoff manufacture the new product himself, or should he get someone else to manufacture it?
- How would the new endeavor be related to the existing business, and to what extent should the other partners be involved?
- Does Suberoff personally have what it takes to persevere with his invention and bring it through to market?

By the time of the feedback session (several months later), a decision had been made to fully integrate the business and do the manufacturing, so this problem was less salient. Given this decision, however, there was a question as to how Suberoff would position his own efforts, and what skills he needed to hire. The problem list was adjusted accordingly.

Feedback dealt with a preestablished set of characteristics. Suberoff was first told that he demonstrated a high need to achieve, no matter what measure was used. Closely related to this achievement motivation was a strong desire to innovate, consistent with his inventor mentality and the creation of new businesses. However, he did not appear to be strongly motivated as a planner, which could create problems.

Suberoff's scores indicated that he did not like to gamble on high risks, and that this risk avoidance was consistent with what we know about successful entrepreneurs. Also, his locus of control was described as heavily internal, with very little feeling of an external locus either from powerful others or chance circumstances. He was described as type A to the point of being somewhat addicted to stress. Questions about his health indicated no evidence of current health problems, however.

Insofar as mental ability is concerned, Suberoff appeared to be quite capable of meeting the challenges he faced. With regard to cognitive style, the most pronounced finding was a strong behavioral emphasis indicating a real empathy for people and a potential talent for sales. Discussion of this feature received strong support from the entrepreneur.

Suberoff scored high on several measures of managerial talent. He showed evidence of being a take-charge person and appeared to work well with authority figures. Unlike many entrepreneurs, he seemed to have the capacity to manage growth, and develop an organization of substantial size. Yet he was in no sense a professional practitioner. He did not possess professional motivation to any marked degree.

Finally, the way Suberoff described his work context was presented to him. In essence, he determined his own work outcomes, and he said that he liked it that way. This is the classic entrepreneurial pattern. Hierarchic, professional, and group processes were less significant in his world.

These test results were then repackaged using the four personality types. As a personal achiever he had many strengths in areas such as achievement motivation, internal locus of control, type A personality, and a high value placed on personal goals and individual accomplishments. Yet he was not a planner and did not particularly enjoy new learning, nor did he possess an especially strong sense of commitment. Overall he was above average as a personal achiever, but this was not a really strong pattern. All this was explained to him.

As a real manager he had many positive characteristics such as supervisory ability, little need for security, positive attitudes to authority, and a desire to exercise power. This is a strong pattern; managing is in his repertoire of skills and he was encouraged to use those skills.

Not surprisingly, for a demonstrated inventor-entrepreneur, a strong expert idea generator pattern was in evidence. He liked to introduce innovative solutions, was concerned about new product development, had a rather high level of intelligence, and did not like to take risks. Along with the managing route, the idea generating route was also open to him. The concept of a complex entrepreneur was explained to him, and he was told he had that type of talent.

The empathic supersalesperson pattern was strong, also. His empathic cognitive style and his desire to help others were the main contributors, but there were other strengths as well. The selling route was clearly one he should follow. Thus a third type was added to his complexity portfolio.

Applying these results to the problems identified earlier, it seemed apparent that Suberoff had what it takes to create and grow a new venture of the kind he had in mind. He was given strong encouragement in this regard. In view of his proclivity for working with people and understanding their needs, plus the basic requirement of this type of business that it do everything possible to generate sales and cash flow initially, it seemed appropriate that he concentrate first on selling his product. Thus, he needed to hire people with skills in the financial and manufacturing areas. Suberoff appeared comfortable with such an agenda. I advised him that later on, as the business grew, it would be best to assume a more general managerial role.

The biggest threat to the whole endeavor would be a lack of planning, which in turn might mean a failure to think through the coordination of various functions. Suberoff was advised either to devote his energies to overcoming his antipathy toward planning or to hire someone who would help in this regard. The latter might be more realistic.

The data gave no clear indication as to how the new endeavor should be related to the existing company, except to suggest that he operate as independently as seemed feasible. Clearly, he wanted to, and could, run his own show. But he was capable of working with others, even those with authority over him. Thus, this was not a major area of concern. Personality considerations could well be subordinated to existing business realities in this area.

Throughout the session the discussion focused on business problems and entrepreneurial characteristics, not test titles and measured scores. As each characteristic was discussed I gave Suberoff an opportunity to provide substantiating data and to raise questions as well. From this process a great deal of support for the interpretations emerged. Suberoff did, however, question the conclusion that he lacked professional motivation. He explained why he felt differently, and we discussed his strong desire to help others, which indeed was not at the same low level as other professional motives. Then we moved on to the findings regarding work context. No attempt was made to force interpretations on him, only to provide such information as the assessment process yielded.

As the session wound up, two hours after it began, I gave Suberoff an opportunity to raise questions that might be answered from the assessment data. He returned to the problem of planning, which he clearly recognized as a source of difficulty. He remembered several instances from the past where a failure to plan got him into trouble. He was told that recognizing weaknesses like this when they appear often can help people to overcome them. He was also told that if he wanted to talk more about this later, we could do so (and we did).

PROFESSIONAL ASSESSMENT TO AID PROSPECTIVE ENTREPRENEURS

When the individual has no venture but is considering entering on an entrepreneurial career, not only is the venture information lacking but there is no list of problems on which to focus the feedback session. Basically, there is only one problem—Does this person have the entrepreneurial talent to be successful in an entrepreneurial venture? If the answer to this question is yes, then there needs to be a discussion of the specific career route or routes to be followed.

To focus this discussion it is sometimes helpful to ask the person to prepare a vision statement describing in as much detail as possible the kind of business that would be most attractive. In many respects this is comparable to a business plan. However, it is not prepared for the purpose of obtaining financing, or operating a business, or facilitating a transition. The idea is to help the person think through what would be involved in starting and operating a specific venture. The vision statement also provides the individual doing the assessment with a picture of how committed the person is to entrepreneurial endeavor and how realistic he or she is about what this would entail.

Often these vision statements are modeled after an existing business with which the person is familiar, but even then, idiosyncratic features tend to enter in. Providing a planning guide of the kind considered in Chapter 7 helps to indicate the various factors that need to be considered.

Vision statements should be prepared so as to be available at the same time tests are completed. The feedback session then considers whether the person has entrepreneurial talent of a kind that would make the vision a reality. The basic process of providing test results and packaging these in terms of the four-way typology is the same as with established entrepreneurs. However, since the vision is only that, and not an established business, it is more easily changed. Thus, the discussion needs to deal with how the vision might be altered to create a better fit with the personality type. In a few cases this is not necessary, but more frequently it is essential. One of the major strengths of plans and visions is that they can serve as trial balloons, and thus be changed easily.

EXAMPLE OF A FEEDBACK SESSION FOR A PROSPECTIVE ENTREPRENEUR

Carolyn Cornwell had worked in a variety of capacities for several advertising agencies in the same local area for over 10 years. Her major in college was history and she had quite a high grade point average at graduation. However, she felt there was no future in pursuing that route any longer, and at her father's urging got her first job in an advertising agency where he had several friends.

The occasion for coming for entrepreneurial assessment was that her present agency was merging with another larger agency, and she had good reason to believe that as a result she would eventually be laid off. She had looked around for another position, but the local advertising industry was in a process of consolidation, and apparently everyone was about to merge or had just done so. There simply were not any positions for an experienced person available in the area. Given this, and the fact that she wanted to remain here where her friends were located, Cornwell had been giving increasing thought to founding her own small advertising agency. She hoped that the assessment would give her some pointers on how to go about doing this.

Since Cornwell expected to use her own funds to start the business, she had not prepared a business plan. Accordingly, I described the idea of a vision statement and provided an outline of the factors she might consider (Table 13.1). She brought in the vision statement for her advertising agency-to-be when she came in for testing.

The feedback session started out with the test results. Cornwell's general intelligence was quite high—at a level commensurate with graduate study. There appeared reason to believe that her verbal skills were particularly strong, and she indicated that in school she always had done better in primarily verbal subjects.

With regard to achievement motivation she was told that she scored at about an average level for entrepreneurs in general, but below what has been found among highly successful entrepreneurs. Most pronounced was a very strong tendency to avoid risks, a characteristic whose value in keeping entrepreneurs from taking too large a gamble was explained to her. Other aspects related to entrepreneurial achievement considered were a desire to personally innovate and introduce changes, and to plan and set future goals; in neither of these respects did she reveal any particular strengths. Cornwell's response to the latter description was that she had found preparing the vision statement difficult, and that maybe this was why.

Her beliefs about control of her own destiny seemed to indicate that she felt largely at the mercy of fate and powerful other people. She did not seem to feel in control of her own outcomes to any large extent. This did not bode well for an independent entrepreneurial start-up, and she was told that.

Cornwell was moderately type A, but not to a point that might pose a health hazard. She also tended to hold onto problems and take them home with her. This was consistent with a kind of tenacious energy that could be valuable to her as an entrepreneur.

As to cognitive style the only thing that stood out was a very marked conceptual orientation of a kind that characterizes very creative people; she seemed to be more of a thinker than a doer. All this was explained to her. Her response was that this is the aspect of advertising that really appeals to her.

Managing did not appear to be Cornwell's forte. She did give some indication of a need for self-actualization and to exercise power over others, but other than that she seemed to have very little motivation to do the things managers do. She said she had always wondered about this. Although she had had various management titles over the years in the advertising agencies, she never really managed much; people just seemed to do their own thing.

What came out most strongly from the whole testing process was Cornwell's high professional motivation. This was emphasized to her. She had a very strong professional commitment and a pronounced need to acquire status, but all components of this type of motivation were up. Actually, she described her own work as primarily professional in nature and she liked that aspect of it. Strangely, the entrepreneurial aspects did not have this same appeal for her.

When put in the form of the typology, this picture became much clearer. As a personal achiever Cornwell was distinctly on the low side. This was not her type at all. Of the characteristics involved she showed no strength at all on the majority. The only really strong showing was on professional commitment.

As might have been expected, the real manager pattern was no better. All that stood out was the desire to exercise power. On most of the measures involved Cornwell exhibited no match to the type of any kind.

The picture as an expert idea generator was somewhat better. There were strengths in Cornwell's conceptual, creative cognitive style, her verbal intelligence, and her desire at least in certain respects to avoid risks. Yet even here her test performance was not at a level that would clearly identify her as of this type.

Finally, as an empathic supersalesperson Cornwell also failed to meet the requirements of the type. Her high value attached to social processes was indicated, but there was very little else of a positive nature. Clearly, selling was somewhat alien to her.

In spite of certain strengths here and there on certain characteristics, Cornwell came out in the end with no strong patterns and thus no indication that she had the talent to be a successful entrepreneur. She was told that, and my advice was that she not undertake the venture she envisioned. Furthermore, it was apparent that her venture statement had not been well thought out, was hastily prepared, and lacked many essential ingredients. This was attributed to lack of interest in planning generally. A question was whether her proposed entrepreneurial activity was not more a function of her desire to stay in the area than of an intense desire to become an entrepreneur.

Cornwell's reaction was uncertain at first, but before long it became clearly apparent that she was relieved. She said that she had had doubts about the venture from the beginning, but saw no other way. Actually, that is why she had come for assessment in the first place.

At this point I brought up her marked professional motivation, as well as her intelligence and creative strengths. Was there a profession that might interest her? Almost immediately she said that she had really always wanted to be a college professor of history and to teach and write in the field. A long discussion followed which, after a total of almost three hours, resulted in what appeared to be a commitment to apply to a local university for admission into the Ph.D. program in history. She could easily put the money she had intended to apply to the advertising agency start-up to this end. I encouraged her to follow this route.

The last I heard from Cornwell she was on the verge of completing her dissertation and obtaining a Ph.D.

PSYCHOLOGICAL ASSESSMENT FOR SELECTION PURPOSES

We have been concerned with the role of entrepreneurial assessment, coupled with feedback to the person assessed, intended to serve the purposes of career development. This is at the present time the most likely use of assessment procedures. However, it is also possible to carry out an assessment the results of which are fed back to someone else who will make a decision regarding investment or employment with regard to the person assessed. Presumably, payment for professional services in these cases would be made by that other person, and the individual assessed would acquiesce to the procedure because he or she wanted something in return from the other person.

Let us start with the use of self-assessment forms such as those contained in Timmons (1989) and Miner (1996a) in these situations. These forms can be completed by other people to describe someone they are interested in hiring or in whom they are considering investing. The only requirement is that knowledge of the target person be sufficient to justify the procedure and permit some meaningful degree of validity.

There are a number of possibilities here. One use involves the evaluation of partners or potential partners, and thus fit with the needs of a venture. Another relates to the assessment of potential successors in a family business, most frequently children. Staffing decisions insofar as corporate ventures are concerned present another situation where the self-assessment form can be applied externally. Those involved in making bank loans can use this type of information both to assess risks and to guide a venture in a manner consistent with the entrepreneur's capabilities. Venture capitalists (and angels) can do the same in evaluating those who apply for funds. Managers in government entities with a mission of economic development and fostering small firm growth can utilize a self-assessment form to evaluate those whom they might support. There are other such situations as well. The key requirement is that the assessor know enough about the person being assessed to make a meaningful and valid evaluation.

People in these situations do in fact utilize personality factors informally in making investment decisions of various kinds. This is well established. But they have rarely, if ever, done so in any systematic manner, as the self-assessment forms would require. Yet it is reasonably easy to take the form and use it to assess another person about whom one has accumulated sufficient information. Furthermore, third parties can use the forms to provide outside input to these decisions, again in a more systematic manner than by simply asking "Does this person appear to have entrepreneurial talent?" In short, if one is going to use information about personality characteristics in any event, this is one method of doing so in a manner that is certainly better than unsystematic intuition.

Yet, there is an even better way—using formal psychological assessment involving tests. When a sizable investment is to be made in a person who is, or might have the potential for being, an entrepreneur, the arguments for some type of objective assessment become quite strong, especially when considerable uncertainty exists in making judgments about a person's personality characteristics. The greater the consequences and the more pronounced the surrounding uncertainty, the more it would seem appropriate to obtain as much information as possible, and to obtain information of the highest possible quality as well.

However, a study of venture capitalists (Sandberg, 1986) indicates that in the early 1980s, feedback from psychological assessments was not used:

The venture capitalists were evenly divided between personal characteristics and experience as the most important factor. There appeared to be no pattern to their preferences,

... as neither size, nor relative exposure in new ventures, nor even the venture capitalist's degree of involvement in venture management explained their priorities.

Despite the importance of the personal characteristics just discussed, the venture capitalists used no formal, psychological tests or measurements to assess what one called "the amalgam of qualities" they considered. Even those who placed experience first relied on their own feel for the quality of an entrepreneur in the absence of a track record. The venture capitalists sometimes relied on references, especially from respected venture capital colleagues, to verify what they sensed (p. 22).

There is no reason to believe this situation has changed since. Yet there is also evidence that venture capitalist–backed firms are not firms that are founded by the most capable entrepreneurs, and that this situation exists because of the inability of venture capitalists to accurately assess entrepreneurial talent (Amit, Glosten, and Muller, 1990). This would seem to argue strongly for the use of selection techniques, such as psychological assessment, that can work.

This same situation appears to exist with regard to other entrepreneurial selection decisions as well. Like venture capitalists, owners of family businesses, managers responsible for staffing corporate ventures and turnarounds, loan officers in banks, government economic development officers, and judges handling bankruptcy proceedings—all of whom make important decisions regarding entrepreneurial talent—rarely seem to use psychological assessments to aid their own judgments. Personality factors are widely recognized as being pivotal in these decisions, but the technology of assessment does not yet enter into the decision-making process. Either this technology is inadequate, or it is of such new vintage as to be far down on the learning curve, or it has not been sold well. I believe the fact of the matter right now is somewhere between the second and third propositions. Assessment technology is new and developing, and like most technologies there has been a tendency among those of us involved to assume that the benefits are so great that it will sell itself (see Chapter 9). Both considerations argue for a more comprehensive treatment of what is involved, so that the reader may be fully informed.

In psychological assessment for selection purposes the individual completes the test battery as previously, and an interview may be conducted also to clarify certain of the test responses and findings. However, there is no feedback session in which the test results are provided to the target person and used to solve his or her problems. The assessment is done so that someone else may make a better decision with regard to the entrepreneurial activities of the target person. Thus, the findings go to this someone else. The most effective approach is to present these within the framework of the four-way typology. Thus, each type is considered in turn and the status of the person on each component characteristic indicated. Personal achiever, real manager, expert idea generator, and empathic supersalesperson scores are reported and interpreted, as are the complexity indexes.

The medium used to report assessment results can vary. When the intent is to provide assessments for selection purposes, some kind of written report seems essential. This can range from a set of scores, with written interpretations, to a lengthy narrative. It is also possible to use telephone reports or one-on-one oral discussions. My personal preference is for a two-way, face-to-face oral discussion, which permits consideration of alternatives, plus a brief written report. But this can be costly. The point is that a number of approaches are available.

The questions involved here are not unique to selection decisions; they can enter into career development efforts as well. In this context many people do indicate a desire for written evaluations in addition to the verbal feedback sessions. The argument against this is that people may not pay as much attention to the feedback discussion as they should because they anticipate the written report. I have had many people start the feedback session taking notes and then shortly put the pad aside, never picking it up again. They want to concentrate on the discussion, and it is best that they do so. I do not make the notes I have prepared prior to the session available. Those are roughly stated for my own use. If a written report on the feedback is desirable, I prepare one specifically for that purpose after the session. In general, my feelings toward written reports are more favorable in the selection context than in the developmental one.

PROFESSIONAL PRACTITIONERS OF ENTREPRENEURIAL ASSESSMENT

Anyone doing assessments of the kind described in this chapter has to have a background in two areas—psychological testing, especially in the personality area, and entrepreneurship. Instead of superimposing a knowledge of testing on a background of psychopathology, as would be the case with a clinical psychologist engaged in diagnostic assessment, a person doing entrepreneurial assessments needs to substitute a knowledge of entrepreneurship practice and the literature of that field for personality theory and psychodynamics.

If one starts as a psychologist with knowledge of testing procedures, the need is to teach oneself or find someone to teach one entrepreneurship. If one starts with a knowledge of entrepreneurship, then one must find a way to learn psychological testing. There are a few people who already have these tandem skills, but not a great many. To my knowledge there is no place right now where one can go and obtain this dual training in a single program—not in a psychology department, and not in a business school either. Most of us who possess this particular mix have learned one area or the other largely on our own.

In any event, as the demand increases for this particular kind of assessment, the availability of the needed training is certain to increase as well. How fast this demand increase will occur is an open question—probably not substantially in my lifetime. But over the long term there seems little doubt that a sizable demand will appear, to the benefit of the varied groups and individuals with a stake in entrepreneurship, and in particular of society as a whole.

CONCLUSION

It is evident that there are different ways of assessing entrepreneurial talent, just as there are different purposes for which these assessments may be used. I have attempted to give the pros and cons associated with the various approaches, so that the reader can make educated decisions on these matters. However, I would like to reassert one major point. People do assess personality strengths and weaknesses—their own and those of others—all the time. Often they do this without being fully aware of the processes they use. To the extent these assessments can be made entirely conscious and more objective, however, and carried out in a systematic manner according to some plan, they are more likely to produce the desired results. That is the goal of psychological assessment of entrepreneurs as described here.

Epilogue

Recently, *Fortune* published a cover story entitled "America's Smartest Young Entrepreneurs" (Dumaine, 1994). These were 40 young people, aged 40 or less, who had started and grown their own firms. These particular firms had generated $17 billion in sales in the previous year and had created nearly 64,000 jobs. To the extent entrepreneurial firms like this grow and create value they are a very important segment of the U.S. economy.

Entrepreneurial firms are a major source of innovation and change. They create jobs, new tax revenues, and other transfers of money. At a time in our society when productivity growth is lagging behind other countries of the world, and our large corporations are cutting back by focusing on core businesses and laying off employees, entrepreneurial firms assume a more significant role; they do what large companies are not doing.

Much has been written about the future of entrepreneurship in this country. Roberts (1991b) predicts a bright future for high-technology entrepreneuring. Schein (1996) emphasizes the expanding opportunities anticipated for entrepreneurs. Others have set forth equally optimistic views.

My own credentials are not quite the equal of these people insofar as predicting the future of the field of entrepreneurship is concerned. Compared to others I am a relative latecomer to the area, although my first research on entrepreneurs was published some 20 years ago (Smith, McCain, and Miner, 1976). Nevertheless, I would like to end this report with some prognostications of my own, looking not only at practice, but at theory and research as well.

THE FUTURE OF ENTREPRENEURSHIP PRACTICE

The predictions of expanding entrepreneurial activity and growing entrepreneurial firms seem warranted, provided something does not happen to lessen the flow and turn down the faucet. One such possibility is that entrepreneurial talent would begin to dry up for some reason. Yet we now know that a wide range of people have the capacity to achieve entrepreneurial success—not just personal achievers, but real managers, expert idea generators, and empathic supersales-people as well. The entrepreneurial horizon is much wider than was previously thought (Miner, 1997a). Furthermore, three of these types are widely employed in non-entrepreneurial occupations. If the talent supply appeared to be dwindling, steps could be taken to redirect more people into the entrepreneurship channel.

A much more likely threat is that just the opposite might happen. Society might act to redirect its abundant entrepreneurial talent away from entrepreneurial activities. Rewards would be even further reduced, freedom would be restricted, burdens would be imposed, cultural values antithetical to entrepreneurship would become ascendant. This threat is real. This has happened in other countries. It is not that an anti-entrepreneurial climate might come to prevail. Rather, other political, economic, and cultural priorities could operate to leave very limited room for entrepreneurship. Other things become more important, or seem more important at the time. The fact that entrepreneurs are a disappearing breed is hardly noticed as society achieves other, valued goals and turns in accomplishments considered superior to those of past generations. Until unemployment becomes widespread, goods and services are not available locally (and must be purchased at a premium from other countries), and our standards of living sink to new lows, nothing untoward is evident.

Should this scenario begin to unfold, or continue to unfold depending on your viewpoint, and perhaps depending on what state you live in as well, the four types would be expected to react somewhat differently. The major engine of small firm growth in this country is reinvested earnings—not bank loans, or venture capital, or initial public offerings. Personal achievers are particularly reliant on this source. If taxes take it away and legislation imposes costs that dry it up, there is no engine of growth and feedback is increasingly perceived as negative.

For any personal achiever this can be a terribly frustrating situation. Entrepreneuring is not fun anymore, but there appears to be no place else to go. Some may find capital elsewhere, some may move the business to a more economically friendly environment (perhaps in another country), some may plan an escape from entrepreneurship to some different career that uses other of their talents. However, the most likely reaction, perhaps after several start-ups that are unable to accomplish much in spite of the personal achiever's best efforts, is to simply give up. When this happens the result is not only business failure, but personal failure also. Personal achievers do not react well under these circumstances. They will lash out at those whom they blame for the situation. They do not accept personal responsibility for failure, and given the extent of their entrepreneurial talents there is no reason that they should. These are people who fight unfavorable climates for entrepreneurship with the greatest vehemence.

Real managers react quite differently. What they want above anything else is to manage something. Perhaps at a point in time this is within entrepreneurship. But at other times they are equally happy managing in other contexts. Without additional strong patterns they are not particularly adept at growing start-up ventures. Their talents tend to clutch-in at a much later point on the growth curve. At this time they can become very concerned about threats to entrepreneurial opportunity. Yet should a new managerial opportunity present itself they will move on. There are other things in this world for them beyond entrepreneurship. Real managers are very adaptive people, and not overly idealistic. It is even conceivable that some might end by managing the controls and restrictions that hold other entrepreneurs in check.

How expert idea generators will react to the threat of venture-stifling actions is more difficult to predict. These are people who can be very idealistic. Thus they may become attached to the very causes that represent a threat. It is unlikely that they would self-destruct in this process, but they can end up supporting positions that are detrimental to other entrepreneurs. Yet along with this idealism goes an intense desire for freedom to carry out their ideas. Many expert idea generators have already escaped to entrepreneurship from some other career that has proven too limiting. Heavy taxation, restrictive legislation, and excessive reporting requirements that occupy their time with routine drudgery can represent a threat to their last retreat. When they view the situation that way, expert idea generators can be expected to resist the controlling factors much as personal achievers would. Their desire to protect their freedom and their idealism become rolled into one.

Empathic supersalespeople, as so often happens in other contexts, can be different in the ways they react to threat. The most likely response is to charge out and sell, sell, sell. Entrepreneurs such as this do not enjoy conflict, and they will do all they can to avoid it. Under these conditions that cut heavily into earnings, they are inclined to do what they do best. Margins may be held to a very low level, and in fact profits may disappear completely, but cash flow can still be maintained for a period. Ultimately, the firm may fail to survive, but empathic supersalespeople tend to keep selling until the end.

My point is that political, economic, and cultural onslaughts on entrepreneurship do not draw the same reactions from the four types. Entrepreneurs cannot all be expected to react as one. Given this, there is some vulnerability. The future looks very promising for entrepreneurship practice, but the line of defense against major threat appears to be somewhat fractured. This is a necessary consequence of the varied types of people who can become successful entrepreneurs. As a group entrepreneurs are much better economic warriors than political ones. It is hoped that society will not cast its entrepreneurs in a role for which they are not best suited. If this should happen both society and entrepreneurship would be the losers.

THE FUTURE OF ENTREPRENEURSHIP THEORY AND RESEARCH

Historically, entrepreneurship in the universities has not had a good image. The field often has been poorly represented in business school curricula, has not been a major research area, and has suffered from a lack of theoretical innovation. As we have seen, many of these conditions are now changing. Thus, it is important to predicate any predictions for the future on a full knowledge of the nature of the present scene. To understand this scene it seems appropriate to look closely at the make-up of bibliographies such as that of this book. Where do we now stand as to theory and research based on the citations included in a book which is in fact dedicated to just these concerns?

Among the journals and annuals cited, two stand out as occurring most frequently with over 10 citations each—*Journal of Business Venturing* and *Entrepreneurship Theory and Practice*. These are the same two journals that dominated a recent analysis of over 16,000 citations in the entrepreneurship literature (Romano and Ratnatunga, 1996), suggesting that using the present bibliography is not at all inappropriate.

The next tier (consisting of journals or annuals with 5 to 10 citations) includes a number at the high end that are dedicated in part or wholly to entrepreneurship subject matter. These are *Entrepreneurship and Regional Development, Strategic Management Journal, Frontiers of Entrepreneurship Research*, and *Journal of Small Business Management*. Also in this tier are *Academy of Management Journal, Academy of Management Review, Journal of Management Studies, Business Horizons*, and *Harvard Business Review*, as well as two major industrial/organizational psychology journals—*Journal of Applied Psychology* and *Personnel Psychology*. Clearly, these general management and psychology publications are accepting a substantial number of articles related to entrepreneurship. Finally, there are six journals (with 3 or 4 citations), similar in their normal content to those above, that appear to be a good outlet for entrepreneurship research. In general management these are *California Management Review* and *Journal of Management*, plus *Organization Studies, Journal of Managerial Psychology, Journal of Occupational and Organizational Psychology*, and *Simulation and Gaming*. There are 44 other journals or annuals with one or two citations. Also, 96 books are cited at least once in the bibliography.

The implications for the current scene are clear. Entrepreneurship is no longer on the outside insofar as research and theory publications are concerned. Articles are appearing regularly not only in publications directed specifically at entrepreneurship, but in many sources outside the field itself, including those with the very highest prestige. Some of these articles are relevant for entrepreneurship, but not actually of the field per se. Yet others deal directly with entrepreneurship subject matter. Furthermore, a number of books have appeared dealing with topics in the field, sufficient to constitute a burgeoning literature.

No reason exists to consider entrepreneurship a second-class citizen insofar as its publications and publication outlets are concerned at the present time. It is indeed attracting major authors from other disciplines who are making contributions to the field for the first time. Increasingly, academics are coming to view entrepreneurship as a fascinating field with unusual potential for innovation. I see no inherent reason why all this should change. The potential for the future seems outstanding.

Furthermore, entrepreneurship science and entrepreneurship practice are much more closely allied than is the case in many other academic areas. This is a major strength. Scholars of entrepreneurship have often had practitioner experience. Many appear to possess one or more of the personality types—especially the expert idea generator type. This close tie between academics and practitioners is important because academics can be and have been leading spokespeople and advocates for practitioner causes. In this instance values seem to be closely aligned. Academics are by nature effective communicators. They can help entrepreneurs ward off threats to their businesses, just as entrepreneurs can help them by providing research sites and stimuli for theoretical speculation.

Yet one threat exists to what otherwise seem grounds for unbridled optimism. Chapter 1 noted that entrepreneurship is still an interdisciplinary field. Its researchers and theoreticians have origins in and identify with a wide range of other disciplines. Among these are economics, sociology, psychology, anthropology, engineering, law, accounting, marketing, finance, organizational behavior, management, policy/strategy, and perhaps other fields of which I am not aware. Entrepreneurship is not yet mature as a discipline, and the glue that holds it together may not be very strong. Other fields that have a longer history, such as organizational behavior and policy/strategy, are still struggling to cope with the divisiveness of multidisciplinary origins. Entrepreneurship is no exception. The possibility that conflict could destroy the field, or at the least retard its development, clearly is a continuing danger.

On the other hand, juxtaposing disciplines in this way offers the opportunity for creative combinations. New ways of thinking can arise out of a process which places key constructs from one discipline in close proximity to key constructs from another, in pursuit of common goals—to understand, predict, and influence entrepreneurship. One can hope that this positive potential will outdistance the power plays and interdisciplinary wrangling, and that the field will avoid its inherent capacity for self-destruction. The chances that this will be the case seem good in the current growth era. Whether this same resilience will be present should the market turn sour is as yet untested.

Bibliography

Aldrich, Howard E. (1995). Entrepreneurial Strategies in New Organizational Populations. In Ivan Bull, Howard Thomas, and Gary Willard (Eds.), *Entrepreneurship:
Perspectives on Theory Building*. Oxford, UK: Pergamon, pp. 91–106.

Aldrich, Howard E., and Gabriele Wiedenmayer (1993). From Traits to Rates: An Eco-
logical Perspective on Organizational Foundings. *Advances in Entrepreneurship,
Firm Emergence, and Growth*, Volume 1, pp. 145–195.

Aldrich, Howard E., and Catherine Zimmer (1986). Entrepreneurship Through Social
Networks. In Donald L. Sexton and Raymond W. Smilor (Eds.), *The Art and
Science of Entrepreneurship*. Cambridge, MA: Ballinger, pp. 3–23.

Amit, Raphael, Lawrence Glosten, and Eitan Muller (1990). Does Venture Capital Foster
the Most Promising Entrepreneurial Firms? *California Management Review*, Volume 32, Number 3, pp. 102–111.

Amit, Raphael, Lawrence Glosten, and Eitan Muller (1993). Challenges to Theory Development in Entrepreneurship Research. *Journal of Management Studies*, Volume 30, Number 5, pp. 815–834.

Arendarski, Andrzej, Tomasz Mroczkowski, and James Sood (1994). A Study of the
Redevelopment of Private Enterprise in Poland: Conditions and Policies for Continuing Growth. *Journal of Small Business Management*, Volume 32, Number 3,
pp. 40–51.

Atkinson, John W., and Joel O. Raynor (1974). *Motivation and Achievement*. New York:
Wiley.

Baldwin, Timothy T., and Margaret Y. Padgett (1993). Management Development: A
Review and Commentary. *International Review of Industrial and Organizational
Psychology*, Volume 8, pp. 35–85.

Basadur, Min, George B. Graen, and Stephen G. Green (1982). Training in Creative
Problem Solving: Effects on Ideation and Problem Finding and Solving in an
Industrial Research Organization. *Organizational Behavior and Human Perfor-
mance*, Volume 30, pp. 41–70.

Baumol, William J. (1993). Formal Entrepreneurship Theory in Economics: Existence and Bounds. *Journal of Business Venturing*, Volume 8, Number 3, pp. 197–210.

Baumol, William J. (1995). Formal Entrepreneurship Theory in Economics: Existence and Bounds. In Ivan Bull, Howard Thomas, and Gary Willard (Eds.), *Entrepreneurship: Perspectives on Theory Building*. Oxford, UK: Pergamon, pp. 17–33.

Begin, James P. (1991). *Strategic Employment Policy: An Organizational Systems Perspective*. Englewood Cliffs, NJ: Prentice-Hall.

Begley, Thomas M., and David P. Boyd (1987). Psychological Characteristics Associated with Performance in Entrepreneurial Firms and Smaller Businesses. *Journal of Business Venturing*, Volume 2, Number 1, pp. 79–93.

Bellu, Renato R. (1988). Entrepreneurs and Managers: Are They Different? *Frontiers of Entrepreneurship Research*, Volume 8, pp. 16–30.

Bellu, Renato R. (1992). Toward a Theory of Entrepreneurial Motivation: Evidence from Female Entrepreneurs. *International Council for Small Business Proceedings*, Volume 37, pp. 195–213.

Bellu, Renato R. (1993). Task Role Motivation and Attributional Style as Predictors of Entrepreneurial Performance: Female Sample Findings. *Entrepreneurship and Regional Development*, Volume 5, Number 4, pp. 331–344.

Bellu, Renato R., Per Davidsson, and Connie Goldfarb (1989). Motivational Characteristics of Small Firm Entrepreneurs in Israel, Italy, and Sweden: A Cross-Cultural Study. *International Council for Small Business Proceedings*, Volume 34, pp. 349–364.

Bellu, Renato R., Per Davidsson, and Connie Goldfarb (1990). Toward a Theory of Entrepreneurial Behavior: Empirical Evidence from Israel, Italy, and Sweden. *Entrepreneurship and Regional Development*, Volume 2, Number 2, pp. 195–209.

Bellu, Renato R., and Herbert Sherman (1993). Predicting Entrepreneurial Success from Task Motivation and Attributional Style: A Longitudinal Study. *Proceedings of the United States Association for Small Business and Entrepreneurship*, Volume 8, pp. 16–23.

Bellu, Renato R., and Herbert Sherman (1995). Predicting Firm Success from Task Motivation and Attributional Style: A Longitudinal Study. *Entrepreneurship and Regional Development*, Volume 7, Number 4, pp. 349–363.

Berman, Frederic E., and John B. Miner (1985). Motivation to Manage at the Top Executive Level: A Test of the Hierarchic Role-Motivation Theory. *Personnel Psychology*, Volume 38, Number 2, pp. 377–391.

Bird, Barbara J. (1989). *Entrepreneurial Behavior*. Glenview, IL: Scott, Foresman.

Bird, Barbara J., and Mariann Jelinek (1988). The Operation of Entrepreneurial Intentions. *Entrepreneurship Theory and Practice*, Volume 13, Number 2, pp. 21–29.

Birley, Sue, and Paul Westhead (1990). Growth and Performance Contrasts between "Types" of Small Firms. *Strategic Management Journal*, Volume 11, Number 7, pp. 535–557.

Block, Zenas, and Ian C. MacMillan (1993). *Corporate Venturing: Creating New Businesses within the Firm*. Boston: Harvard Business School Press.

Bouchikhi, Hamid (1993). A Constructivist Framework for Understanding Entrepreneurship Performance. *Organization Studies*, Volume 14, Number 4, pp. 549–570.

Boyd, Brian K. (1991). Strategic Planning and Financial Performance: A Meta-Analytic Review. *Journal of Management Studies*, Volume 28, Number 4, pp. 353–374.

Bracker, Jeffrey S., John N. Pearson, Barbara W. Keats, and John B. Miner (1992).

Entrepreneurial Intensity, Strategic Planning Process Sophistication, and Firm Performance in a Dynamic Environment. *Working Paper*, University of Louisville.

Bramlette, Carl A., Donald O. Jewell, and Michael H. Mescon (1977). Designing for Organizational Effectiveness: A Better Way; How It Works. *Atlanta Economic Review*, Volume 27, Numbers 5 and 6, pp. 35–41, 10–15.

Brockhaus, Robert H., and Pamela S. Horwitz (1986). The Psychology of the Entrepreneur. In Donald L. Sexton and Raymond W. Smilor (Eds.), *The Art and Science of Entrepreneurship*. Cambridge, MA: Ballinger, pp. 25–48.

Brush, Candida G. (1992). Research on Women Business Owners: Past Trends, a New Perspective and Future Directions. *Entrepreneurship Theory and Practice*, Volume 16, Number 4, pp. 5–30.

Burgelman, Robert A., and Leonard R. Sayles (1986). *Inside Corporate Innovation: Strategy, Structure, and Managerial Skills*. New York: Free Press.

Burns, Tom, and G. M. Stalker (1961). *The Management of Innovation*. London, UK: Tavistock Publications.

Buttner, E. Holly (1993). Female Entrepreneurs: How Far Have They Come? *Business Horizons*, Volume 36, Number 2, pp. 59–65.

Buttner, E. Holly, and Nur Gryskiewicz (1993). Entrepreneurs' Problem Solving Styles: An Empirical Study Using the Kirton Adaptation/Innovation Theory. *Journal of Small Business Management*, Volume 31, Number 1, pp. 22–31.

Caird, Sally P. (1993). What Do Psychological Tests Suggest about Entrepreneurs? *Journal of Managerial Psychology*, Volume 8, Number 6, pp. 11–20.

Campbell, Donald J., and Cynthia Lee (1988). Self-Appraisal in Performance Evaluation: Development versus Evaluation. *Academy of Management Review*, Volume 13, Number 2, pp. 302–314.

Carsrud, Alan L., Kenneth W. Olm, and James B. Thomas (1989). Predicting Entrepreneurial Success: Effects of Multi-dimensional Achievement Motivation, Levels of Ownership, and Cooperative Relationships. *Entrepreneurship and Regional Development*, Volume 1, Number 3, pp. 237–244.

Center for Entrepreneurial Leadership (undated). [Brochure] Buffalo, NY: State University of New York at Buffalo, School of Management.

Center for Entrepreneurial Leadership Inc. (1993, 1994, 1995). *Outstanding Innovations in Entrepreneurship Education*. Kansas City, MO: Ewing Marion Kauffman Foundation.

Chia, Robert (1996). Teaching Paradigm Shifting in Management Education: University Business Schools and the Entrepreneurial Imagination. *Journal of Management Studies*, Volume 33, Number 4, pp. 409–428.

Churchill, Neil C., and Virginia L. Lewis (1983). The Five Stages of Small Business Growth. *Harvard Business Review*, Volume 61, Number 3, pp. 30–50.

Collins, Orvis F., and David G. Moore (1964). *The Enterprising Man*. East Lansing: Bureau of Business and Economic Research, Graduate School of Business Administration, Michigan State University.

Cooper, Arnold C., and F. Javier Gimeno Gascón (1992). Entrepreneurs, Processes of Founding, and New-Firm Performance. In Donald L. Sexton and John D. Kasarda (Eds.), *The State of the Art of Entrepreneurship*. Boston: PWS-Kent, pp. 301–340.

Cornwall, Jeffrey R., and Baron Perlman (1990). *Organizational Entrepreneurship.* Homewood, IL: Irwin.

Covin, Jeffrey G. (1991). Entrepreneurial versus Conservative Firms: A Comparison of Strategies and Performance. *Journal of Management Studies*, Volume 28, Number 5, pp. 439–462.

Crant, J. Michael (1996). The Proactive Personality Scale as a Predictor of Entrepreneurial Intentions. *Journal of Small Business Management*, Volume 34, Number 3, pp. 42–49.

Daily, Catherine M., and Dan R. Dalton (1992). Financial Performance of Founder-Managed versus Professionally Managed Small Corporations. *Journal of Small Business Management*, Volume 30, Number 2, pp. 25–34.

Davidsson, Per (1988). Type of Man and Type of Company Revisited: A Confirmatory Cluster Analysis Approach. *Frontiers of Entrepreneurship Research*, Volume 8, pp. 88–105.

Davidsson, Per (1989a). *Continued Entrepreneurship and Small Firm Growth.* Stockholm, Sweden: Stockholm School of Economics.

Davidsson, Per (1989b). Entrepreneurship—and After? A Study of Growth Willingness in Small Firms. *Journal of Business Venturing*, Volume 4, Number 3, pp. 211–226.

Dill, William R., Thomas L. Hilton, and Walter R. Reitman (1962). *The New Managers: Patterns of Behavior and Development.* Englewood Cliffs, NJ: Prentice-Hall.

Doty, D. Harold, and William H. Glick (1994). Typologies as a Unique Form of Theory Building: Toward Improved Understanding and Modeling. *Academy of Management Review*, Volume 19, Number 2, pp. 230–251.

Duchesneau, Donald A., and William B. Gartner (1990). A Profile of New Venture Success and Failure in an Emerging Industry. *Journal of Business Venturing*, Volume 5, Number 5, pp. 297–312.

Dumaine, Brian (1994). America's Smartest Young Entrepreneurs. *Fortune*, Volume 129, Number 6, pp. 34–48.

Dumas, Colette (1992). Integrating the Daughter into Family Business Management. *Entrepreneurship Theory and Practice*, Volume 16, Number 4, pp. 41–55.

Dyer, W. Gibb (1992). *The Entrepreneurship Experience: Confronting Career Dilemmas of the Start-up Executive.* San Francisco, CA: Jossey-Bass.

Dyer, W. Gibb (1994). Toward a Theory of Entrepreneurial Careers. *Entrepreneurship Theory and Practice*, Volume 19, Number 2, pp. 7–21.

Eggers, John H. (1995). Developing Entrepreneurs: Skills for the "Wanna Be," "Gonna Be," and "Gotta Be Better" Employees. In Manuel London (Ed.), *Employees, Careers, and Job Creation.* San Francisco, CA: Jossey-Bass, pp. 165–184.

Ehringer, Ann G. (1995). *Make Up Your Mind: Entrepreneurs Talk about Decision Making.* Santa Monica, CA: Merritt Publishing.

Eisenhardt, Kathleen M., and Claudia B. Schoonhoven (1996). Resource-based View of Strategic Alliance Formation: Strategic and Social Effects in Entrepreneurial Firms. *Organization Science*, Volume 7, Number 2, pp. 136–150.

Elizur, Dov (1984). Facets of Work Values: A Structural Analysis of Work Outcomes. *Journal of Applied Psychology*, Volume 69, Number 3, pp. 379–389.

Elliott, Clifford J., Jack S. Goodwin, and James C. Goodwin (1994). MBA Programs and Business Needs: Is There a Mismatch? *Business Horizons*, Volume 37, Number 4, pp. 55–60.

Fagenson, Ellen A. (1993). Personal Value Systems of Men and Women Entrepreneurs versus Managers. *Journal of Business Venturing*, Volume 8, Number 5, pp. 409–430.

Farh, Jiing-Lih, and Gregory H. Dobbins (1989). Effects of Comparative Performance Information on the Accuracy of Self-Ratings and the Agreement between Self- and Supervisor Ratings. *Journal of Applied Psychology*, Volume 74, Number 4, pp. 606–610.

Farh, Jiing-Lih, Gregory H. Dobbins, and Bor-Shiuan Cheng (1991). Cultural Relativity in Action: A Comparison of Self-Ratings Made by Chinese and U.S. Workers. *Personnel Psychology*, Volume 44, Number 1, pp. 129–147.

Fast, Norman D. (1978). *The Rise and Fall of Corporate New Venture Divisions*. Ann Arbor, MI: University Microfilms International Research Press.

Feeser, Henry R., and Gary E. Willard (1990). Founding Strategy and Performance: A Comparison of High and Low Growth High Tech Firms. *Strategic Management Journal*, Volume 11, Number 2, pp. 87–98.

Fiedler, Fred E., and Martin M. Chemers (1984). *Improving Leadership Effectiveness: The Leader Match Concept*. New York: Wiley.

Fiedler, Fred E., and Joseph E. Garcia (1987). *New Approaches to Effective Leadership: Cognitive Resources and Organizational Performance*. New York: Wiley.

Filley, Alan C., and Ramon J. Aldag (1978). Characteristics and Measurement of an Organizational Typology. *Academy of Management Journal*, Volume 21, Number 4, pp. 578–591.

Filley, Alan C., and Ramon J. Aldag (1980). Organizational Growth and Types: Lessons from Small Institutions. *Research in Organizational Behavior*, Volume 2, pp. 279–320.

Fisher, Roger, and William Ury (1981). *Getting to Yes*. Boston: Houghton-Mifflin.

Freear, John, Jeffrey E. Sohl, and William J. Wetzel (1995). Angels: Personal Investors in the Venture Capital Market. *Entrepreneurship and Regional Development*, Volume 7, Number 1, pp. 85–94.

Frishkoff, Patricia A., and Bonnie M. Brown (1993). Women on the Move in Family Business. *Business Horizons*, Volume 36, Number 2, pp. 66–70.

Galbraith, Jay (1982). New Venture Planning—The Stages of Growth. *Journal of Business Strategy*, Volume 3, Number 1, pp. 70–79.

Gartner, William B. (1985). A Conceptual Framework for Describing the Phenomenon of New Venture Creation. *Academy of Management Review*, Volume 10, Number 4, pp. 696–706.

Gartner, William B. (1988). "Who Is an Entrepreneur?" Is the Wrong Question. *American Journal of Small Business*, Volume 12, Number 4, pp. 11–32.

Gartner, William B. (1989). Some Suggestions for Research on Entrepreneurial Traits and Characteristics. *Entrepreneurship Theory and Practice*, Volume 14, Number 1, pp. 27–37.

Gartner, William B., Terence R. Mitchell, and Karl H. Vesper (1989). A Taxonomy of New Business Ventures. *Journal of Business Venturing*, Volume 4, Number 3, pp. 169–186.

Gartner, William B., and Karl H. Vesper (1994). Experiments in Entrepreneurship Education: Successes and Failures. *Journal of Business Venturing*, Volume 9, Number 3, pp. 179–187.

Gasse, Yvon (1982). Elaborations on the Psychology of the Entrepreneur. In Calvin A.

Kent, Donald L. Sexton, and Karl H. Vesper (Eds.), *Encyclopedia of Entrepreneurship*. Englewood Cliffs, NJ: Prentice-Hall, pp. 57–71.

George, Jennifer M. (1992). The Role of Personality in Organizational Life: Issues and Evidence. *Journal of Management*, Volume 18, Number 2, pp. 185–213.

Gersick, Kelin E., John A. Davis, Marion M. Hampton, and Ivan Lansberg (1997). *Generation to Generation: Life Cycles of the Family Business*. Boston: Harvard Business School Press.

Ghiselli, Edwin E. (1971). *Explorations in Managerial Talent*. Pacific Palisades, CA: Goodyear.

Gillin, L. Murray, Marcus Powe, Alison L. Dews, and W. Ed McMullan (1996). An Empirical Assessment of the Returns to Investment in Entrepreneurial Education. *Frontiers of Entrepreneurship Research*, Volume 16, pp. 638–639.

Ginn, Charles W., and Donald L. Sexton (1990). A Comparison of the Personality Type Dimensions of the 1987 *Inc.* 500 Company Founders/CEOs with Those of Slower-Growth Firms. *Journal of Business Venturing*, Volume 5, Number 5, pp. 313–326.

Greenwood, Royston, and C. R. Hinings (1993). Understanding Strategic Change: The Contribution of Archetypes. *Academy of Management Journal*, Volume 36, Number 5, pp. 1052–1081.

Guth, William (1991). Director's Corner—Research in Entrepreneurship. *The Entrepreneurship Forum*, Winter, p. 11.

Hackman, Richard, and Greg C. Oldham (1980). *Work Redesign*. Reading, MA: Addison-Wesley.

Hagan, Oliver, Carol Rivchun, and Donald L. Sexton (1989). *Women-Owned Businesses*. Westport, CT: Praeger.

Harnett, Donald L., and Larry L. Cummings (1980). *Bargaining Behavior: An International Study*. Houston, TX: Dame.

Harnett, Donald L., Larry L. Cummings, and G. D. Hughes (1968). The Influence of Risk-Taking Propensity on Bargaining Behavior. *Behavioral Science*, Volume 13, pp. 1–11.

Harris, Michael M., and John Schaubroeck (1988). A Meta-Analysis of Self-Supervisor, Self-Peer, and Peer-Supervisor Ratings. *Personnel Psychology*, Volume 41, Number 1, pp. 43–62.

Herrnstein, Richard J., and Charles Murray (1994). *The Bell Curve: Intelligence and Class Structure in American Life*. New York: Free Press.

Herron, Lanny, and Richard B. Robinson (1993). A Structural Model of the Effects of Entrepreneurial Characteristics on Venture Performance. *Journal of Business Venturing*, Volume 8, Number 3, pp. 281–294.

Herzberg, Fred (1976). *The Managerial Choice: To Be Efficient and to Be Human*. Homewood, IL: Dow-Jones-Irwin.

Hetzner, William A., Louis G. Tornatzky, and K. J. Klein (1983). Manufacturing Technology in the 1980s: A Survey of Federal Programs and Practices. *Management Science*, Volume 29, Number 8, pp. 951–961.

Hines, George H. (1973). Achievement Motivation, Occupations, and Labor Turnover in New Zealand. *Journal of Applied Psychology*, Volume 58, Number 3, pp. 313–317.

Hisrich, Robert D., and Candida G. Brush (1986). *The Woman Entrepreneur: Starting,*

Financing, and Managing a Successful New Business. Lexington, MA: Lexington Books.

Hisrich, Robert D., and Mikhail V. Grachev (1995). The Russian Entrepreneur: Characteristics and Prescriptions for Success. *Journal of Managerial Psychology*, Volume 10, Number 2, pp. 3–9.

Hisrich, Robert D., and Barra O'Cinneide (1996). Entrepreneurial Activities in Europe-oriented Institutions. *Journal of Managerial Psychology*, Volume 11, Number 2, pp. 45–64.

Hisrich, Robert D., and Michael P. Peters (1995). *Entrepreneurship: Starting, Developing, and Managing a New Enterprise.* Chicago, IL: Irwin.

Hoffman, Calvin C., Barry R. Nathan, and Lisa M. Holden (1991). A Comparison of Validation Criteria: Objective versus Subjective Performance Measures and Self- versus Supervisor Ratings. *Personnel Psychology*, Volume 44, Number 3, pp. 601–619.

Hofstede, Geert H. (1980). *Culture's Consequences: International Differences in Work-Related Values.* Beverly Hills, CA: Sage.

Hornaday, John, and Karl Vesper (1982). Alumni Perceptions of Entrepreneurship Courses after Six to Ten Years. In Terry D. Webb, Thelma A. Quince, and David S. Watkins (Eds.), *Small Business Research: The Development of Entrepreneurs.* London, UK: Gower, pp. 29–45.

Hoy, Frank, Thomas G. Monroy, and Jay Reichert (1993, 1994). *The Art and Science of Entrepreneurship Education.* Berea, OH: Baldwin-Wallace College.

Ivancevich, John M. (1991). A Traditional Faculty Member's Perspective on Entrepreneurship. *Journal of Business Venturing*, Volume 6, Number 1, pp. 1–7.

Johnson, Bradley R. (1990). Toward a Multidimensional Model of Entrepreneurship: The Case of Achievement Motivation and the Entrepreneur. *Entrepreneurship Theory and Practice*, Volume 14, Number 3, pp. 39–54.

Kao, John J. (1995). *Entrepreneurship, Creativity, and Organization.* Englewood Cliffs, NJ: Prentice-Hall.

Katzenbach, Jon R., and Douglas K. Smith (1993). *The Wisdom of Teams: Creating the High-Performance Organization.* Boston: Harvard Business School Press.

Kaufmann, Patrick J., Dianne H. B. Welsh, and Nicholas V. Bushmarin (1995). Locus of Control and Entrepreneurship in the Russian Republic. *Entrepreneurship Theory and Practice*, Volume 20, Number 1, pp. 43–56.

Keats, Barbara W., and Jeffrey S. Bracker (1988). Toward a Theory of Small Firm Performance: A Conceptual Model. *American Journal of Small Business*, Volume 12, Number 4, pp. 41–58.

Ketchen, David J., and Christopher L. Shook (1996). The Application of Cluster Analysis in Strategic Management Research: An Analysis and Critique. *Strategic Management Journal*, Volume 17, Number 6, pp. 441–458.

Kets de Vries, Manfred F. R. (1977). The Entrepreneurial Personality: A Person at the Cross Roads. *Journal of Management Studies*, Volume 14, Number 1, pp. 34–57.

Kirchhoff, Bruce A. (1996). Self-Employment and Dynamic Capitalism. *Journal of Labor Research*, Volume 17, Number 4, pp. 627–643.

Koh, Hian Chye (1996). Testing Hypotheses of Entrepreneurial Characteristics: A Study of Hong Kong MBA Students. *Journal of Managerial Psychology*, Volume 11, Number 3, pp. 12–25.

Korman, Abraham K. (1988). *The Outsiders: Jews and Corporate America.* Lexington, MA: Lexington Books.

Kram, Kathy E., and Douglas T. Hall (1989). Mentoring as an Antidote to Stress During Corporate Trauma. *Human Resource Management*, Volume 28, Number 4, pp. 493–510.

Lafuente, Alberto, and Vicente Salas (1989). Types of Entrepreneurs and Firms: The Case of New Spanish Firms. *Strategic Management Journal*, Volume 10, Number 1, pp. 17–30.

Lammers, Cornelis J. (1978). The Comparative Sociology of Organizations. *Annual Review of Sociology*, Volume 4, pp. 485–510.

Langan-Fox, Janice, and Susanna Roth (1995). Achievement Motivation and Female Entrepreneurs. *Journal of Occupational and Organizational Psychology*, Volume 68, Part 3, pp. 209–218.

Lee, Cynthia, Susan J. Ashford, and Philip Bobko (1990). Interactive Effects of ''Type A'' Behavior and Perceived Control on Worker Performance, Job Satisfaction, and Somatic Complaints. *Academy of Management Journal*, Volume 33, Number 4, pp. 870–881.

Lessner, M., and R. R. Knapp (1974). Self-Actualization and Entrepreneurial Orientation among Small Business Owners: A Validation Study of the P.O.I. *Educational and Psychological Measurement*, Volume 34, pp. 455–460.

Levenson, Hanna (1972). Distinctions within the Concept of Internal-External Control: Development of a New Scale. *Proceedings, American Psychological Association Annual Convention*, 80th Convention, pp. 261–262.

Levenson, Hanna (1974). Activism and Powerful Others: Distinctions within the Concept of Internal-External Control. *Journal of Personality Assessment*, Volume 38, Number 4, pp. 377–383.

Levinson, Harry (1994). Why the Behemoths Fall: Psychological Roots of Corporate Failure. *American Psychologist*, Volume 49, Number 5, pp. 428–436.

Liles, F. (1974). Who Are the Entrepreneurs? *MSU Business Topics*, Volume 22, Winter Issue, pp. 5–14.

Livesay, Harold C. (1982). Entrepreneurial History. In Calvin A. Kent, Donald L. Sexton, and Karl H. Vesper (Eds.), *Encyclopedia of Entrepreneurship*. Englewood Cliffs, NJ: Prentice-Hall, pp. 7–15.

Locke, Edwin A. (1967). Motivational Effects of Knowledge of Results: Knowledge or Goal Setting. *Journal of Applied Psychology*, Volume 51, pp. 324–329.

Locke, Edwin A., and Gary P. Latham (1990). *A Theory of Goal Setting and Task Performance*. Englewood Cliffs, NJ: Prentice-Hall.

Low, Murray, S. Venkataraman, and V. Srivatsan (1994). Developing an Entrepreneurship Game for Teaching and Research. *Simulation and Gaming*, Volume 25, Number 3, pp. 383–401.

Low, Murray B., and Ian C. MacMillan (1988). Entrepreneurship: Past Research and Future Challenges. *Journal of Management*, Volume 14, Number 2, pp. 139–161.

Lumpkin, G. T., and Gregory G. Dess (1996). Clarifying the Entrepreneurial Orientation Construct and Linking It to Performance. *Academy of Management Review*, Volume 21, Number 1, pp. 135–172.

Luthans, Fred, Richard M. Hodgetts, and Stuart A. Rosenkrantz (1988). *Real Managers*. Cambridge, MA: Ballinger.

Lynn, Richard (1969). An Achievement Motivation Questionnaire. *British Journal of Psychology*, Volume 60, Number 4, pp. 529–534.

Matteson, Michael T., and John M. Ivancevich (1982a). *Managing Job Stress and Health: The Intelligent Person's Guide*. New York: Free Press.

Matteson, Michael T., and John M. Ivancevich (1982b). Type A and B Behavior Patterns and Self-Reported Health Symptoms and Stress: Examining Individual and Organizational Fit. *Journal of Occupational Medicine*, Volume 24, pp. 585–589.

Matteson, Michael T., and John M. Ivancevich (1983). Note on Tension Discharge Rate as an Employee Health Status Predictor. *Academy of Management Journal*, Volume 26, Number 3, pp. 540–545.

Matthews, Charles H., and Steven B. Moser (1995). Family Background and Gender: Implications for Interest in Small Firm Ownership. *Entrepreneurship and Regional Development*, Volume 7, Number 4, pp. 365–377.

McCaskey, Michael B. (1982). *The Executive Challenge: Managing Change and Ambiguity*. Boston: Pitman.

McClelland, David C. (1961). *The Achieving Society*. Princeton, NJ: D. Van Nostrand.

McClelland, David C. (1962). Business Drive and National Achievement. *Harvard Business Review*, Volume 40, Number 4, pp. 99–112.

McClelland, David C. (1965). N Achievement and Entrepreneurship: A Longitudinal Study. *Journal of Personality and Social Psychology*, Volume 1, pp. 389–392.

McClelland, David C. (1975). *Power: The Inner Experience*. New York: Irvington.

McClelland, David C., John W. Atkinson, Russell A. Clark, and Edgar L. Lowell (1953). *The Achievement Motive*. New York: Appleton-Century-Crofts.

McClelland, David C., and David G. Winter (1969). *Motivating Economic Development*. New York: Free Press.

McDougall, Patricia, and Richard B. Robinson (1990). New Venture Strategies: An Empirical Identification of Eight ''Archetypes'' of Competitive Strategies for Entry. *Strategic Management Journal*, Volume 11, Number 6, pp. 447–467.

McGrath, Rita G., Ian C. MacMillan, and Sari Scheinberg (1992). Elitists, Risk-takers, and Rugged Individualists? An Exploratory Analysis of Cultural Differences between Entrepreneurs and Non-entrepreneurs. *Journal of Business Venturing*, Volume 7, Number 2, pp. 115–135.

McKelvey, Bill (1982). *Organizational Systematics: Taxonomy, Evolution, Classification*. Berkeley: University of California Press.

Meindl, James R., Raymond G. Hunt, and Wonsick Lee (1989). Individualism-Collectivism and Work Values: Data from the United States, China, Taiwan, Korea, and Hong Kong. *Research in Personnel and Human Resources Management*, Supplement 1, pp. 59-77.

Merchant, John (1992). *Economic Performance Index for Cities*. Louisville, KY: Bureau of Economic Research, University of Louisville.

Meyer, Herbert H., and Michael S. Raich (1983). An Objective Evaluation of a Behavior Modeling Training Program. *Personnel Psychology*, Volume 36, Number 4, pp. 755–761.

Miles, Raymond E., and Charles C. Snow (1978). *Organizational Strategy, Structure and Process*. New York: McGraw-Hill.

Miller, Danny (1990). *The Icarus Paradox: How Exceptional Companies Bring about Their Own Downfall*. New York: Harper Business.

Miller, Danny (1996). Configurations Revisited. *Strategic Management Journal*, Volume 17, Number 7, pp. 505–512.

Miller, Danny, and Peter H. Friesen (1984). *Organizations: A Quantum View*. Englewood Cliffs, NJ: Prentice-Hall.

Miller, Danny, Manfred F. R. Kets de Vries, and Jean-Marie Toulouse (1982). Top Executive Locus of Control and Its Relationship to Strategy-Making, Structure, and Environment. *Academy of Management Journal*, Volume 25, pp. 237–253.

Milne, Tom, and John Lewis (1982). Models and Approaches to Teaching Entrepreneurship. In Terry D. Webb, Thelma A. Quince, and David S. Watkins (Eds.), *Small Business Research: The Development of Entrepreneurs*. London, UK: Gower, pp. 61–83.

Miner, John B. (1961). On the Use of a Short Vocabulary Test to Measure General Intelligence. *Journal of Educational Psychology*, Volume 52, Number 3, pp. 157–160.

Miner, John B. (1964). *Scoring Guide for the Miner Sentence Completion Scale—Form H*. Eugene, OR: Organizational Measurement Systems Press.

Miner, John B. (1973a). The Real Crunch in Managerial Manpower. *Harvard Business Review*, Volume 51, Number 6, pp. 146–158.

Miner, John B. (1973b). *Intelligence in the United States*. Westport, CT: Greenwood.

Miner, John B. (1980). *Theories of Organizational Behavior*. Hinsdale, IL: Dryden.

Miner, John B. (1981). *Scoring Guide for the Miner Sentence Completion Scale—Form P*. Eugene, OR: Organizational Measurement Systems Press.

Miner, John B. (1985). *People Problems: The Executive Answer Book*. New York: Random House.

Miner, John B. (1986). *Scoring Guide for the Miner Sentence Completion Scale—Form T*. Eugene, OR: Organizational Measurement Systems Press.

Miner, John B. (1989). *Supplement—Scoring Guide for the Miner Sentence Completion Scale—Form H*. Eugene, OR: Organizational Measurement Systems Press.

Miner, John B. (1990). Entrepreneurs, High Growth Entrepreneurs, and Managers: Contrasting and Overlapping Motivational Patterns. *Journal of Business Venturing*, Volume 5, Number 4, pp. 221–234.

Miner, John B. (1991a). Individuals, Groups, and Networking: Experience with an Entrepreneurship Development Program. *International Council for Small Business Proceedings*, Volume 2, pp. 82–90.

Miner, John B. (1991b). Psychological Assessment in a Developmental Context. In Curtiss P. Hansen and Kelley A. Conrad (Eds.), *A Handbook of Psychological Assessment in Business*. Westport, CT: Quorum, pp. 225–236.

Miner, John B. (1992). *Industrial-Organizational Psychology*. New York: McGraw-Hill.

Miner, John B. (1993). *Role Motivation Theories*. New York: Routledge.

Miner, John B. (1996a). *The 4 Routes to Entrepreneurial Success*. San Francisco, CA: Berrett-Koehler.

Miner, John B. (1996b). *How Honesty Testing Works*. Westport, CT: Quorum.

Miner, John B. (1996c). Routes to Entrepreneurial Success: Guidelines from Research. In George T. Solomon, K. Mark Weaver, and John Bebris (Eds.), *Keys to the Future of American Business*. Buffalo, NY: Creative Education Foundation, pp. 1–18.

Miner, John B. (1996d). Rhyme and Reason for Entrepreneurial Success. *At Work: Stories of Tomorrow's Workplace*, Volume 5, Number 4, pp. 12–15.

Miner, John B. (1996e). Evidence for the Existence of a Set of Personality Types, Defined by Psychological Tests, that Predict Entrepreneurial Success. *Frontiers of Entrepreneurship Research*, Volume 16, pp. 62–76.

Miner, John B. (1997a). The Expanded Horizon for Achieving Entrepreneurial Success. *Organizational Dynamics*, Volume 25, Number 3, pp. 54–67.

Miner, John B. (1997b). Becoming a Successful Franchisee: Four Kinds of People, Four Different Routes. *Franchising Research: An International Journal*, Volume 2, Number 2, pp. 64–74.

Miner, John B. (1997c). A Psychological Typology and Its Relationship to Entrepreneurial Success. *Entrepreneurship and Regional Development*, Volume 9, Number 3, forthcoming.

Miner, John B., and Donald P. Crane (1995). *Human Resource Management: The Strategic Perspective*. New York: HarperCollins.

Miner, John B., Donald P. Crane, and Robert J. Vandenberg (1994). Congruence and Fit in Professional Role Motivation Theory. *Organization Science*, Volume 5, Number 1, pp. 86–97.

Miner, John B., Norman R. Smith, and Jeffrey S. Bracker (1989). Role of Entrepreneurial Task Motivation in the Growth of Technologically Innovative Firms. *Journal of Applied Psychology*, Volume 74, Number 4, pp. 554–560.

Miner, John B., Norman R. Smith, and Jeffrey S. Bracker (1992a). Defining the Inventor Entrepreneur in the Context of Established Typologies. *Journal of Business Venturing*, Volume 7, Number 2, pp. 103–113.

Miner, John B., Norman R. Smith, and Jeffrey S. Bracker (1992b). Predicting Firm Survival from a Knowledge of Entrepreneur Task Motivation. *Entrepreneurship and Regional Development*, Volume 4, Number 2, pp. 145–153.

Miner, John B., Norman R. Smith, and Jeffrey S. Bracker (1994). Role of Entrepreneurial Task Motivation in the Growth of Technologically Innovative Firms: Interpretations from Follow-up Data. *Journal of Applied Psychology*, Volume 79, Number 4, pp. 627–630.

Miner, John B., and Susan Stites-Doe (1994). Applying an Entrepreneurship Development Program to Economic Problems in the Buffalo Area. In Abraham K. Korman (Ed.), *Human Dilemmas in Work Organizations: Strategies for Resolution*. New York: Guilford, pp. 243–271.

Mintzberg, Henry (1979). *The Structuring of Organizations*. Englewood Cliffs, NJ: Prentice-Hall.

Mintzberg, Henry (1984). Power and Organizational Life Cycles. *Academy of Management Review*, Volume 9, pp. 207–224.

Mintzberg, Henry (1994). *The Rise and Fall of Strategic Planning*. New York: Free Press.

Miron, David, and David C. McClelland (1979). The Impact of Achievement Motivation Training on Small Business. *California Management Review*, Volume 21, Number 4, pp. 13–28.

Mosakowski, Elaine (1993). A Resource-Based Perspective on the Dynamic Strategy-Performance Relationship: An Empirical Examination of the Focus and Differentiation Strategies in Entrepreneurial Firms. *Journal of Management*, Volume 19, Number 4, pp. 819–839.

Mowday, Richard T., Lyman W. Porter, and Richard M. Steers (1982). *Employee-

Organization Linkages: The Psychology of Commitment, Absenteeism, and Turnover. New York: Academic Press.

Naffziger, Douglas (1995). Entrepreneurship: A Person-Based Theory Approach. *Advances in Entrepreneurship, Firm Emergence, and Growth,* Volume 2, pp. 21–50.

Naman, John L., and Dennis P. Slevin (1993). Entrepreneurship and the Concept of Fit: A Model and Empirical Tests. *Strategic Management Journal,* Volume 14, Number 2, pp. 137–153.

New York State Department of Economic Development (1990). *New York State 1990 County Profiles.* Albany, NY: Author.

Noe, Raymond A. (1988). An Investigation of the Determinants of Successful Assigned Mentoring Relationships. *Personnel Psychology,* Volume 41, Number 3, pp. 457–479.

Oakes, Guy (1990). *The Soul of the Salesman: The Moral Ethos of Personal Sales.* Atlantic Highlands, NJ: Humanities Press International.

O'del, John N. (1997). *Polish Entrepreneurs and American Entrepreneurs: A Comparative Study of Role Motivations.* New York: Garland.

Oliver, John E. (1981). *Scoring Guide for the Oliver Organization Description Questionnaire.* Eugene, OR: Organizational Measurement Systems Press.

Oliver, John E. (1982). An Instrument for Classifying Organizations. *Academy of Management Journal,* Volume 25, Number 4, pp. 855–866.

Osborne, Richard L. (1994). Second Phase Entrepreneurship: Breaking through the Growth Wall. *Business Horizons,* Volume 37, Number 1, pp. 80–86.

Palich, Leslie E., and D. Ray Bagby (1995). Using Cognitive Theory to Explain Entrepreneurial Risk-Taking: Challenging Conventional Wisdom. *Journal of Business Venturing,* Volume 10, Number 6, pp. 425–438.

Pandey, Janek, and N. B. Tewary (1979). Locus of Control and Achievement Values of Entrepreneurs. *Journal of Occupational Psychology,* Volume 52, Part 2.

Paradiso, James (1990). An Interview with Dr. Roman Galar: The Impact of Deregulation on Small Business in Poland. *Journal of Small Business Management,* Volume 28, Number 3, pp. 81–85.

Parasuraman, Saroj, Yasmin S. Purohit, and Veronica M. Godshalk (1996). Work and Family Variables, Entrepreneurial Career Success, and Psychological Well-Being. *Journal of Vocational Behavior,* Volume 48, Number 3, pp. 275–300.

Peters, Thomas J. (1987). *Thriving on Chaos.* New York: Alfred A. Knopf.

Peterson, Rein, and Norman R. Smith (1986). Entrepreneurship: A Culturally Appropriate Combination of Craft and Opportunity. *Frontiers of Entrepreneurship Research,* Volume 6, pp. 1–11.

Porter, Lyman W., and Lawrence E. McKibbin (1988). *Management Education and Development: Drift or Thrust Into the 21st Century.* New York: McGraw-Hill.

Preisendorfer, Peter, and Thomas Voss (1990). Organizational Mortality of Small Firms: The Effects of Entrepreneurial Age and Human Capital. *Organization Studies,* Volume 11, Issue 1, pp. 107–129.

Ransom, S., C. R. Hinings, and Royston Greenwood (1980). The Structuring of Organizational Structures. *Administrative Science Quarterly,* Volume 25, Number 1, pp. 1–17.

Ray, Dennis M. (1993). Understanding the Entrepreneur: Entrepreneurial Attributes, Experience, and Skills. *Entrepreneurship and Regional Development*, Volume 5, Number 4, pp. 345–357.

Rich, Philip (1992). The Organizational Taxonomy: Definition and Design. *Academy of Management Review*, Volume 17, Number 4, pp. 758–781.

Richards, Max D. (1973). An Exploratory Study of Strategic Failure. *Academy of Management Proceedings*, Volume 33, pp. 40–46.

Roberts, Edward B. (1989). The Personality and Motivations of Technological Entrepreneurs. *Journal of Engineering and Technology Management*, Volume 6, Number 1, pp. 5–23.

Roberts, Edward B. (1991a). High Stakes for High-Tech Entrepreneurs: Understanding Venture Capital Decision Making. *Sloan Management Review*, Volume 32, Number 2, pp. 9–20.

Roberts, Edward B. (1991b). *Entrepreneurs in High Technology: Lessons from MIT and Beyond*. New York: Oxford University Press.

Robinson, Peter B., Jonathan C. Huefner, and H. Keith Hunt (1991). Entrepreneurial Research on Student Subjects Does Not Generalize to Real World Entrepreneurs. *Journal of Small Business Management*, Volume 29, Number 2, pp. 42–50.

Romano, Claudio, and Janek Ratnatunga (1996). A Citation Analysis of the Impact of Journals on Contemporary Small Enterprise Research. *Entrepreneurship Theory and Practice*, Volume 20, Number 3, pp. 7–21.

Rose, R. M., C. D. Jenkins, and M. W. Hurst (1978). *Air Traffic Controller Health Change Study: A Prospective Investigation of Physical, Psychological, and Work-Related Changes*. Austin: University of Texas Press.

Rowe, Alan J., and Richard O. Mason (1987). *Managing with Style: A Guide to Understanding, Assessing, and Improving Decision Making*. San Francisco, CA: Jossey-Bass.

Runco, Mark A., and Robert S. Albert (1990). *Theories of Creativity*. Newbury Park, CA: Sage.

Sanchez, Julio C. (1993). The Long and Thorny Way to an Organizational Taxonomy. *Organization Studies*, Volume 14, Issue 1, pp. 73–92.

Sandberg, William R. (1986). *New Venture Performance: The Role of Strategy and Industry Structure*. Lexington, MA: Lexington Books.

Schaubroeck, John, Daniel C. Ganster, and Barbara E. Kemmerer (1994). Job Complexity, "Type A" Behavior, and Cardiovascular Disorder: A Prospective Study. *Academy of Management Journal*, Volume 37, Number 2, pp. 426–439.

Schein, Edgar H. (1994). Commentary: What Is an Entrepreneur? *Entrepreneurship Theory and Practice*, Volume 19, Number 2, pp. 87–88.

Schein, Edgar H. (1996). Career Anchors Revisited: Implications for Career Development in the 21st Century. *Academy of Management Executive*, Volume 10, Number 4, pp. 80–88.

Scherer, Robert F., James D. Brodzinski, and Frank A. Wiebe (1991). Examining the Relationship between Personality and Entrepreneurial Career Preference. *Entrepreneurship and Regional Development*, Volume 3, Number 2, pp. 195–206.

Scrace, Ronald H. (1991). *Tomorrow's Jobs, Tomorrow's Workers: Western New York*. Albany, NY: New York State Department of Labor.

Sexton, Donald L., and Nancy Bowman-Upton (1990). Female and Male Entrepreneurs: Psychological Characteristics and Their Role in Gender-Related Discrimination. *Journal of Business Venturing*, Volume 5, Number 1, pp. 29–36.

Sexton, Donald L., and Nancy B. Bowman-Upton (1991). *Entrepreneurship: Creativity and Growth.* New York: Macmillan.

Sexton, Donald L., and John D. Kasarda (1992). *The State of the Art of Entrepreneurship.* Boston: PWS-Kent.

Shane, Scott (1996). Explaining Variation in Rates of Entrepreneurship in the United States: 1899–1988. *Journal of Management,* Volume 22, Number 5, pp. 747–781.

Shaver, Kelly G., and Linda R. Scott (1991). Person, Process, Choice: The Psychology of New Venture Creation. *Entrepreneurship Theory and Practice,* Volume 16, Number 2, pp. 23–45.

Shefsky, Lloyd (1994). *Entrepreneurs Are Made Not Born.* New York: McGraw-Hill.

Shure, G. H., and J. P. Meeker (1967). A Personality Attitude Schedule for Use in Experimental Bargaining Studies. *Journal of Psychology,* Volume 65, pp. 233–252.

Slevin, Dennis P., and Jeffrey G. Covin (1990). Juggling Entrepreneurial Style and Organizational Structure—How to Get Your Act Together. *Sloan Management Review,* Volume 31, Number 2, pp. 43–53.

Slocum, John W., and Don Hellriegel (1983). A Look at How Managers' Minds Work. *Business Horizons,* Volume 26, Number 4, pp. 58–68.

Smith, Norman R. (1967). *The Entrepreneur and His Firm: The Relationship between Type of Man and Type of Company.* East Lansing: Bureau of Business and Economic Research, Graduate School of Business Administration, Michigan State University.

Smith, Norman R., Jeffrey S. Bracker, and John B. Miner (1987). Correlates of Firm and Entrepreneur Success in Technologically Innovative Companies. *Frontiers of Entrepreneurship Research,* Volume 7, pp. 337–353.

Smith, Norman R., Kenneth G. McCain, and John B. Miner (1976). The Managerial Motivation of Successful Entrepreneurs. *Oregon Business Review,* Volume 34, p. 3.

Smith, Norman R., and John B. Miner (1983). Type of Entrepreneur, Type of Firm, and Managerial Motivation: Implications for Organizational Life Cycle Theory. *Strategic Management Journal,* Volume 4, Number 4, pp. 325–340.

Smith, Norman R., and John B. Miner (1984). Motivational Considerations in the Success of Technologically Innovative Entrepreneurs. *Frontiers of Entrepreneurship Research,* Volume 4, pp. 488–495.

Smith, Norman R., and John B. Miner (1985). Motivational Considerations in the Success of Technologically Innovative Entrepreneurs: Extended Sample Findings. *Frontiers of Entrepreneurship Research,* Volume 5, pp. 482–488.

Smyntek, George P. (1991). Focus on Western New York . . . The Right Place at the Right Time. *Employment in New York State,* December, p. 2.

Smyntek, George P., Ronald H. Scrace, and Lissa M. Swinarski (1990). *Labor Market Assessment—Occupational Supply and Demand: Buffalo-Niagara Falls CMSA.* Albany, NY: New York State Department of Labor.

Solomon, Charlene M. (1990). What an Idea: Creativity Training. *Personnel Journal,* Volume 69, Number 5, pp. 65–71.

Solomon, George T., and Lloyd W. Fernald (1991). Trends in Small Business Management and Entrepreneurship Education in the United States. *Entrepreneurship Theory and Practice,* Volume 15, Number 3, pp. 25–39.

Solomon, George T., K. Mark Weaver, and Lloyd W. Fernald (1994). A Historical Examination of Small Business Management and Entrepreneurship Pedagogy. *Simulation and Gaming*, Volume 25, Number 3, pp. 338–352.

Sonnenfeld, Jeffrey (1988). *The Hero's Farewell: What Happens When CEOs Retire.* New York: Oxford University Press.

Spector, Paul E., and Brian J. O'Connell (1994). The Contribution of Personality Traits, Negative Affectivity, Locus of Control, and Type A to the Subsequent Reports of Job Stressors and Job Strains. *Journal of Occupational and Organizational Psychology*, Volume 67, Part 1, pp. 1–11.

Steiner, George A., and John B. Miner (1986). *Management Policy and Strategy.* New York: Macmillan.

Stevenson, Howard H., and J. Carlos Jarillo (1990). A Paradigm of Entrepreneurship: Entrepreneurial Management. *Strategic Management Journal*, Volume 11, Special Issue, Summer, pp. 17–27.

Stewart, Alex (1989). *Team Entrepreneurship.* Newbury Park, CA: Sage.

Strube, Michael J. (1991). *Type A Behavior.* Newbury Park, CA: Sage.

Tannenbaum, Scott I., and Gary Yukl (1992). Training and Development in Work Organizations. *Annual Review of Psychology*, Volume 43, pp. 399–441.

Taylor, Calvin W. (1972). *Climate for Creativity.* Elmsford, NY: Pergamon Press.

Thorndike, Robert L. (1942). Two Screening Tests of Verbal Intelligence. *Journal of Applied Psychology*, Volume 26, pp. 128–135.

Thorndike, Robert L., and George H. Gallup (1944). Verbal Intelligence of the American Adult. *Journal of General Psychology*, Volume 30, pp. 75–85.

Ticknor, Samuel H. (1985). *The Economic History of Buffalo: 1825–1984.* Buffalo, NY: M&T Bank.

Tikoo, Surinder (1996). Assessing the Franchise Option. *Business Horizons*, Volume 39, Number 3, pp. 78–82.

Timmons, Jeffry (1971). Black Is Beautiful—Is It Bountiful? *Harvard Business Review*, Volume 49, Number 6, pp. 81–94.

Timmons, Jeffry A. (1989). *The Entrepreneurial Mind.* Acton, MA: Brick House Publishing.

Timmons, Jeffry A. (1990a). *New Venture Creation: Entrepreneurship in the 1990s.* Homewood, IL: Irwin.

Timmons, Jeffry A. (1990b). *Planning and Financing the New Venture.* Acton, MA: Brick House Publishing.

Tornatzky, Louis G., and Mitchell Fleischer (1990). *The Processes of Technological Innovation.* Lexington, MA: Lexington Books.

Trist, Eric L., and K. W. Bamforth (1951). Some Social and Psychological Consequences of the Longwall Method of Coal-getting. *Human Relations*, Volume 4, pp. 3–38.

Vesper, Karl H. (1980, 1990). *New Venture Strategies.* Englewood Cliffs, NJ: Prentice-Hall.

Vesper, Karl H. (1993). *Entrepreneurship Education 1993.* Los Angeles: Entrepreneurial Studies Center, Anderson School, University of California, Los Angeles.

Vesper, Karl H., and W. Ed McMullan (1988). Entrepreneurship: Today Courses, Tomorrow Degrees? *Entrepreneurship Theory and Practice*, Volume 13, Number 1, pp. 7–13.

Waldinger, Roger, Howard Aldrich, and Robin Ward (1990). *Ethnic Entrepreneurs: Immigrant Business in Industrial Societies.* Newbury Park, CA: Sage.

Wallace, Jean E. (1993). Professional and Organizational Commitment: Compatible or

Incompatible. *Journal of Vocational Behavior*, Volume 42, Number 3, pp. 323–349.

Wallace, Phyllis A. (1989). *MBAs on the Fast Track: Career Mobility of Young Managers*. New York: Ballinger.

Walton, Richard E. (1972). How to Counter Alienation in the Plant. *Harvard Business Review*, Volume 50, Number 6, pp. 70–81.

Ward, J. L. (1987). *Keeping the Family Business Healthy*. San Francisco, CA: Jossey-Bass.

Weber, Max (1947). *The Theory of Social and Economic Organization*. New York: Free Press.

Weidenbaum, Murray (1996). The Chinese Family Business Enterprise. *California Management Review*, Volume 38, Number 4, pp. 141–156.

Whitely, William, Thomas J. Dougherty, and George F. Dreher (1991). Relationship of Career Mentoring and Socioeconomic Origin to Managers' and Professionals' Early Career Progress. *Academy of Management Journal*, Volume 34, Number 2, pp. 331–351.

Willard, Gary E., David A. Krueger, and Henry R. Feeser (1992). In Order to Grow, Must the Founder Go: A Comparison of Performance between Founder and Non-Founder Managed High-Growth Manufacturing Firms. *Journal of Business Venturing*, Volume 7, Number 3, pp. 181–194.

Wolfe, Joseph, and Garry Bruton (1994). On the Use of Computerized Simulations for Entrepreneurship Education. *Simulation and Gaming*, Volume 25, Number 3, pp. 402–415.

Woo, Carolyn Y., Arnold C. Cooper, and William C. Dunkelberg (1988). Entrepreneurial Typologies: Definitions and Implications. *Frontiers of Entrepreneurship Research*, Volume 8, pp. 165–176.

Woo, Carolyn Y., Arnold C. Cooper, and William C. Dunkelberg (1991). The Development and Interpretation of Entrepreneurial Typologies. *Journal of Business Venturing*, Volume 6, Number 2, pp. 93–114.

Woo, Carolyn, Urs Daellenbach, and Charlene Nicholls-Nixon (1994). Theory Building in the Presence of "Randomness": The Case of Venture Creation and Performance. *Journal of Management Studies*, Volume 31, Number 4, pp. 507–524.

Name Index

Subject Index

About the Author

JOHN B. MINER currently has a professional practice in Eugene, Oregon, specializing in entrepreneurship, human resource management, and industrial psychology. He has an undergraduate degree in psychology from Princeton University, a master's degree in clinical psychology from Clark University, and a Ph.D. in personality theory and clinical psychology from Princeton. After holding research positions at Columbia University and the Atlantic Refining Company, he served on the business faculties at the University of Oregon, the University of Maryland, Georgia State University, and the State University of New York (SUNY) at Buffalo. At SUNY he was director of the Center for Entrepreneurial Leadership, held the Donald S. Carmichael chair in human resources, and chaired his department. He has been awarded the honor of Fellow status by five professional organizations, has been editor of the *Academy of Management Journal*, and was president of the Academy of Management. His prior publications include 38 books and monographs (many of which appeared in multiple editions), 125 articles and book chapters, and a number of psychological tests and testing materials.

ISBN 1-56720-115-6

90000>

EAN

9 781567 201154

HARDCOVER BAR CODE